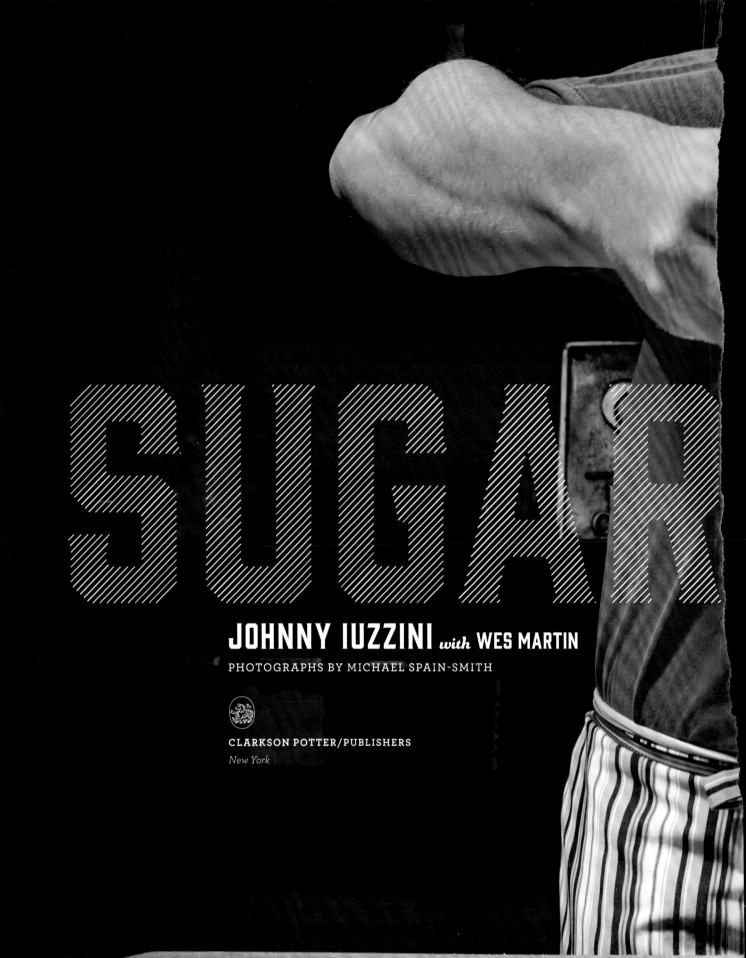

SUGAR

JOHNNY IUZZINI *with* WES MARTIN

PHOTOGRAPHS BY MICHAEL SPAIN-SMITH

CLARKSON POTTER/PUBLISHERS
New York

RUSH

Master Tips, Techniques, and Recipes for Sweet Baking

Published in the United States by Clarkson Potter/
Publishers, an imprint of the Crown Publishing Group, a
division of Random House LLC, a Penguin Random House
Company, New York.
www.crownpublishing.com
www.clarksonpotter.com

CLARKSON POTTER is a trademark and POTTER with
colophon is a registered trademark of Random House LLC.

Library of Congress Cataloging-in-Publication Data
Iuzzini, Johnny.
   Sugar rush : master tips, techniques, and recipes for sweet
baking / Johnny Iuzzini. — First edition.
      pages cm
   Includes bibliographical references and index.
1. Desserts. 2. Baking. I. Title.
   TX773. I985 2014
   641.86—dc23

                              2013038727

ISBN 978-0-7704-3369-7
eBook ISBN 978-0-7704-3370-3

Printed in China

Book and cover design by Marysarah Quinn
Photographs by Michael Spain-Smith
Cover photographs by Michael Spain-Smith

10 9 8 7 6 5 4 3 2 1

First Edition

I dedicate this book to my father and namesake,

JOHN JOSEPH IUZZINI, Jr.

He has taught me many lessons in life, but the
greatest lesson of all was to work hard and do
whatever you have to do to achieve your goals.
Without that work ethic, this book wouldn't exist.
Love ya, Pops.

Contents

Introduction

Before you even think about making Killer Chocolate Chip Cookies (page 220) or Chipotle Churros with Dulce de Leche Cream (page 124), grab some coffee, settle into your favorite spot, and give yourself up to the pleasures of reading this book from cover to cover. My guess is that when you've finished, you'll not only be happy, but you'll also have bookmarked dozens of pages and be raring to head into the kitchen for a long and delicious time.

It's what I did. First I roasted white chocolate, something I've wanted to do for years, but needed Johnny's encouragement to attempt, and turned it into panna cotta. Then I cranked up the oven and roasted oranges, a new technique for me, and made Bitter Orange Ice Cream (page 38). And I didn't even try to resist the call of Smack Caramel Corn (page 165).

Sugar Rush is the book I've always hoped Johnny would write. It's got his voice, his passion, his distinctive take on everything from meringues to motorcycles, and his genius recipes.

It's a great basic baking book.

I know it looks glamorous and sexy and everything except basic, but looks tell only a small piece of the story: Everything in this book is as right for home bakers as it is for accomplished pastry chefs. Consider it a stealth primer.

The more I read *Sugar Rush,* the more I kept thinking that I would have given anything to have had this book when I was teaching myself how to bake almost forty years ago.

But books like this didn't exist. There were books for professionals that assumed you knew a lot (some were just lists of ingredients), and books for home bakers that assumed you didn't need to know. A shame, since pastry is made up of building blocks: Understand the how and why of a master recipe, learn it, and it's yours to riff on endlessly. Pastry chefs teach this to their apprentices; Johnny teaches us.

If there weren't books like this, there certainly weren't chefs like Johnny. He straddles two worlds: He's a pastry chef's pastry chef who's won every prize in the field, and a pro who understands those of us who bake at home. He gets us because he remembers being a student (a mischievous one).

And I remember him as a student. I met him when he was an eighteen-year-old pastry cook in Daniel Boulud's kitchen. It was near impossible to keep up with him as he raced around finishing his work, then staying on so he could peer over the shoulders of the chefs to learn more.

Today young cooks peer over his shoulders and he's always generous with them. And with his friends, which explains why the following story has a happy ending.

Five years ago my son, Joshua, and I decided to create a weeklong cookie boutique to celebrate Valentine's Day. We rented a huge kitchen with equipment we didn't know how to operate and rounded up a team to bake with us. We spent the first day in that kitchen making mountains of dough and our plan was to spend the next days baking like mad. Neither Joshua nor I had ever made more that a few hundred cookies for parties and now, with our team, we were going to bake a few thousand every day. Except no one on the team showed up. No one. Everyone stayed home to watch the Super Bowl.

I sat in the middle of the kitchen and did the most useless thing: I cried. Joshua did the best thing: He called Johnny.

Within twenty minutes we could hear the roar of his Ducati. His motorcycle jacket was half off as he walked into the kitchen and, after picking me up off the floor, giving me a pep talk, a hug, and orders to fire up the ovens, he put on his chef's whites. Had he been a cartoon character, you'd have seen him grow three feet taller. You would also have seen those lines that tell you that someone is moving at warp speed.

For the next five hours, that kitchen was as busy as Santa's Workshop. In between rolling, cutting, chilling, baking, and cooling cookies with us—and coming up with an ingenious way to salvage the chocolate cookies that refused to keep their shape—Johnny gave us a master class in baking.

He may have been a prankster student, but he's a terrific teacher. I've learned from him and you will, too, on every page of this book.

Keep reading. And then keep baking.

—Dorie Greenspan

GETTING STARTED

I was a typical kid, building bike jumps, sneaking out late at night, getting lost in the woods, and generally wreaking havoc with my brother in upstate New York. The decision to take culinary classes in my high school vocational program, though, snapped me right into focus. I found a place to put all of my teenage energy; desserts turned out to be life defining—and I never looked back. I love being a pastry chef because of the endless opportunity for creativity.

Although I have many passions in life, they don't bring me the satisfaction that creating desserts does. Motorcycles, my other true love, work one way, with the same parts, every time. You can't take a spark plug out of the engine and expect the bike to start. But with desserts, switching one ingredient for another or serving something cold instead of hot can be an entirely unexpected, killer experience. Once you grasp some fundamentals, you are limited only by your imagination.

This book contains master recipes that form the foundation of the pastry kitchen; they are the building blocks for all the desserts I make. I'll take you, step by step, through the key methods behind traditional recipes and then show you how to change the spark plug to turn the classics into something completely new.

We'll start off with custard, the primary element for ice cream, crème brûlée, and a lot of popular creamy desserts—all of which require proper technique to get their smooth, ethereal textures. Then we'll dive further into eggs, whipping them to make mousse and meringue to serve on their own or to lighten cake batter, for example. Caramel, a flavor that is indispensable to rich, complex combinations, will be our next stop. It can elevate or ruin a dessert if not cooked correctly. In subsequent chapters, we'll get to desserts that are primarily about texture and construction—such as cakes, cupcakes, brownies, muffins, cookies, tea cakes, and biscuits—picking up on what we've covered in prior chapters. Tarts, cobblers, and crisps showcase both fruit and other types of fillings, as well as a contrast of textures between buttery and flaky or crunchy crusts and toppings and smooth interiors. There's nothing to fear about yeast doughs, especially once you have my key tips for success in your back pocket. Basics, such as glazes, frostings, fillings, and sauces, round out the recipes. A final chapter on plated desserts shows you how to put everything together and gives a peek into how I construct restaurant-quality finishes to a great meal.

This collection of recipes and techniques, which I have spent years perfecting, will teach you the basics of successful baking. But the book is just that—a foundation and scaffolding; use the recipes, along with your own creative touch, to concoct new and even more exciting desserts.

Before You Begin

Make sure you have plenty of time when you decide to bake or create desserts. Read the recipe carefully so you know how long you'll need. Be sure to account for any cooking or resting times.

Next pull out everything you will need—all ingredients, tools, and equipment. I'm talking spoons, spatulas, parchment paper, ice bath, everything. The time it takes for you to rifle through the junk drawer to find your thermometer when you have bubbling hot sugar on the stove could be the difference between fluffy Italian meringue and setting off the fire alarm.

Working with the Recipes

I am a multitasker; I thrive on juggling many things at once. That is reflected in the way I cook and bake. Instead of standing around waiting for egg whites to whip, I move on to something else while the mixer does its job. In fact, good pastry technique often requires this—you cannot make Italian meringue by whipping the egg whites first, then cooking the sugar, and then going back to the whites; the whites and sugar must be prepped simultaneously so they are ready at the same time. Don't freak out about this; I'll guide you through the steps. You can do it.

INGREDIENTS

It should go without saying: quality ingredients make quality desserts. The better the butter, eggs, chocolate, fruits, herbs, spices, et cetera, the better your cakes, cookies, custards, and other desserts will be. If you use inexpensive chocolate loaded with cocoa butter, sugar, and additives, your chocolate desserts will not taste deep and rich. They will taste store-bought. And don't expect to make a tasty peach tart in February just because you found peaches at the supermarket. If they aren't ripe when you start the recipe, they won't taste ripe in the dessert. Use the best ingredients you can find and afford. Pair them with good technique and you're on your way.

You will notice that I give weights for most of the ingredients. This is because using a scale is the most precise way to measure. If you had four people measure 1 cup of flour and then weighed it, you would have four different amounts. That said, I give both options here so you can work in whichever way you are comfortable. Here are some key things to keep in mind regarding ingredients:

- Measure everything before you start. Much of baking is about timing, and if you have to stop to measure something midrecipe, it can affect the final dessert.

- To measure flour, sugar, spices, and other dry ingredients with measuring cups, use a large spoon to stir the ingredient well to lighten it. Then spoon the ingredient into the measuring cup until it is overflowing. Finally, scrape across the top of the cup with a straight edge to level it. *Never* scoop with the measuring cup—it will compact the ingredient, giving you too much of it, and will affect the outcome of the recipe.

- If you are using a scale, weigh each ingredient *separately*. Piling dry ingredients on top of one another in a bowl on a scale and pressing the tare button each time is risky. If you make a mistake, there is no way you can pick the baking soda out of a mound of flour and feel confident that the ratios are correct.

- If a recipe says to use something cold, at room temperature, or warm, do it. Many desserts require the emulsification of fats and liquids, and temperature is important. Usually the strongest emulsification results when the separate ingredients are the same temperature.

EQUIPMENT

Working in the finest restaurants in New York and around the world gave me the opportunity to work with the best equipment available. But honestly, you need only basic equipment and tools to produce world-class desserts.

Oven

Every oven on the planet is different. Some have convection settings; some have built-in microwaves; some even have low temperature settings for proofing (rising) bread dough. All you really need, though, is a reliable oven with even heat. Electric ovens are best, as the temperature range tends to be a little more precise than with gas ovens. No matter what kind of oven you have in your home, though, you'll want to make sure it is heating to the right temperature. Grab a couple of inexpensive oven thermometers the next time you are at the supermarket so you can test your oven. Is 375°F on the dial or digital display really 375°F inside?

Keep in mind that all ovens also have hot spots; you've likely noticed this if you've ever toasted a sheet pan of sliced almonds or shredded coconut and some areas darken more quickly than others. That's why rotating a baking pan 180 degrees in the oven midway through baking times is so important, especially when baking delicate items like meringue, soufflés, or foam cakes. If you are baking a cake and one side of the pan gets hotter than the other, it can cause the cake to bake unevenly, and your cake could rise higher on the hotter side.

Convection setting: Some gas or electric ovens have fans built into them that circulate the hot air around the oven while you bake. In general, convection ovens bake things more quickly and evenly and at a lower temperature than conventional ovens. *The recipes in this book have been developed for a regular oven without the convection setting.* Most oven manuals and recipes say that you should lower the temperature by 25 degrees if using the convection setting for a recipe developed for a conventional oven. There is no exact rule for this, however. Consult your oven manual if you have a convection setting you would like to use for baking. For the best results, though, train yourself to know when things are baked properly, according to how they look and feel to the touch. The fact that a recipe says to bake something for 20 minutes doesn't mean that will work perfectly every time. Many variables affect baked goods, from the temperature and humidity in your kitchen to the material your baking pans are made of. I will always give you a visual cue test to tell when something is ready to come out of the oven. Soon you will get to know by sight, smell, and touch when a cake is finished baking or meringue is ready to use. Timing is a guideline; with so many factors affecting baking, it's wise to learn to rely on your senses as well.

My Favorite Countertop Appliances

- **Standing mixer with whisk, paddle, and dough hook attachments:** for mixing batters, whipping meringue, and kneading dough. Handheld mixers will work in a pinch, but standing mixers, such as KitchenAid, allow you to monitor cooking sugar, melting chocolate, and such simultaneously, so investing in a standing mixer is wise.

- **Food processor:** for grinding and chopping ingredients like nuts and making some doughs like tart crust.

- **Blender:** I like Vitamix for its sheer power.

- **Immersion blender:** for smoothing chocolate ganache and mixing thin batters like crepe batter.

- **Digital scale:** for accurate measurements, look for one with both ounce and single gram settings.

- **Spice grinder:** freshly ground spices have more vibrant flavor.

Tools

The real key to stress-free baking, in my opinion, is having plenty of spatulas, spoons, and mixing bowls within reach. If you have to stop and wash something while you are in the middle of making meringue for a mousse or folding melted chocolate into a batter, you'll increase the odds of things not turning out right.

Here's a list of suggested tools to execute the recipes in this book:

- **Balloon whisks**
- **Wooden spoons:** various sizes
- **Metal spoons:** both large and small, for stirring, and slotted spoons for straining
- **Rubber spatulas:** Silicone ones are heatproof and are great for stirring hot pots. You can never have enough of these. I like flat ones in various sizes for folding, scraping, stirring, and mixing.
- **Offset metal spatulas:** These narrow, straight-edged spatulas that have a 1-inch-wide blade are crucial for spreading batters evenly and icing and moving cakes. Have various sizes at hand—sometimes you need a smaller one to work in tighter corners and smaller desserts. I use my baby offset all the time—it is about 3 inches long and ½ inch wide.
- **Large flat metal spatulas:** These have uses beyond flipping burgers. They are great for releasing and moving baked cakes, cookies, et cetera, from pans to racks and platters.
- **Metal tongs**
- **Pastry brushes:** These are important to the pastry kitchen. Remember to wash them well and keep them clean and free of oil. Oily residue in a brush can ruin cooked sugar.
- **Knives:** a large chef's knife, paring knives, and a large serrated knife for cutting cakes

- **Graters:** I like both a basic box grater and a Microplane grater for zesting citrus and grating ginger.
- **Mandoline slicer:** Useful for slicing fruits and vegetables uniformly; small plastic ones are inexpensive and found in most kitchen stores.
- **Fine-mesh strainer:** for straining custards and sifting dry ingredients
- **Metal cake tester:** The skewer portion is superthin so you won't make large holes in cakes when checking for doneness. Thin toothpicks or wooden skewers also work.
- **Oven thermometers:** See page 16.
- **Thermometers:** for monitoring frying oil and sugar temperatures especially. Make sure your thermometer can handle the level of heat of your recipes; standard meat thermometers tap out at 220°F. I like digital-read probe thermometers, which can reach even shallow levels of cooking sugar, unlike candy thermometers, which can be cumbersome. You can also set some digital thermometers to beep when the liquid reaches a specific temperature.
- **Pastry scrapers:** I like both plastic (the curved edge is really helpful for scraping out bowls) and metal, which are really great for cutting doughs cleanly and for scraping work surfaces when you are working with a sticky dough.

- **Silicone baking mats:** These are an amazing invention, and worth investing in. You can pour hot caramel on them and bake on them at any temperature.
- **Parchment paper:** You'll use tons of this, so go to a restaurant supply store and get a box of sheets. The sheets are easier to handle than parchment on rolls and will lie flat on the pans. You'll also save money in the long run. *Do not* bake with wax paper or aluminum foil on sheet pans.
- **Teflon-coated baking paper:** This is a relatively new product that functions like a silicone baking mat but is much more flexible and lighter. It can easily be cut to line any shape of pan, can be wiped clean, and is reusable.
- **Pastry bags:** canvas or plastic bags both large and small with several sizes of tips
- **Digital kitchen timer**
- **Dry and liquid measuring cups and spoons**

Bakeware

There is a huge array of new nonstick bakeware and pans designed to make things easier: nonstick angel food pans, cookie sheets, and muffin tins. The problem is that most of these pans are made of a darker metal composite than regular stainless steel and behave differently from the pans I have used all of my life. Darker metal pans conduct heat more quickly and can overcook the edges of cakes and baked goods before the center is cooked through. Cookies can burn in no time on a nonstick sheet pan.

You can find inexpensive stainless bakeware in restaurant supply stores, and the pans are typically cheaper there than at department stores. If you follow the instructions in recipes for greasing and flouring pans, you'll have little need for nonstick bakeware.

When using dark nonstick pans, you may need to set your oven to a lower temperature so things bake evenly, typically 25 degrees cooler. There is no hard and fast rule to this; you will simply need to pay extra attention.

The majority of recipes in this book have been developed in basic stainless-steel baking pans. That said, I use nonstick pans in a few places for better caramelization, which requires more concentrated heat, so read recipes closely and be sure to use the pan I suggest.

Here are the pans I own and use most regularly:

- **Sheet pans:** I use standard 13 × 18-inch stainless-steel sheet pans for baking, which are what you will find in every professional kitchen. Look for them at restaurant supply stores—you'll be surprised; you can sometimes find them for just five bucks apiece, much cheaper than at fancy kitchen stores, which also stock them.

- **Cake pans:** Use round, plain stainless straight- and high-sided pans. Again, try to find professional-grade ones for the best results. Be careful when buying cake pans at the supermarket—they are sometimes slope-sided and not deep enough for most recipes. They are designed for boxed cake mixes and should be used only for that.

  - Two 8-inch and two 9-inch round cake pans
  - Two 8-inch square (brownie) pans
  - One 9 × 13-inch pan (preferably metal and straight-sided as opposed to glass with sloped sides)
  - One 9-inch and one 10-inch springform pan

- **Loaf pans:** two 4½ × 8½-inch standard pans

- **Muffin tins:** The recipes in this book use the following sizes:
  - Two standard 12-portion tins
  - Two 12-portion minimuffin tins
  - One 12-portion nonstick minimuffin tin
  - Two 6-portion jumbo-muffin tins

- **Tart pans:**
  - Two fluted 8-inch and two fluted 9-inch removable-bottom pans
  - Twelve fluted 4-inch removable-bottom pans

- **Miscellaneous bakeware:**
  - 9 × 13-inch glass or ceramic baking dish
  - 8 × 11-inch glass or ceramic baking dish
  - Two 9-inch pie plates
  - Eight 4-ounce ramekins
  - Eight 6-ounce ramekins
  - Eight 6-ounce crème brûlée dishes (1 inch deep)

CHAPTER 1

CUSTARDS *and* CRE

AMY DESSERTS

There wasn't a lot of sugar to be found in my house while I was growing up—Mom didn't allow it. But the one thing she did break down and buy, once a week, was ice cream. We each got our favorite flavor in a half-gallon box, and it was ours alone. Dad liked butter pecan, my younger brother chocolate. My choice was Breyers Mint Chocolate Chip. There were always at least three flavors of ice cream in the freezer at any given time, and if mine ran out before the weekly supermarket haul, I was dipping into everyone else's.

Out of all the sweets I craved, I was most eager to learn how to make ice cream as a young cook, and it was incredibly rewarding the very first time I made my own. It was just plain vanilla, but I made it with real vanilla beans and it tasted freakin' amazing. Once I understood the basics of how to make ice cream, I couldn't wait to push the envelope with different flavors.

CUSTARD

Custard, the mother sauce of ice cream, is a crucial technique and the foundation of so many desserts, so that's where we'll start. Once you have mastered making a basic custard, the flavors and types of creamy desserts you can make—like ice cream, pastry cream, dessert sauces, chilled and frozen desserts, flans, and crème brûlée—are endless.

The basic ingredients of custard are egg yolks, sugar, milk or cream, and sometimes starch, and by heating these ingredients together you make a thick, rich emulsification that has a multitude of uses. Depending on the ratio of yolks to sugar and milk, the mixture can be cooked to different consistencies. Milk-based egg custard, in French culinary terminology, is called *crème anglaise*, or "English cream," and is used primarily as a sauce. Here in the United States, it is sometimes referred to as *boiled custard* (even though it should not be boiled) and is used mostly for freezing in an ice cream maker. If you let an all-natural ice cream with no stabilizing agents melt, what's left in the container is crème anglaise, or milk custard.

Custard is made by whisking sugar and yolks together and then introducing hot milk or cream. The sugar helps prevent the yolks from setting too firmly the moment the hot liquid touches them. Egg yolks are also an emulsion of protein and water, so when they are heated with milk or cream, they help set the texture of the sauce, much like mustard and vinegar hold a salad dressing together when whisked with oil. Adding sugar to custard allows you to heat the yolk and milk mixture to a higher temperature, which helps make a stronger emulsion without scrambling the eggs and guarantees bacteria will be destroyed by the heat.

The thickness of a custard can be manipulated in several ways: by adding more yolks, increasing the cooking time, or adding starch, which creates pastry cream. The fun of this mother of all sweet recipes is that you can play with flavors and textures as much as you like. If using pastry cream as a filler for a cake or tart, you might make it "tighter" (thicker and stronger), so that it will not run or get gloppy, but if you're filling an éclair or layering it in a delicate dessert, you might fold some softly whipped cream into it to make it thinner and softer. Manipulating the textures of custards is half of the game, next to figuring out what flavor combinations really excite you.

PASTRY CREAM

Pastry cream is a very thick custard that has both egg yolks and starch, such as flour or cornstarch, in it. The process is essentially the same as for making crème anglaise, but the starch is whisked into the egg yolks with sugar before the eggs are tempered. The mixture is also then brought to a rolling boil and whisked for a minute or two to activate the starch-thickening agents properly. To cool, pastry creams should be strained onto a small sheet pan or into a cake pan, the surface covered directly with plastic wrap, cooled to room temperature, and then immediately refrigerated. Pastry cream can be used to fill cream puffs, cakes, or tarts or thinned with whipped cream as a dessert on its own.

OTHER TYPES *of* CUSTARD

Other custards, including flan, crème brûlée, crème caramel, and pots de crème, begin with the same technique of heating the dairy with a portion of the sugar and carefully tempering it into the egg yolks and sugar. But instead of being stirred and cooked on the stovetop, the custard is baked to finish the cooking process. This technique, as with basic cream sauces, also lends itself to countless flavoring additions—the tempered custard mixture can be made with milk or cream that is steeped with other flavors like spices, nuts, or herbs. Most of the recipes for these dessert types call for resting the custard overnight, with the whole spices or herbs still in them, for maximum flavor punch.

EGGLESS CUSTARD

Creamy desserts can also be made without eggs. Panna cotta may be the easiest one to make in this category. Thickened with gelatin, it does not need to be cooked on the stovetop. It's a great entry-level dessert—simple enough for a weeknight dinner but elegant enough for guests.

Puddings are cooked custard thickened with starch instead of egg yolks. I usually serve pudding as a freestanding dessert, while I use pastry cream, which has eggs, as a filling. Puddings are made by sifting sugar and cornstarch into cold milk, cream, or half-and-half and then heating the mixture gently until it begins to thicken. These "custards" are mixed completely with a whisk and are brought to a full boil for 1 to 2 minutes to hydrate, cook, and set the starch. Sometimes butter is added after cooking to make them smoother and richer. Puddings should also be pressed through a fine-mesh strainer with a rubber spatula to smooth them and catch any impurities and cooled in an ice bath before refrigerating. Once a pudding has cooled and set, if it is whisked or stirred it will not return to its original thickness.

CRUSTLESS TARTS

The fancy-schmancy French name for this dessert is *clafouti,* which is a custard tart without a crust, usually with fresh fruit like cherries in it. It is made of a custard base fortified with some flour that is poured over fruit; it sets up firm enough in the oven to slice once cool. I make clafouti when I need a quick dessert and don't have time to roll out and bake tart shells or piecrusts. They're a nice one-dish family-style dessert.

VANILLA CREAM SAUCE *(Crème Anglaise)*

This was the very first recipe I cooked for my friends back in high school, who called me "Johnny Crocker." I was enrolled in a vocational cooking program through my school and brought a pound cake home from class. I decided to make crème anglaise flavored with orange zest to pour over slices of it for my buddies while they watched. They gave me endless grief, but I knew then that I already had a love for the kitchen and wanted to make it my career. **MAKES ABOUT 2¼ CUPS**

---

6 tablespoons sugar (72 g)

2 cups whole milk (480 g)

1 vanilla bean, split and scraped

6 large egg yolks

⅛ teaspoon kosher salt

Prepare an ice bath in a large bowl.

In a medium saucepan, whisk 1½ tablespoons of the sugar with the milk and vanilla bean and seeds. Heat the milk over medium heat for about 3 minutes, only until it is steaming and beginning to bubble at the edges of the pan (called a *scald*). Do not let the milk come to a boil.

When the milk is hot, whisk the remaining 4½ tablespoons sugar, egg yolks, and the salt together in a bowl until very light and fluffy and the whisk begins to create a trail, or "ribbon," in the yolks. Do not do this before the milk is hot, as the yolk proteins can actually start cooking and coagulating if the sugar is introduced too soon.

While whisking, very slowly pour about half of the warm milk into the yolks and whisk this mixture until everything is dissolved and equally homogenous. This is known as *tempering*, or bringing the egg temperature up to that of the warm milk.

Off the heat, slowly whisk the egg yolk mixture into the remaining milk in the saucepan until combined. Switch to a spatula. Return the pan to medium-low heat and stir constantly until the mixture is hot to the touch and the custard holds a trail without running when you dip the spatula into it, which happens when the custard hovers around 180°F; this should take about 5 minutes. To test this, dip the spatula into the mixture and hold it horizontally over the pan. Pull your finger across the spatula; if the cream sauce does not drip or run into the trail you created, it is ready. If it runs easily, it needs to be cooked further. Do not boil the custard.

Turn off the heat. Pour the mixture through a fine-mesh strainer into a clean bowl and set the bowl into the ice bath; discard the vanilla bean. Stir occasionally until cool; cover and refrigerate immediately.

See technique photos, pages 28–29

VANILLA CREAM SAUCE: 1 *Scrape seeds from vanilla bean and heat seeds and bean with milk.* **2** *Whisk sugar, yolks, and salt until light, fluffy, and hold the whisk trail.* **3** *Whisk yolks while slowly adding hot liquid to temper eggs.* **4** *Return the entire mixture to saucepan and cook over medium-low heat.* **5** *Sauce is ready when custard holds the trail of your finger without running.* **6** *Strain and chill immediately in an ice bath.*

Vanilla Ice Cream

MAKES ABOUT 3 CUPS

Vanilla Cream Sauce (page 27) makes a great ice cream base as well. Simply increase the sugar to ½ cup (100 g). Make the custard and chill it overnight for the best flavor before churning in an ice cream maker.

Blackberry-Vanilla CREAM SAUCE

Blackberries are one of my favorite berries because they are not terribly sweet and are great in desserts. When perfectly ripe, they still have a nice tartness, but if you eat them out of season, they taste the worst of any berry. Avoid blackberries in the fall or winter; make this at the height of summer and you'll understand why. **MAKES ABOUT 2 CUPS**

2 cups fresh blackberries (245 g)

1 cup whole milk (240 g)

1 vanilla bean, split and scraped

4 large egg yolks

¼ cup sugar (50 g)

¼ teaspoon kosher salt (1 g)

Put the blackberries and milk into a blender and purée on low speed just until liquefied. Do not overblend—pulverizing the seeds can make the mixture bitter. Pour the mixture into a medium saucepan, add the vanilla bean and seeds, and heat the mixture over medium heat until very hot and steaming but not boiling.

Continue with the master recipe (page 27), using the egg yolks, sugar, and salt as directed.

➡ *Tips for* SUCCESSFUL CUSTARD:

- Start with room-temperature egg yolks. Cold yolks can seize more easily when warm liquid is introduced to them.

- Heat milk only until it is steaming; do not boil. If it is just warm when added to the yolks, the mixture will heat and cook together more evenly, creating a stronger emulsion and a smoother sauce with a more velvety mouthfeel.

- Do not whisk custards when cooking them. Whisking creates foam, which can weaken the emulsification and cause the custard to cook unevenly.

- You can tell when crème anglaise is almost cooked by the bubbles; when the color of the bubbles at the surface matches the color of the base, it is nearly cooked through.

- The best way to know when custard is ready is to check the temperature with a thermometer. If you cook the mixture to 180°F, the sauce will be properly emulsified, thick, and pasteurized.

- Always strain custards through a fine-mesh strainer into a clean bowl to remove any impurities or possible cooked egg bits or shell pieces.

- Cool custard down in an ice bath as quickly as possible to prevent bacteria growth. Once the custard is cool to the touch, it should be refrigerated immediately.

- Custards and cream sauces should be used within 3 days. In general, custard bases and sauces taste better the day after they are made. This is especially true if you have cooked or added spices or herbs in the mixture for flavored ice cream, crème brûlée, flan, or other custard-based desserts.

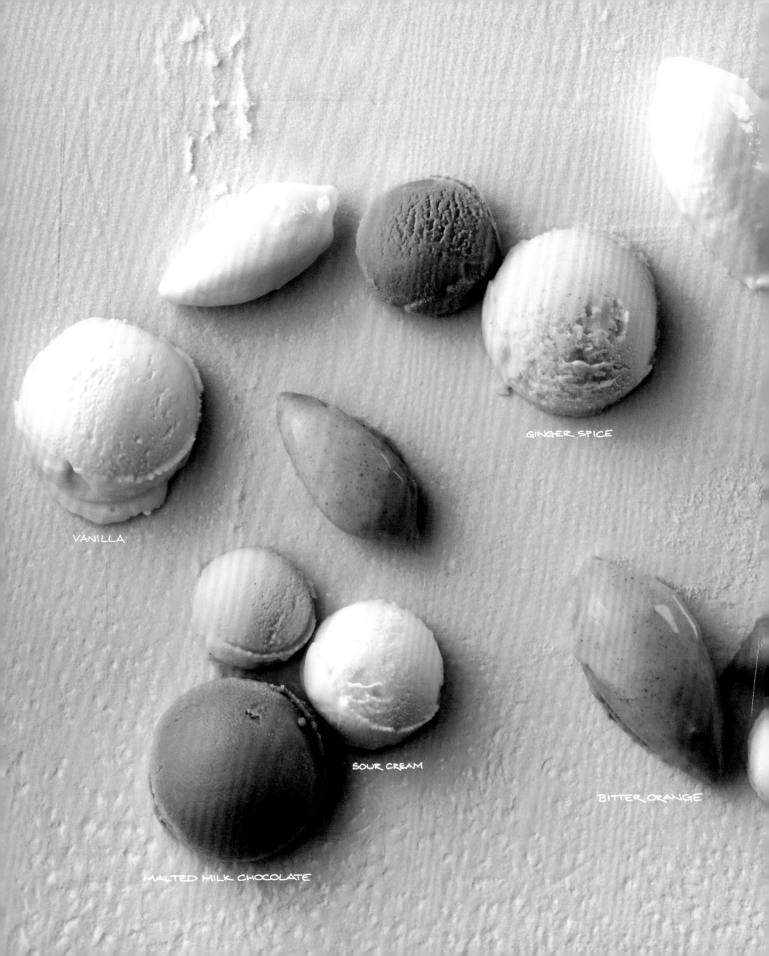

GINGER SPICE

VANILLA

SOUR CREAM

BITTER ORANGE

MALTED MILK CHOCOLATE

Ice Cream & Sorbet

Ginger Spice ICE CREAM

One of my favorite family pastimes while growing up was building gingerbread houses. We each chose our favorite candies and cookies and designed the style of house we wanted. I always started out with a mansion in mind but ended up with a shed because I would eat up all the gingerbread pieces before the walls even went up. I like ginger because of its intense flavor and love combining it with other spices associated with fall and winter, like cinnamon, nutmeg, and cloves. Tasting those warm spices in a frozen texture, which is a little unexpected, is really sexy to me. **MAKES ABOUT 1 QUART**

2 cups heavy cream (480 g)

1 cup whole milk (240 g)

¼ cup honey (80 g)

1 tablespoon molasses (25 g)

1 6-inch piece of fresh ginger, peeled

7 large egg yolks

⅓ cup (packed) dark brown sugar (75 g)

1 teaspoon ground cinnamon (2 g)

¼ teaspoon ground star anise

¼ teaspoon ground cardamom

¼ teaspoon freshly grated nutmeg

¼ teaspoon freshly ground black pepper

⅛ teaspoon ground cloves

½ teaspoon kosher salt (2 g)

In a medium saucepan, heat the cream, milk, honey, and molasses gently over medium heat, stirring, for about 4 minutes, until the honey is dissolved and the liquid is steaming. Using the large holes of a box grater, grate the ginger directly into the hot cream. Remove from the heat, cover, and let stand for 10 minutes.

Prepare an ice bath in a large bowl.

Meanwhile, whisk the egg yolks, brown sugar, cinnamon, star anise, cardamom, nutmeg, pepper, cloves, and salt together in a mixing bowl. Continue as directed in the recipe for Vanilla Cream Sauce (page 27).

Freeze the custard in an ice cream maker according to the manufacturer's instructions, transfer to an airtight container, and freeze for up to 2 weeks.

Malted Milk Chocolate ICE CREAM

My favorite movie snack is malted milk balls. The flavor of real malt, though, is much more sophisticated than that of the addictive candy. Barley malt syrup is an intense flavor that works well in desserts and, of course, milk shakes. **MAKES ABOUT 1½ QUARTS**

---

3 cups whole milk (720 g)

1 cup heavy cream (240 g)

12 large egg yolks

¾ cup sugar (150 g)

5 tablespoons barley malt syrup (113 g)

½ teaspoon kosher salt (2 g)

3½ ounces milk chocolate, chopped (100 g)

Prepare an ice bath in a large bowl.

In a large saucepan, heat the milk and cream over medium-low heat until hot and steamy but not boiling, about 4 minutes. In a medium bowl, whisk the egg yolks, sugar, malt syrup, and salt together until lightened. Put the chocolate into a clean bowl and set aside. Continue as directed in the recipe for Vanilla Cream Sauce (page 27), straining the hot custard through a fine-mesh strainer into the bowl of chocolate. Stir until the chocolate is completely melted and smooth. Set the bowl in the ice bath and let stand until completely cool.

Refrigerate the custard overnight or freeze it immediately in an ice cream maker according to the manufacturer's instructions, transfer it to an airtight container, and freeze for up to 2 weeks.

Bitter Orange ICE CREAM

One day when I was working at River Café in Brooklyn, I smelled an unfamiliar odor coming from the pastry kitchen. I opened the oven and saw charred pieces of orange wedges. Thinking something was wrong, I took them out of the oven and chucked them into the garbage. I recut fresh oranges and put them in the oven, saving the day. I was wrong—I got yelled at for the one-hour setback to the pastry chef's special that night. By roasting oranges and their peel at intense heat, you toast the essential oils, changing their flavor. It brings out the appealing natural bitter elements in an otherwise sweet fruit. This ice cream is amazing with almond, chocolate, vanilla, and other neutral-flavored desserts that could use something to jazz them up.

MAKES ABOUT 1 QUART

---

2 large navel oranges, unpeeled, washed, and quartered lengthwise

2 cups whole milk (480 g)

2 cups heavy cream (480 g)

¾ cup sugar (150 g)

6 large egg yolks

½ teaspoon kosher salt (2 g)

Preheat the oven to 450°F. Line a baking sheet with aluminum foil and set a rack on it.

Set the oranges, cut side down, on the rack and roast until the skins are blackened and crisp, about 45 minutes, flipping the oranges halfway through the cooking time. Remove from the oven and cool.

Prepare an ice bath in a large bowl.

Put the cooled orange pieces into a blender with 1 cup of the milk and purée until smooth, adding more milk if needed to liquefy it. Pour the mixture into a medium saucepan and add the remaining milk, the cream, and ¼ cup of the sugar. Heat the mixture over medium heat, stirring, for about 4 minutes, until very hot and steaming but not boiling.

Meanwhile, in a medium bowl, whisk the egg yolks, remaining ½ cup sugar, and salt together until lightened. Continue as directed in the recipe for Vanilla Cream Sauce (page 27). Strain the custard the next day instead of after cooking. Press on the mixture in the strainer with a rubber spatula to remove the orange pulp. Discard the solids and freeze the custard in an ice cream maker according to the manufacturer's instructions, transfer it to an airtight container, and freeze for up to 2 weeks.

Sour Cream SHERBET

This is not technically custard, since it does not contain eggs, but it's a simple way to make a cold, rich, creamy, and sophisticated treat without much work. If a cake, tart, or fruit dessert like cobbler is on the sweeter side, a scoop of a tart ice cream or sherbet like this one helps balance out the flavors.

MAKES ABOUT 1 QUART

2½ cups sour cream (650 g)

⅔ cup sugar (135 g)

½ cup water (120 g)

2 tablespoons honey (40 g)

½ teaspoon kosher salt (2 g)

Grated zest and juice of 1 lemon

Prepare an ice bath in a large bowl.

Put the sour cream into a mixing bowl. In a medium saucepan, whisk the sugar, water, honey, and salt together and bring to a boil over medium heat. While whisking, pour the hot liquid over the sour cream and whisk until combined and smooth. Add the lemon zest and juice and whisk well.

Set the bowl in the ice bath and let stand, stirring occasionally, until very cold. Refrigerate the sherbet base overnight.

Freeze the mixture in an ice cream maker according to the manufacturer's instructions, transfer it to an airtight container, and freeze for up to 2 weeks.

PEANUT BUTTER

COFFEE-CARDAMOM

VANILLA

CHOCOLATE

BANANA

VANILLA PASTRY CREAM

This is a staple recipe and major building block of the pastry kitchen. It can be flavored as you like and used in fillings for all types of pastries and cakes and as a base for soufflés. **MAKES ABOUT 2 CUPS, ENOUGH TO FILL ABOUT 1½ DOZEN 3-INCH ÉCLAIRS OR 3 DOZEN SMALL CREAM PUFFS**

2 cups whole milk (480 g)

2 vanilla beans, split and scraped

⅓ cup sugar (65 g)

3 tablespoons cornstarch (27 g)

¼ teaspoon kosher salt (1 g)

6 large egg yolks

3 tablespoons cold unsalted butter, diced (42 g)

In a medium saucepan, heat the milk and vanilla beans and seeds over medium heat, stirring occasionally, for about 4minutes, until the milk is very hot and steaming but not boiling.

Meanwhile, in a small bowl, whisk the sugar, cornstarch, and salt together.

In a medium bowl, whisk the egg yolks until well mixed and homogenous. Whisk the sugar mixture into the eggs until lightened and fluffy.

While whisking, pour about a third of the hot milk over the yolk mixture and whisk very well until combined. Add another third of the hot milk and whisk well. Whisk in the remaining milk and pour the mixture back into the saucepan. Return the pan to medium heat and whisk constantly until the

mixture begins to boil. Once it is bubbling, whisk the mixture vigorously at a boil for 2 full minutes.

Remove the pan from the heat and whisk in the butter, a little at a time. Pass the mixture through a fine-mesh strainer into a small baking sheet or cake pan, pressing the cream in the strainer to remove any cooked egg bits. Discard the vanilla bean or reserve for another use. Spread the pastry cream into a thin layer on the sheet; lay a sheet of plastic wrap directly on the surface. Cool the pastry cream to room temperature; refrigerate for at least 2 hours and preferably overnight.

When ready to use, transfer the pastry cream to a bowl and stir with a rubber spatula to loosen it. Pastry cream should be used within 3 days.

See technique photos, page 42

PASTRY CREAM: 1 *Whisk yolks with combined sugar, cornstarch, and salt.* **2** *Whisk until mixture is very light, fluffy, and holds a ribbon.* **3** *Very slowly whisk one-third of the hot milk into yolks to temper.* **4** *Whisk remaining milk into yolks and return entire mixture to pan.* **5** *Bring to a boil and whisk vigorously at a boil for 2 minutes.*

Chocolate Pastry Cream

Finely chop 4 ounces bittersweet chocolate (66 to 72% cacao). Prepare Vanilla Pastry Cream (page 41), whisking in the chocolate (1, 2) after the pastry cream has boiled and before whisking in the butter (3). Pour hot pastry cream into a fine-mesh strainer (4) into a shallow pan, pressing with a rubber spatula (5). Discard the vanilla bean. Cover with plastic wrap, let cool, and then refrigerate.

Banana PASTRY CREAM

I loved bananas as a kid and ate them almost every day. I especially enjoyed the combination of bananas and dark chocolate. My mother used to cut them in half, skewer them with Popsicle sticks, and freeze them. Then she would dip them in melted chocolate and roll them in Shredded Wheat crumbs from the bottom of the cereal box. To this day I love bananas and chocolate together and like to make this to fill a rich chocolate cake. **MAKES ABOUT 2 CUPS**

2 bananas, peeled

½ cup whole milk, plus more as needed (120 g)

⅓ cup sugar (65 g)

3 tablespoons cornstarch (27 g)

⅛ teaspoon kosher salt

4 large egg yolks

2 tablespoons (¼ stick) cold unsalted butter, diced (28 g)

2 tablespoons dark rum (optional) (30 g)

Put the bananas and ½ cup milk into a blender and purée until smooth. Pour the mixture into a glass measuring cup and add enough milk to make 2 cups. Transfer the mixture to a medium saucepan over medium heat and cook, stirring frequently, for about 3 minutes, until very hot and steaming but not boiling.

Continue with the recipe for Vanilla Pastry Cream (page 41), using the sugar, cornstarch, salt, egg yolks, and butter as directed and mixing in the rum, if using, once the butter has been incorporated.

Piña Colada PASTRY CREAM

Anyone who knows me knows I love a good cocktail. Growing up, our go-to vacation spot was the Caribbean, where Dad always ordered himself a piña colada and virgin versions for my brother and me. We used to try the old switcheroo at the table when he looked away. Sometimes we were successful, and his, of course, tasted even better. This pastry cream is great for cakes or meringues with coconut as a base flavor—no umbrella needed. **MAKES ABOUT 2 CUPS**

---

1 cup pineapple juice (240 g)

1 cup coconut milk (240 g)

½ cup sugar (100 g)

3 tablespoons cornstarch (24 g)

¼ teaspoon kosher salt (1 g)

4 large egg yolks

1 large egg

2 tablespoons (¼ stick) cold unsalted butter, diced (28 g)

2 tablespoons light rum (optional) (30 g)

In a medium saucepan, whisk the pineapple juice and coconut milk together. Heat over medium heat, stirring occasionally, for about 3 minutes, until the liquid is hot and steaming but not boiling. Continue with the recipe for Vanilla Pastry Cream (page 41), using the sugar, cornstarch, salt, egg yolks, whole egg, and butter as directed and boiling the mixture for 3 to 4 full minutes. (Due to the acid in the pineapple juice, the pastry cream should be boiled longer to make sure the starch sets.) Mix in the rum, if using, after the butter has been incorporated.

Coffee-Cardamom PASTRY CREAM

This probably seems like a weird flavor combination, but it's an awesome mash-up. I first tasted these flavors together when traveling in Turkey and tried Turkish coffee when I was about twenty-two years old. There they stir coffee and cardamom into boiling water and bring it to your café table, where you wait for the grounds to settle before you slurp the dark bitter coffee from the top. Try this smeared on some chocolate crepes with a little lemon zest—it's like eating the best espresso ever. **MAKES ABOUT 2½ CUPS**

---

2 cups whole milk, plus more as needed (480 g)

½ cup coffee beans, crushed (40 g)

15 cardamom pods, crushed

½ cup sugar (100 g)

3 tablespoons cornstarch (27 g)

¼ teaspoon kosher salt (1 g)

6 large egg yolks

3 tablespoons cold unsalted butter, diced (42 g)

In a medium saucepan, bring the milk, coffee beans, and cardamom pods to a simmer over medium heat. Immediately turn off the heat, cover, and let stand for at least 30 minutes. Pour the mixture through a fine-mesh strainer into a glass measuring cup and press on the solids in the strainer with a rubber spatula to remove all of the milk. Replace any milk that has evaporated with fresh milk so you have a total of 2 cups again. Return the infused milk to the saucepan. Continue with the recipe for Vanilla Pastry Cream (page 41), using the sugar, cornstarch, salt, egg yolks, and butter as directed.

CHOCOLATE

COFFEE-CARDAMOM

PEANUT BUTTER

Peanut Butter PASTRY CREAM

Like most kids, my favorite sandwich was a PB and J. But as I grew up and started cooking, my palate evolved and so did my appreciation for how different nuts taste. I still love peanut butter, but now I like it with less sugar—or paired with honey, which intensifies its roasted caramel notes. **MAKES ABOUT 2 CUPS**

2 cups whole milk (480 g)

½ cup natural unsweetened creamy peanut butter (125 g)

⅓ cup honey (110 g)

¼ teaspoon kosher salt (1 g)

2 tablespoons sugar (24 g)

2 tablespoons cornstarch (18 g)

4 large egg yolks

Put the milk and peanut butter into a blender and purée until smooth. Transfer the mixture to a medium saucepan and add the honey and salt. Put the pan over medium-low heat and warm slowly, stirring frequently, for about 3 minutes, until very hot and steaming but not boiling. Continue with the recipe for Vanilla Pastry Cream (page 41), using the sugar, cornstarch, and egg yolks as directed. The peanut butter pastry cream is rich enough that it doesn't need added butter.

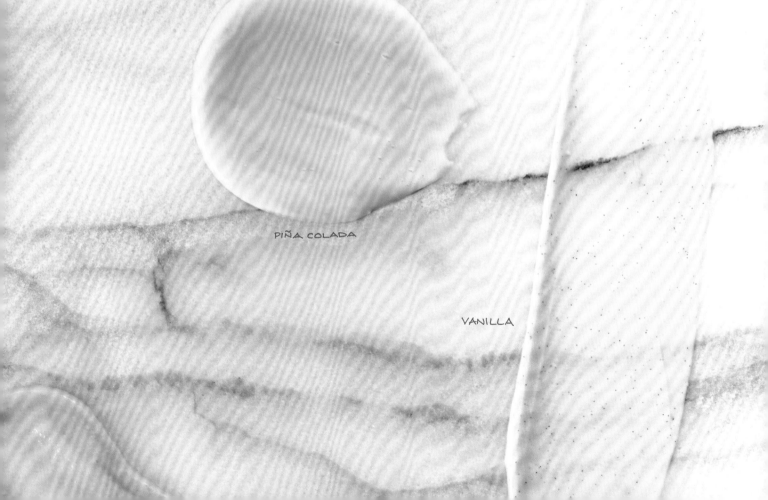

PIÑA COLADA

VANILLA

Tarragon-Vanilla PASTRY CREAM

I use herbs whenever I can to accentuate the best fruit and produce of a particular season. Tarragon is one of my favorites since it has a licorice-like quality that is awesome with berries and even melon. This pastry cream is great with fruit desserts and has a delicious, fresh flavor. MAKES ABOUT 1¼ CUPS

---

1 cup whole milk, plus more as needed (240 g)

1 cup chopped fresh tarragon leaves (30 g)

1 vanilla bean, split and scraped

3 tablespoons sugar (36 g)

1½ tablespoons cornstarch (12 g)

¼ teaspoon kosher salt (1 g)

3 large egg yolks

2 tablespoons (¼ stick) cold unsalted butter, diced (28 g)

In a small saucepan, heat the milk, tarragon, and vanilla bean and seeds over medium heat, stirring occasionally, for about 3 minutes, until the milk is very hot and steaming but not boiling. Remove from the heat, cover, and let stand until room temperature.

Remove the vanilla bean and transfer the mixture to a blender. Purée until very smooth. Set a very-fine-mesh strainer over a liquid measuring cup and strain the mixture into it, pressing on the solids with a rubber spatula to extract as much liquid as possible. Discard the solids. Add enough fresh milk to bring the quantity back to 1 cup. Return the milk to the saucepan over medium heat and cook until very hot and steaming but not boiling, about 3 minutes. Continue with the recipe for Vanilla Pastry Cream (page 41), using the sugar, cornstarch, salt, egg yolks, and butter as directed.

Blackberry PASTRY CREAM

This is an unusual flavor for pastry cream, and it does take quite a lot of blackberries to make. It is well worth the expense, though, and is awesome to fill cream puffs, spread into tart shells, or use as a base for a soufflé. Don't waste the money on out-of-season berries; since there is no milk in this pastry cream, the berry flavor is intensified, so if you are going to spend the money to make this, do it when they are at their peak. **MAKES ABOUT 2 CUPS**

1½ pounds fresh ripe blackberries (750 g)

Juice of 1 lime

7 tablespoons sugar (84 g)

4 tablespoons cornstarch (36 g)

1 large egg

2 tablespoons (¼ stick) cold unsalted butter, diced (28 g)

Put the blackberries into a blender and purée until liquefied; do not overblend (the seeds can make the juice bitter if pulverized). Pour through a fine-mesh strainer set over a liquid measuring cup; press on the solids with a rubber spatula to extract as much liquid as possible. Discard the solids. Measure 2 cups of purée; reserve the remainder for another use.

In a medium saucepan, heat the blackberry purée, lime juice, and 3½ tablespoons (42 g) of the sugar over medium heat for about 3 minutes, until warm and steaming but not boiling. Continue with the recipe for Vanilla Pastry Cream (page 41), using the remaining 3½ tablespoons sugar, cornstarch, egg, and butter. The blackberry purée takes the place of the milk.

Crème Brûlées

VANILLA CRÈME BRÛLÉE

To this day, this dessert is the anchor of most dessert menus. It also happens to be a favorite of Fran, my dad's wife, my second mom. When I make it for her, I put an extra layer of caramelized sugar on it. She can't get enough of that crunchy shell with the rich creamy custard beneath it. This is one spot not to skimp on using real vanilla bean. **SERVES 4**

---

2 cups half-and-half (480 g)

1 vanilla bean, split and scraped

⅓ cup plus 1 tablespoon granulated sugar (77 g)

7 large egg yolks

½ teaspoon kosher salt (2 g)

Raw sugar (turbinado), as needed

Prepare an ice bath in a large bowl.

Put the half-and-half, vanilla bean and seeds, and 3 tablespoons of the granulated sugar into a saucepan and bring to a simmer over medium heat.

Meanwhile, in a medium bowl, whisk the egg yolks, remaining granulated sugar, and salt together. While whisking, slowly add about a third of the hot liquid to the eggs and whisk for at least 30 seconds to combine. Slowly whisk the remaining hot cream into the eggs until combined. Set the bowl in the ice bath and let stand, stirring occasionally, until cold. Cover the bowl with plastic wrap and refrigerate overnight.

Preheat the oven to 300°F. Strain the custard base through a fine-mesh strainer, discard the vanilla bean, and let it come to room temperature.

Put four 6-ounce, 1-inch-deep ramekins into a large baking dish and divide the custard evenly among the ramekins. Fill the baking dish with hot water until it comes halfway up the sides of the ramekins. Bake in the center of the oven for 35 to 40 minutes, until the custards are just set but still slightly jiggly in the center. Remove the baking dish from the oven and let the custards cool completely in the dish in the water.

Remove the custards from the water bath and refrigerate for at least 4 hours.

To serve, sprinkle about 1 tablespoon raw sugar onto the top of a custard (1, 2), pick up the dish, and rotate it to cover the surface evenly with sugar and shake out the excess. Using a blowtorch, slowly run the flame, moving it constantly, over the surface of the sugar until it liquefies completely and begins to caramelize (3). Sprinkle another tablespoon of sugar over the top of the brûlée (4) and shake out the excess. Torch the surface again until the sugar melts and continue moving the flame over the surface until it turns an even deep caramel color. Let stand for a few minutes to allow the sugar to harden.

Repeat with the remaining custards and serve immediately.

Note: *To protect your work surface or sheet pans from the torch flame, set a cooling rack in a sheet pan and pour a little water into the pan. Set the custards on top of the rack to caramelize the sugar without scorching your countertops.*

Strawberry-Tomato CRÈME BRÛLÉE

There is a fine line between a tomato being a fruit or vegetable. A ripe, in-season tomato is quite sweet, and plays well with sweet berries; their flavors echo each other. I especially love roasting small, ripe cherry tomatoes with a little honey and then mixing them with fresh berries for a nice summer fruit salad. Here, the two "fruits" make a bold compote in the bottom of the crème brûlée, and you get all of the flavors in every single bite. **SERVES 4**

Unbaked Vanilla Crème Brûlée custard
   (page 52)

2 pints ripe fresh strawberries, hulled (450 g)

2 medium vine-ripened tomatoes (about
   6 ounces each) (340 g)

Raw sugar (turbinado), as needed

Prepare the custard base and chill overnight.

Preheat the oven to 250°F. Line a baking sheet with parchment paper or a silicone baking mat.

Quarter the strawberries and cut each tomato into 8 wedges and remove the seeds. Scatter the fruit evenly over the lined baking sheet and roast in the oven for 1 hour and 15 minutes. The fruit will be dehydrated but still soft.

Put the strawberry and tomato pieces into a food processor and purée until smooth. Use immediately or refrigerate the fruit paste until ready to bake the custards.

When ready to bake, preheat the oven to 300°F.

Divide the strawberry-tomato paste among four 6-ounce, 1-inch-deep ramekins and spread it very evenly over the surface of the bottom of each ramekin. Gently pour the custard base evenly into each ramekin and transfer them to a large baking dish. Fill the baking dish with hot water until it comes halfway up the sides of the ramekins.

Continue with the recipe for Vanilla Crème Brûlée (page 52), baking and then caramelizing the sugar on top as directed.

Chai CRÈME BRÛLÉE

I first tasted chai with my mom in a strip mall coffee house in upstate New York. She ordered coffee, and while she wouldn't let me have that, she let me order chai, which seemed much more grown up than regular tea. Later when I traveled through Asia and tasted real high-quality chai, I realized what a great complex flavor it can be for dessert, especially when you use whole spices instead of premixed tea bags. **SERVES 6**

2½ cups half-and-half (600 g)

1 vanilla bean, split and scraped

4 3-inch cinnamon sticks

1 heaping tablespoon crushed whole star anise pieces

12 cardamom pods, smashed

8 whole cloves

30 whole black peppercorns

7 large egg yolks

½ cup (packed) light brown sugar (116 g)

1 tablespoon molasses (25 g)

½ teaspoon kosher salt (2 g)

Raw sugar (turbinado), as needed

Prepare an ice bath in a large bowl.

In a medium saucepan, bring the half-and-half, vanilla bean and seeds, cinnamon sticks, star anise, cardamom pods and seeds, cloves, and peppercorns to a simmer over medium heat.

Meanwhile, whisk the egg yolks, brown sugar, molasses, and salt together in a medium bowl. While whisking, slowly add about a third of the hot liquid to the eggs and whisk for at least 30 seconds to combine. Slowly whisk the remaining hot cream, spices and all, into the eggs until combined. Set the bowl in the ice bath and let stand, stirring occasionally, until cold. Cover the bowl with plastic wrap and refrigerate overnight (with the whole spices still in it).

Continue with the recipe for Vanilla Crème Brûlée (page 52), straining the spices from the custard and then dividing it among six 6-ounce, 1-inch-deep ramekins and caramelizing the raw sugar on top as directed.

Toasted Almond–Cinnamon PANNA COTTA

This dessert is based on the flavor of horchata, the Mexican rice and cinnamon drink. I didn't taste it until I was in college, when a friend ordered it at a Mexican restaurant; I instantly fell in love with it. This is a play on those flavors, without using rice. It has a warm, toasty flavor, but the dessert is as light and soft as air. Don't discard the deeply toasted almonds after straining them; they can be dried in a warm oven and sprinkled over your morning oatmeal. **SERVES 6**

1 cup slivered almonds (130 g)

3½ cups whole milk, plus more as needed (840 g)

4 large strips orange zest (about 1 × 3 inches)

3 3-inch cinnamon sticks

3 tablespoons sugar (36 g)

¼ teaspoon kosher salt (1 g)

2 teaspoons powdered gelatin (6 g)

Grated orange zest, for garnish

¼ cup Crystallized Nuts, using almonds (page 145), chopped, for garnish (optional)

TOASTED ALMOND-CINNAMON

Preheat the oven to 375°F.

Spread the slivered almonds on a baking sheet and toast in the oven, stirring often, for about 15 minutes, until deep golden brown. They will seem darker than normal; if you snap an almond in half, it should be golden brown all the way through.

Meanwhile, in a medium saucepan, heat the milk, strips of orange zest, cinnamon sticks, sugar, and salt over medium heat for about 5 minutes, until the sugar is dissolved and the milk is just beginning to boil. Pour the warm toasted nuts into the milk, stir, cover, and remove from the heat. Let stand for at least 2 hours.

Pour the infused milk through a fine-mesh strainer set over a large measuring cup; press on the solids with a rubber spatula to remove as much liquid as possible. Add more milk to bring the liquid level to 3 cups.

Pour about ½ cup of the milk into a small saucepan and sprinkle the gelatin evenly over the top; let stand for 10 minutes. Put the pan over medium heat and whisk until the gelatin is completely dissolved. Whisk the gelatin mixture into the rest of the infused milk.

Divide the mixture among six 4-ounce straight-sided ramekins or glass bowls set on a small sheet pan. Pop any bubbles that rise to the surface with a knife. Refrigerate the panna cotta until completely set and cold, at least 4 hours and preferably overnight.

To unmold, fill a small bowl with hot water. Dip each ramekin in the water up to the rim for 10 seconds, until the panna cotta releases itself from the sides. Wipe the surface of the ramekin dry with a towel before inverting the panna cotta onto a serving plate. Garnish with grated orange zest and chopped crystallized almonds, if using, and serve immediately.

ROASTED WHITE CHOCOLATE

Roasted White Chocolate PANNA COTTA

Roasting white chocolate was a popular technique a few years back in a lot of pastry kitchens. I don't use white chocolate a lot because it is so sweet, but roasting it first caramelizes the sugar and toasts the milk solids to give it a nutty flavor, like brown butter, that balances its high sugar content. **SERVES 6**

---

8 ounces white chocolate, chopped (227 g)

2 cups whole milk (480 g)

1½ teaspoons powdered gelatin (5 g)

¾ teaspoon kosher salt (3 g)

1 cup cold heavy cream (240 g)

Preheat the oven to 250°F.

Put the chocolate into an 8 × 11-inch glass baking dish and transfer to the oven. Stir every 10 minutes with a rubber spatula until it turns a nutty brown color, about 1 hour. (The chocolate may be lumpy and not completely smooth; that's fine.) Remove the chocolate from the oven and spread it out on a sheet of parchment paper. Cool to room temperature and then transfer to a heatproof bowl.

Pour the milk into a wide saucepan and sprinkle the gelatin evenly over the surface. Let stand for 10 minutes. Heat the milk over medium heat, whisking, until it just begins to boil. Add the salt and whisk until the gelatin is completely dissolved.

Pour about a third of the hot milk over the chocolate and stir slowly until the chocolate is completely melted. Add the remaining milk and whisk until completely combined and smooth. Add the cream and whisk until combined; let stand until room temperature.

Divide the mixture among six 6-ounce glass bowls or ramekins set on a small sheet pan. Pop any bubbles that come to the surface with the tip of a knife.

Refrigerate the panna cotta until completely set and cold, at least 2 hours and preferably overnight.

To unmold, fill a small bowl with hot water. Dip the bottom of each bowl in the water for 10 seconds. Wipe the surface of the bowl dry before inverting onto a serving plate.

Note: *Roasted white chocolate curls make a great garnish for this and other desserts. Simply roast some chopped white chocolate as directed, pour it into a small plastic container, and let it cool until hardened. Pop the brick out of the container and use a vegetable peeler to peel curls of chocolate from the outside edge and use to garnish tarts, puddings, or mousse.*

Chocolate PUDDING

I'm a pudding person—especially chocolate. It is luxurious and creamy, and I love the richness and complexity of it. It can be used to fill cakes, tarts, and pastries and should have a bold flavor on its own. For my rich, decadent pudding, I use a dark, natural cocoa powder, not the standard inexpensive baking cocoa. That, paired with bittersweet chocolate, makes this old-fashioned recipe really amazing. **MAKES ABOUT 1 QUART; SERVES 6**

---

1 quart half-and-half (960 g)

½ cup sugar (100 g)

¼ cup plus 1 teaspoon cornstarch (39 g)

6 tablespoons dark cocoa powder (36 g)

½ teaspoon kosher salt (2 g)

3 ounces bittersweet chocolate (68% cacao), chopped (85 g)

1 tablespoon vanilla extract (15 g)

Prepare an ice bath in a large bowl.

Pour the half-and-half into a medium saucepan. Sift the sugar, cornstarch, cocoa, and salt directly into the liquid and whisk to combine. Cook over medium heat, whisking constantly, for about 5 minutes, until very hot, steaming, and beginning to thicken.

Add the chocolate and vanilla and cook, whisking, until the chocolate is melted. Switch to a rubber spatula and stir constantly until the mixture begins to boil; continue stirring while it boils for 2 full minutes.

Pour the mixture through a fine-mesh strainer into a bowl, pressing on the pudding with a rubber spatula to remove any solids. Put plastic wrap directly on the surface and set the bowl in the ice bath until the pudding is completely cool. Refrigerate for at least 2 hours before serving.

To serve, stir the pudding gently with a wooden spoon to loosen it.

MANGO LASSI

Puddings

Red Berry PUDDING

This combination, with the addition of lime juice, which helps accentuate the tartness of the fruit, is awesome. It's like eating lemon curd that tastes like strawberries and raspberries.

MAKES ABOUT 2 CUPS; SERVES 3 TO 4

6 ounces raspberries (170 g)

1 pint strawberries (8 ounces), hulled and halved (227 g)

½ cup heavy cream (120 g)

½ cup sugar (100 g)

3 tablespoons cornstarch (27 g)

⅛ teaspoon kosher salt

Juice of 1 lime

2 tablespoons (¼ stick) unsalted butter, diced (28 g)

Prepare an ice bath in a large bowl.

Put the berries in a blender and purée for 30 seconds, until liquefied; do not overblend, as it will pulverize the seeds and make the pudding bitter. Pour the mixture through a fine-mesh strainer set over a saucepan, pressing on the solids with a rubber spatula to remove as much liquid as possible. Discard the solids. Whisk the cream into the fruit purée.

In a small bowl, whisk the sugar, cornstarch, and salt together; sift the mixture into the berry purée in the pan and whisk well to combine.

Put the pan over medium heat and cook, whisking constantly, for about 5 minutes, until very hot and the mixture begins to boil. Once it begins to boil, cook, whisking constantly, for 2 full minutes. Remove from the heat, whisk in the lime juice, and then whisk in the butter, a few pieces at a time, until completely melted and combined.

Pour the mixture through a fine-mesh strainer into a bowl, pressing with a rubber spatula to remove any solids; put plastic wrap directly on the surface of the pudding. Chill the mixture in the ice bath until cool. Refrigerate for at least 2 hours before serving.

To serve, stir the pudding gently with a wooden spoon to loosen it.

Mango Lassi PUDDING

As a young, curious cook, on my single day off each week, I would try to eat in unfamiliar restaurants. The first time I had a meal in an Indian restaurant, the waiter suggested trying a lassi. I loved the texture and the way the flavors of sweet, tart yogurt and mango melded together, yet you could still taste each ingredient. It was rich and bold, but also crisp, soothing, and refreshing. I knew I had to find a way to turn the combination into a dessert. This pudding is great paired with richer items like carrot cake, charred pineapple, or heavily spiced desserts. Or serve it on its own with some toasted pistachios (see page 142) sprinkled over the top.

MAKES ABOUT 3 CUPS; SERVES 5 TO 6

2 large mangos, peeled and cut into chunks

1 banana, peeled and sliced

Juice of 2 large limes

1 tablespoon honey (20 g)

1¼ cups nonfat Greek yogurt (312 g)

½ cup sugar (100 g)

3 tablespoons cornstarch (27 g)

½ teaspoon ground cinnamon (1 g)

⅛ teaspoon kosher salt

3 tablespoons unsalted butter, diced (42 g)

¼ teaspoon rose water (optional)

Prepare an ice bath in a large bowl.

Put the mangos, banana, lime juice, and honey into a blender and purée until liquefied.

Pour the mixture through a fine-mesh strainer into a measuring cup, pressing on the solids with a rubber spatula to remove as much liquid as possible. Measure 1½ cups of fruit purée (reserve the rest for another use) and pour it into a medium saucepan.

Whisk the yogurt into the fruit purée. In a small bowl, whisk together the sugar, cornstarch, cinnamon, and salt; sift the mixture into the fruit purée in the pan and whisk well to combine.

Put the pan over medium heat and cook, whisking constantly, for about 5 minutes, until very hot and the mixture begins to boil. Once it begins to boil, cook, whisking constantly, for 2 full minutes. Remove from the heat and whisk in the butter and rose water, if using, until smooth.

Pour the mixture through a fine-mesh strainer into a bowl, pressing with a rubber spatula to remove any solids; put plastic wrap directly on the surface of the pudding. Chill the mixture in the ice bath until completely cool. Refrigerate for at least 2 hours before serving.

To serve, stir the pudding gently with a wooden spoon to lighten it.

Apricot

Fresh apricots, of all the stone fruits, have the shortest season of optimal flavor. And, even at their ripest, they're still a little tart. That's why I love them. They also bake well; they have a lower water content than peaches or nectarines, and they maintain their shape in the oven. Because of their acidity, apricots are the perfect match for a sweet custard, making this a very satisfying one-dish dessert. Apricots pair well with almond and marzipan or other nut flavors.

APRICOT CUSTARD TART

MAKES ONE 10-INCH TART; SERVES 10 TO 12

Softened butter, for greasing the pan

Confectioners' sugar, for dusting

14 fresh apricots, halved and pitted

¾ cup granulated sugar (150 g)

2 large eggs

6 tablespoons all-purpose flour (48 g)

½ cup heavy cream (120 g)

½ cup whole milk (120 g)

1 cup almond flour (95 g)

½ cup shelled pistachios, roughly chopped (70 g)

Preheat the oven to 350°F. Butter a 10-inch spring-form pan and dust it with confectioners' sugar.

Put the apricots in a bowl and sprinkle ¼ cup of the granulated sugar over them (1). Toss lightly (2) and let stand for 10 minutes.

In a medium bowl, whisk the eggs and remaining ½ cup granulated sugar until light and fluffy. One by one, whisk in the all-purpose flour, cream, milk, and almond flour, beating well after each addition. Arrange the apricots in the prepared pan, cut side down, slightly leaning and overlapping each other, in 2 concentric circles (3). Gently push the outer circle of apricot halves into the center so there is at least ½ inch of space between the outer edge of apricots and the pan. Pour the custard mixture into the spaces in the pan, taking care not to pour it directly on the fruit (4).

Bake in the center of the oven for 20 minutes. Carefully remove the pan, sprinkle the pistachios evenly over the top (5), and return the tart to the oven. Continue baking for about 40 minutes more, until light golden. Cool the tart completely in the pan before running a thin spatula around the edge to release it and remove the outer ring.

Dust with confectioners' sugar before cutting and serving at room temperature.

CHAPTER 2

EGGS *and* MERINGUE

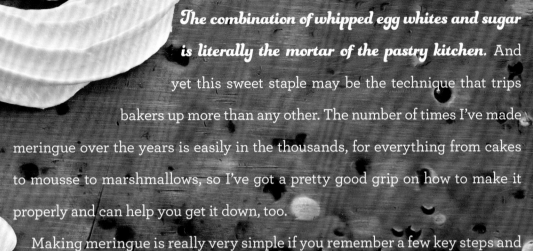

The combination of whipped egg whites and sugar is literally the mortar of the pastry kitchen. And yet this sweet staple may be the technique that trips bakers up more than any other. The number of times I've made meringue over the years is easily in the thousands, for everything from cakes to mousse to marshmallows, so I've got a pretty good grip on how to make it properly and can help you get it down, too.

Making meringue is really very simple if you remember a few key steps and don't try to rush it. You know what can happen if you slap up a brick wall without properly spreading and packing the mortar between the bricks—disaster! The same will happen with desserts that are built with weak meringue: Cakes will fall, mousse will break, and marshmallows will be gooey and not set.

There are three basic types of meringue: French, Swiss, and Italian. Each is used in different ways, from dried in a low oven to make simple crunchy cookies to whipped into a silky, glossy icing for a cake or lemon-curd-filled pie.

- Start with the freshest eggs possible. Protein strands in fresh eggs are tighter and, when pulled apart and whipped into meringue, create a stronger structure.

- It is easier to separate eggs when they are cold. Separate eggs, one at a time, into a small bowl in case any yolk or shell gets into the whites. If you see any trace of yolk in the white, dump that one white and start over with a fresh egg.

- Keep the whites chilled: When you whip cold whites, the proteins are tougher and break down more slowly, which, once acid and sugar are introduced, results in stronger meringue.

- Completely clean equipment is essential—any trace of fat or soap in a mixing bowl or on a whisk can prevent whites from gaining ultimate volume.

- Slow and steady is better. Always start whipping whites at low speeds, increasing the speed as the volume creeps up. This helps make a more stable meringue.

- Remember, meringue cannot be "fixed" if you whip it too long and the egg whites get dry and grainy. At this point, the water is seeping out of the egg white foam and the whites will separate. This meringue is unusable, and you must start over. Keep a close eye on the mixer once you start whipping egg whites.

A sturdy meringue is also the scaffolding for many kinds of cakes and chilled desserts, adding structure and lightness at the same time. Once you understand the differences among the types and know what proper meringue should feel and look like, you'll *immediately* be a better baker. There's nothing to be afraid of. It's just egg whites and sugar.

When you whip egg whites, you are breaking them down and then rebuilding them, putting them to work for you. Egg whites are made of bundles of protein and water, and when you whisk them, you unfold the protein strands. The water in the whites and the bubbles of air introduced by whipping inch their way in between the strands, creating foam. The more you whip, the more air squeezes in and the more volume you create. Egg whites, when whipped properly, can expand to nearly *eight times* their original size. Whipped whites alone, though, will not hold. The water begins to seep out of the bubbles you created, and they will separate. That's where sugar and cream of tartar come in.

Introducing sugar to whipped egg whites helps strengthen the new protein bubbles. Sugar in meringue also absorbs water when baked, solidifying and holding the structure in place. If you whip heavy cream past the point of creamy peaks, it will eventually solidify into butter—leaving the liquid (buttermilk) behind. Egg whites do the same thing; if you overwhip them, you'll be left with dry, grainy whites sitting on top of a pool of water. Adding a touch of acid to the whites when you start whipping them helps keep the protein from rebonding and destroying your meringue. I use cream of tartar, an acidic compound that is a by-product of winemaking, but a few drops of lemon juice or vinegar also work. Acid helps strengthen the proteins, creating more volume and stability when the meringue is baked.

When a recipe calls for meringue, it should be used immediately, so be sure to have any other components of the recipe ready, whether it's softened butter for buttercream, batter for a sponge cake, or the base of a mousse. Have them standing by so you can keep moving with the recipe once the meringue is finished and you are ready to assemble.

French MERINGUE

This is the quickest, lightest type of meringue to make and is used for everything from mousses to cakes and soufflés. It also bakes into the airiest, crunchiest meringue on its own, so it is great for cookies or molding into shapes with the addition of confectioners' sugar. Be sure to have your recipe components ready for the meringue, as this type is the least stable and must always be used immediately.

Making FRENCH MERINGUE:

- Following the recipe ingredient amounts, put the whites, cream of tartar, and one third of the granulated sugar in the bowl of a standing mixer with the whisk and turn the mixer on to medium. Whip until the whites are foamy and then increase the speed slightly. Continue whipping for 2 to 3 minutes, until the whites have tripled in volume and are fluffy but still soft. The whites should just be starting to hold the trail of the whisk along the sides.

- With the motor running, very slowly sprinkle another third of the sugar onto the whites between the bowl and the edge of the whisk. Increase the mixer speed slightly and whip until the whites start to turn glossy but are still soft, another 1 to 2 minutes. Slowly sprinkle in the remaining sugar and increase the speed to medium-high. Whip for 2 to 3 minutes longer, until firm and glossy but not dry.

- The meringue is now ready to fold into mousse, cake batter, or soufflé base, or to have confectioners' sugar added to make crunchy, light-as-air cookies.

Swiss MERINGUE

Do you remember your grandmother's seven-minute icing? That's exactly what Swiss meringue is: The egg whites and sugar are actually cooked over a water bath before being whipped. It is used to decorate cakes, but I mainly use it to fold into batters and mousses that need more structure than what French meringue provides. It is stronger and denser than French meringue, holds up longer, and doesn't dissolve as easily. You can also use Swiss meringue to make decorations, especially if you need to make a lot of them. Swiss meringue holds well in a piping bag if you are making cookies, small shapes, or other items. When I need to make hundreds of meringue mushrooms for Yule logs at Christmas, I always use Swiss meringue.

MASTER TECHNIQUE

Making SWISS MERINGUE:

- Following the recipe ingredient amounts, whisk the sugar and egg whites together in a standing mixer bowl until the sugar is well incorporated and the whites have thickened (1). Fill a saucepan one-third full of water and bring to a simmer over medium-low heat (2).

- Set the mixer bowl over the simmering water, making sure the water doesn't touch the bottom of the bowl, and whisk the whites constantly (3, 4) until the sugar is completely dissolved and the mixture is hot to the touch (about 160°F) (5).

- Transfer the bowl to the standing mixer with the whisk attachment and whip on high speed for 5 minutes. The meringue should be stiff and glossy. Continue whipping for 3 to 5 minutes longer, until the mixture is cool to the touch. If the level of the meringue begins to recede in the bowl, stop whipping immediately.

- The meringue is now ready to fold into a mousse, cake batter, or soufflé base or can be transferred to a piping bag with a tip to pipe shapes, bowls, or baskets and dried in the oven.

- The meringue can also be used to ice cooled baked cakes, but work fast while you spread it; when in contact with air, it will begin to set quickly and will tear if it gets too dry while you are icing the cake.

Italian MERINGUE

This is the trickiest type of meringue to make, but it is also the most stable once finished. Rather than whipping the sugar and whites together, you cook the sugar separately in a saucepan to the firm-ball stage while the whites are whipping. The hot sugar is poured directly into the whipping whites, and then the mixture is whipped into a fluffy meringue. This is the meringue I use for topping tarts or coating ice cream molds (think baked Alaska) when I want to toast the meringue with a blowtorch or in the oven under a broiler. If you are making lemon meringue pie, this is the recipe you want. It is also used for making buttercream and icing cakes or for mixing into some mousse, cake, and soufflé recipes.

The trick to making perfect Italian meringue is in the timing—you want the whites to be whipped with enough volume and be fluffy and shiny at the same time that the sugar is cooked to the correct temperature. If you overwhip the whites before you add the sugar, you'll end up with grainy meringue or worse. Just be sure to use a reliable thermometer to monitor the cooking sugar and keep your eyes on the egg whites so they don't whip too quickly.

MASTER TECHNIQUE

Making ITALIAN MERINGUE:

- Following the recipe ingredient amounts, put the whites, cream of tartar, and a couple of tablespoons of the sugar into the bowl of a standing mixer with the whisk attachment and turn it on to low.

- Put the remaining sugar into a small saucepan and add the water the recipe calls for. Use a clean finger to stir the sugar until evenly moistened and sandy (1). Wet your finger and wipe down the sides of the pan, rinsing down any sugar crystals stuck to the pan, and put the pan over medium heat. When the sugar is melted and begins to bubble, with a very clean pastry brush, brush down the sides of the pan with cool water in case any sugar crystals remain (2).

- When the sugar reaches a rolling boil, increase the mixer speed to medium.

- Continue cooking the sugar, brushing the pan sides if any crystals form, until it reaches 250°F (firm-ball stage) (3). You can easily test this without a thermometer by dropping a little of the cooked sugar into a glass of ice water. Use your fingers to squeeze the mass together; if it holds together in a firm, tight ball and doesn't come apart, the sugar is ready.

- Increase the mixer speed to medium-high. The whites should be fluffy and shiny but still soft. With the motor running, carefully pour in the hot sugar syrup in a slow, steady stream—pour it directly onto the whites between the mixer bowl edge and outer reach of the whisk so it doesn't splatter or create lumps (4). Increase the mixer speed to high and whip the meringue for 6 to 8 minutes, until cool to the touch (5). If the meringue level begins to recede in the mixing bowl, immediately stop whipping.

- The meringue is now ready to use (6).

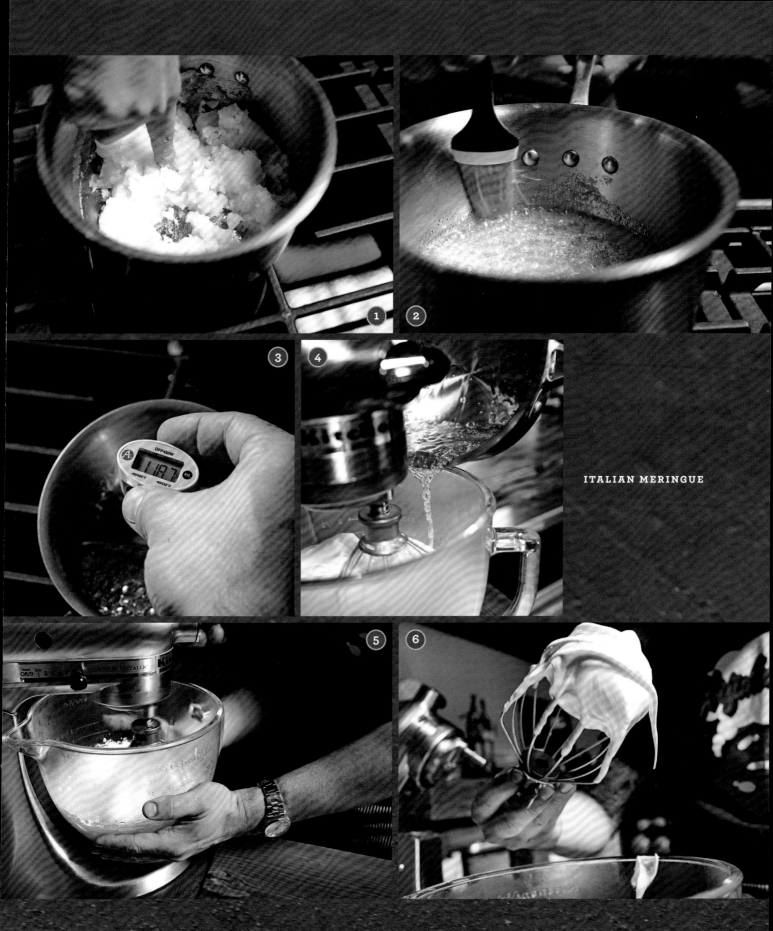

ITALIAN MERINGUE

SABAYON

Sabayon, or zabaglione in Italian, is simply egg yolks and sugar whipped over a simmering pot of water until frothy and foamy. Making sabayon is a great way to witness how agitating eggs by whisking them constantly (by hand this time) and adding sugar creates a silky, stable foam. Most people think only egg whites can give great volume, but yolks can, too.

Sabayon can be flavored many ways, with different liqueurs, citrus zest, extracts, or even chocolate. The Italians flavor it with Marsala and serve it over berries or fold it into mascarpone cheese for tiramisù. The only tricky part to making sabayon is sticking with it—it can take a while to reach the fluffy, thick foam that reminds me of a blanket of fresh snow on the roof of a house.

SEMIFREDDO

Semifreddo, translated from Italian as "semifrozen," is an absolute favorite of mine. I love it because it is not as dense as ice cream but has an even creamier texture due to the whole eggs in it, making it terrific alone or as a component of a plated dessert. To make semifreddo, you cook whole eggs, yolks, and sugar over a pot of simmering water, and then whip it until cool before folding in whipped cream and flavorings. It can be frozen into any shape, from loaves that are sliced to individual portions in cups or even Popsicle molds.

MOUSSE

The word *mousse* probably means something different to everyone, but generally it's a creamy, fluffy dessert served cold or frozen. The actual translation of this French word is "foam," which to me means one thing: bubbles. Bubbles are what make mousse so light and airy, and how you produce them depends on what base you're working with, be it fruit purée, chocolate, or even cream cheese. To produce the bubbles in any mousse, you can use either whipped heavy cream, which has bubbles of air in it from whisking; egg whites that have been whipped with sugar into meringue; whole eggs that are cooked over a water bath with sugar and whipped into foam; gelatin, which will hold any whipped mousse in place once chilled; or a combination of these methods. I incorporate all techniques, depending on how heavy the base is or how much fat content the primary mousse ingredient has. Fruit purées have no fat, so you usually add some whipped cream and meringue to them to hold the bubbles in place and give it that airy texture. Sometimes I'll add gelatin, too, if I need a boost in holding that delicate foam in place. Chocolate and fresh cheeses, however, contain fat, so they usually require whipped whole eggs or whites and whipped cream to produce an airy foam.

One of the few things my mother would bake when I was a kid was a Black Forest cake for my father. The chocolate mousse filling was rich and dense, with little specks of chocolate throughout, which I thought were intentional. Later, in culinary school, I realized that the specks were a mistake, even though the cake still tasted great. Mousses—chocolate or otherwise—should be completely smooth throughout. To achieve this, it's important that the ingredients all be at the right temperature and that you don't overwhip any one component.

Chocolate mousse can be made in several ways, and the recipes in this chapter reflect that. Since different chocolates have varying amounts of cocoa solids (fat), the structure of the mousse itself changes.

In my opinion, dark chocolate mousse is best made with a cooked egg and sugar foam called a *pâté à bombe* in French, folded together with whipped cream to match its richer flavor and higher cocoa fat content. Milk chocolate, with much less cocoa content, benefits from the addition of gelatin to help it set up; there are simply not enough fat solids in the chocolate to reset once the cream and egg foam are introduced to it. White chocolate, with no cocoa solids at all, can be made into a mousse with the addition of just whipped cream, but this mixture is actually much more temperamental than mousses made with either milk or dark chocolate.

Pay close attention to the temperature guidelines for any type of chocolate you are using to make mousse. This is the key to success—the chocolate, fruit purée, or cheese cannot be too warm or too cool or you can end up with broken mousse. Or, at the least, specks of hardened chocolate or clumps of cream cheese in your dessert, which, props to you, Mom, can be equally delicious if not technically perfect.

CREPES

Another useful and easy dessert component (once you get the hang of making them) is crepes, which are made from a loose milk and flour batter bound together by eggs. They have no leavening in them, so they don't puff like pancakes, but the batter still needs whole eggs to make them moist and stretchy.

When I worked for François Payard, occasionally he would put crepes on the dessert menu. It required me to use four pans at a time and get the rhythm down to make hundreds of crepes daily. If they weren't just perfect, he would give them to the cooks for snacks. Making crepes is easy; it just takes practice and patience. Remember to plan ahead and make your batter the day before you want to cook the crepes—if the batter has not rested long enough, bubbles will form on the surface when you cook it. Also remember to keep the pan moving from the moment you start pouring batter into the hot pan until you have a superthin layer spread out over the bottom. Practice, practice, practice!

SOUFFLÉ

This dish intimidates and scares most home bakers and professionals alike. There are many old wives' tales about soufflés (such as not opening the oven while they bake), but if you understand how meringue works, they are not difficult at all. If you follow my guidelines, you will have no problems. Remember that practice makes perfect.

Soufflés are probably so popular due to their texture: cakelike outside and soft, gooey inside. To create even more dimension, I often like to add fresh fruit or cubed sponge cake to the soufflé dishes before pouring in the soufflé mixture.

The components of a soufflé differ from one recipe to the next, but essentially there is a base (typically a pastry cream or other thick sauce) that flavors the dessert, to which you add French or Italian meringue. You can cut down on the stress of soufflé baking by creating a more stable baking environment in your oven; I always bake my soufflés in a water bath, which helps distribute the heat evenly to the batter and creates a stronger, more even texture as the soufflé rises.

Soufflés are, of course, temperamental, so be sure you are ready to serve the moment they come out of the oven; there are just a few minutes in the window between a light, airy soufflé and something more akin to hot cake batter in a ramekin. Either is delicious, though, so if you have trouble getting a big rise out of your soufflé, have another drink and serve it anyway—it will still taste great.

PÂTE À CHOUX

My first memory of pâte à choux was in pastry school, where we piped trays and trays of cream puff swans. Although it has been many years since I made a swan (and likely never will again), I do enjoy the precision of making a perfectly round, crisp ball of pâte à choux to fill with something as simple as whipped cream or to use them to construct an ornate croquembouche, the famous "cream puff tree" bound together with caramel and spun sugar.

This dough, pronounced *pat-ah-SHOE,* is used mainly for cream puffs, éclairs, profiteroles, and beignets. It starts with a simple flour, water, and butter paste that is made on the stovetop, and once the paste cools, eggs are beaten into it to make an elastic, firm dough that is either piped onto baking sheets and baked or dropped into hot oil and fried. When the dough cooks, it puffs and becomes relatively hollow, leaving room for all types of fillings. The longer you bake these pastries, the crisper and drier they get; I like mine to be very deep golden brown, hollow, and very dry, because I like even a cream puff or éclair to have a little bit of crunch to play against the creamy filling.

Pâte à choux dough itself isn't very sweet, which gives you a lot of flexibility with flavors or toppings; it can be taken in savory or sweet directions. The technique is straightforward, but making the perfect puff can be tricky. Don't be upset if your pastry cracks, which can happen if your dough is too dry. The texture of the final batter is key—it must be stretchy and loose enough to pipe but still firm enough to hold its shape, which is all determined by the amount of egg added to the base flour/water paste. If they aren't perfect at first, keep trying. No one will complain if your cream puffs have holes.

Crunchy MERINGUE COOKIES

When you go to Europe, virtually every bakery has at least ten types of dried meringues. American bakeries don't have them, and I don't know why. Crispy, chewy, crunchy meringues are satisfying on their own and can also be used in countless ways: You can sandwich jams or icings between them, top them with whipped cream and fruit, or crumble them over finished desserts to add great texture.

This is a simple French meringue with confectioners' sugar folded in to fortify it and make the cookies even lighter and crunchier. You can form these into any shape you want using a piping bag, spoon, or spatula.

MAKES ABOUT 6 DOZEN 2-INCH COOKIES

---

5 large egg whites

⅛ teaspoon cream of tartar

¾ cup granulated sugar (150 g)

1½ cups confectioners' sugar (180 g)

Preheat the oven to 200°F. Line 2 baking sheets with parchment paper.

Put the egg whites, cream of tartar, and ¼ cup of the granulated sugar in the bowl of a standing mixer with the whisk and turn the mixer on to medium. Whip until the whites are foamy and then slightly increase the speed. Continue whipping until the whites have tripled in volume and are fluffy but still soft. The whites should just be starting to hold the trail of the whisk along the sides of the bowl.

With the motor running, very slowly sprinkle another ¼ cup of the granulated sugar onto the whites between the bowl and the edge of the whisk. Slightly increase the mixer speed and whip until the whites start to turn glossy but are still soft. Slowly sprinkle in the remaining ¼ cup granulated sugar and increase the heat to medium-high. Whip for 2 to 3 minutes longer, until very stiff and glossy but not dry. Transfer the whites to a very large mixing bowl.

Put the confectioners' sugar into a fine-mesh strainer. Sift about one quarter of it onto the whipped whites. Using the largest rubber spatula you have, gently fold the sugar into the meringue, drawing the spatula through the meringue and pulling it up and over itself from the sides of the bowl in. Move slowly and precisely so you don't knock the air out of the whites. Continue sifting and folding in the sugar in 2 or 3 more additions. Once the whites are smooth with no lumps of confectioners' sugar, they are ready.

The meringue can be transferred to a pastry bag with a star tip or into a resealable plastic food bag with the corner snipped and used to pipe stars, circles, or any shape you like onto the lined baking sheets. You can make the cookies as small as dimes to sprinkle over ice cream or large enough to sandwich ice cream between them. Or use 2 spoons to mound the meringue into pillows.

Bake for 1 hour, rotating and switching the pans halfway through. Baking time may vary depending on the size of the meringues; the cookies should feel dry, light, and hollow and have no give when you press on them. If they still feel soft, bake for 15 minutes longer and test again. Turn the oven off and let the meringues cool completely in the oven. Store the cooled meringues in an airtight container for up to 2 weeks.

Pineapple-Coconut MERINGUE TORTE

As much as I like a pavlova, this dessert takes that classic combination and blows it out of the water. Piña Colada Pastry Cream lightened with softly whipped cream, layered with caramelized fresh pineapple, crunchy-chewy French meringue, and crisp strips of toasted coconut is textural nirvana. Searing fresh pineapple in a skillet adds caramel flavor to balance very sweet fruit. This is a showstopper. **SERVES 12**

Batter for Crunchy Meringue Cookies
(page 80)

½ fresh pineapple, peeled and cored

Olive oil, as needed

Coarse salt, as needed

½ cup heavy cream (120 g)

2 tablespoons confectioners' sugar (16 g)

Piña Colada Pastry Cream (page 45)

½ cup unsweetened flaked coconut, lightly toasted (36 g)

Preheat the oven to 200°F. Line 2 baking sheets with parchment paper.

Prepare the meringue cookie batter as directed. Using a piping bag with a ½-inch plain tip, or using a spoon, form the meringue into three 8-inch disks on the lined baking sheets, each about ½ inch thick. Bake for about 45 minutes, until crisp on the outside but still moist in the center. Cool completely in the oven.

Halve the pineapple lengthwise and cut the pieces crosswise into ¼-inch-thick slices. Heat a very thin layer of oil in large nonstick skillet or griddle over medium-high heat and add the pineapple. Cook for 4 to 5 minutes, until seared and golden, then flip the pieces and sear the other side. Transfer the pieces to a plate and sprinkle them lightly with salt; cool to room temperature.

Whip the cream until soft peaks form; sift the confectioners' sugar over it and whip until combined and the cream forms medium-firm peaks. Put the pastry cream in a large bowl and whisk to loosen it.

Add about a third of the whipped cream and whisk it into the pastry cream to lighten it. Using a large spatula, add the remaining whipped cream and fold it into the pastry cream until just combined. Reserve about ½ cup of the cream and transfer the remainder to a piping bag fitted with a ½-inch plain tip.

Put one meringue disk onto a serving plate and pipe a spiral of pastry cream (using a little less than half of it) over it, covering it completely but leaving a ½-inch border around the edge. Blot the pineapple pieces with a paper towel and arrange half of them, fanning them in a concentric circle, over the pastry cream. Put another meringue disk on top and repeat with the remaining pastry cream and pineapple. Top with the remaining meringue disk and, using a small offset spatula, spread the reserved pastry cream in a thin even layer over the top. Sprinkle the coconut evenly over the top.

The torte can be sliced immediately and served but is better if refrigerated for at least 1 hour and no longer than 3 hours to soften the meringue.

See technique photos, pages 84–85

PREPARING PINEAPPLE: 1 *Slice bottom off pineapple so fruit stands upright. Use chef's knife to cut away peel and eyes.* **2** *Halve pineapple lengthwise. Halve one piece again lengthwise; save other half for another use.* **3** *Cut woody core away from wedges.* **4** *Slice pineapple crosswise into ¼-inch-thick slices.* **5** *Sear slices in single layer in nonstick pan until golden.* **6** *Drain on paper towels.*

CHAMPAGNE SABAYON

A French classic, champagne sabayon pairs beautifully with ripe strawberries or raspberries or ladled over a slice of pound cake. **MAKES ABOUT 1¼ CUPS**

3 large egg yolks

¼ cup sugar (50 g)

Pinch of kosher salt

¾ cup champagne (180 g)

¼ teaspoon vanilla extract

⅛ teaspoon rose water (optional)

Fill a saucepan half full of water and bring it to a boil over medium-high heat. In a heatproof glass bowl large enough to fit into the saucepan without touching the water, whisk together the egg yolks, sugar, and salt (1) for about 1 minute, until combined and lightened. Add a couple of tablespoons of the champagne, whisk well, and then slowly whisk in the remaining champagne until combined (2).

Set the bowl over the water and whisk constantly and vigorously for about 5 minutes, until the mixture has tripled in volume and the temperature reaches 180°F (3). The sabayon should be thick enough to hold the trail of the whisk; if the volume in the bowl begins to recede while whisking, remove it from the heat immediately. You can also lift the bowl and look at the bottom (4)—if there is liquid separated in the bottom of the bowl, it needs further cooking time. Whisk in the vanilla and the rose water, if using.

Pour the sabayon through a fine-mesh strainer set over a bowl to remove any cooked egg bits (5). Serve immediately or let stand until room temperature before refrigerating and using within 1 day.

Citrus SABAYON

If you are a person who doesn't like overly sweet or heavy desserts, this is for you. This tart, velvety foam pairs nicely with fresh orange segments and perhaps biscotti on the side. **MAKES ABOUT 1¼ CUPS**

4 large egg yolks

¼ cup sugar (50 g)

Pinch of kosher salt

½ cup fresh orange juice (120 g)

2 tablespoons fresh lemon juice (30 g)

2 tablespoons fresh lime juice (30 g)

Follow the recipe for Champagne Sabayon (above), adding the juices before heating the yolks.

Bittersweet Chocolate MOUSSE

Dark chocolate mousse, when made properly, is one of those desserts that can make people's eyes roll back in their heads. There's almost nothing like its velvety, rich-yet-light texture. Cooked egg foam adds the pillowy, mouth-coating richness, while whipped cream gives it the smooth, unctuous, and, dare I say, orgasmic texture. Be sure to use quality chocolate and get ready for moans and groans in the dining room. **MAKES ABOUT 6 CUPS; SERVES 8**

1⅔ cups heavy cream (400 g)

1 teaspoon vanilla extract (5 g)

11 ounces bittersweet chocolate (70% cacao), chopped (311 g)

5 large egg yolks

2 large eggs

½ cup sugar (100 g)

1 teaspoon kosher salt (4 g)

¼ cup water (60 g)

In a medium bowl with a whisk, whip the cream and vanilla to medium-firm peaks and refrigerate until needed.

Fill a small saucepan one-third full of water and bring it to a boil over medium-high heat. Put the chocolate in a large heatproof bowl and set it on the saucepan, being sure the bowl doesn't touch the water. Reduce the heat to low, so that the water simmers, and melt the chocolate, stirring occasionally. When the chocolate is completely smooth and hot to the touch, remove the bowl from the water bath.

Return the saucepan of water to a simmer over medium heat. Put the egg yolks, whole eggs, sugar, salt, and water into a standing mixer bowl, set it over the simmering water, and whisk constantly until the sugar is melted and the mixture is hot to the touch (about 165°F). Attach the bowl and whisk to the mixer and whip at medium-high speed until the mixture triples in volume and is cool. (Stop the mixer if the volume begins to recede.)

Remove the whipped cream from the refrigerator. Check the chocolate—it should feel warm to the touch but not hot (about 113°F). With a large rubber spatula, add about ½ cup of the whipped cream to the center of the bowl of chocolate and stir it in small circles from the center, working outward into the chocolate with the spatula until the cream is completely mixed in. Fold the mixture around the outer edges of the bowl once to combine; the mixture should be thick but smooth. If it looks grainy, add a little more cream to the center of the bowl and stir outward again; fold until the chocolate is smooth. This will lower the chocolate temperature and strengthen the emulsification with the whipped eggs.

Add all of the whipped egg mixture to the chocolate and fold until streaky; add the remaining whipped cream and fold until just combined, with no streaks remaining. Do not overmix.

Transfer the mousse to a large container or individual glasses and chill until set, at least 2 hours. The mousse can be made up to 1 day ahead.

Mocha Mousse

Dissolve 1 tablespoon (6 g) instant espresso powder in the water before whipping it with the eggs and sugar.

MILK
CHOCOLATE

BITTERSWEET
CHOCOLATE

WHITE
CHOCOLATE

Milk Chocolate MOUSSE

Milk chocolate has a lower cacao content and is softer than bittersweet. It also has more milk solids, flavorings, and sugar so I add gelatin to this mousse to help it set. **MAKES ABOUT 4 CUPS; SERVES 6**

½ cup plus 5 tablespoons heavy cream (175 g)

2 tablespoons water (30 g)

¾ teaspoon powdered gelatin (2 g)

9½ ounces milk chocolate (31 to 34% cacao), chopped (270 g)

3 large egg yolks

1 large egg

2 tablespoons sugar (24 g)

¼ teaspoon kosher salt (1 g)

In a medium bowl with a whisk, whip the cream to medium-firm peaks and refrigerate until needed.

Pour the water into a small glass bowl and sprinkle the gelatin evenly over it.

Fill a small saucepan one-third full of water and bring to a boil over medium-high heat. Put the chocolate in a large heatproof bowl and set it on the saucepan, being sure the bowl doesn't touch the water. Reduce the heat to low, so that the water simmers, and melt the chocolate, stirring occasionally. When the chocolate is completely smooth and very warm to the touch, remove the bowl from the water bath. Do not let milk chocolate get too warm, or it can seize.

Quickly melt the softened gelatin in the microwave for 20 to 30 seconds until smooth or set the bowl into the hot water in the saucepan until the gelatin is liquefied. Return the saucepan of water to a simmer over medium heat. Put the egg yolks, whole egg, sugar, and salt into a standing mixer bowl, set it over the simmering water, and whisk constantly until the sugar is melted and the mixture is hot to the touch (about 165°F). Whisk in the melted gelatin. Attach the bowl and whisk to the mixer and whip at medium-high speed until the mixture triples in volume and is cool (stop the mixer if the volume begins to recede).

Remove the whipped cream from the refrigerator. Check the chocolate—it should feel slightly warm to the touch but not hot (about 104°F). With a large rubber spatula, add about one quarter of the whipped cream to the center of the bowl of chocolate and stir it in small circles from the center, working outward into the chocolate with the spatula until the cream is completely mixed in. Fold the mixture around the outer edges of the bowl once to combine; the mixture should be thick but smooth. If it looks grainy, add a little more cream to the center of the bowl and stir outward again; fold until the chocolate is smooth. This will lower the chocolate temperature and strengthen the emulsification with the whipped eggs.

Add all of the whipped egg mixture to the chocolate and fold until streaky; add the remaining whipped cream and fold until just combined, with no streaks remaining. Do not overmix.

Transfer the mousse to a large container or individual glasses and chill until set, at least 2 hours.

White Chocolate MOUSSE

Although this is the simplest method of the three types of mousse and has no eggs, be careful when working with white chocolate, which contains no cocoa solids and is more temperamental than dark chocolate. In general, it should be melted more slowly and worked with at a cooler temperature, because it can easily seize up. Use good-quality white chocolate, such as Callebaut or Valrhona, for this recipe. This mousse is also great frozen or poured into plastic-lined muffin tins or ramekins for individual servings. **MAKES ABOUT 5 CUPS; SERVES 6 TO 7**

---

9 ounces white chocolate, chopped (255 g)   2¼ cups heavy cream (540 g)

Fill a small saucepan one-third full of water and bring to a boil over medium-high heat. Put the chocolate in a large heatproof bowl and set it on the saucepan, being sure the bowl doesn't touch the water. Turn off the heat, stir occasionally with a rubber spatula, and let stand until melted and smooth. The chocolate should be melted but just above room temperature and not hot (about 105°F).

Meanwhile, in a small saucepan, heat ¾ cup of the cream until very hot, steaming, and beginning to bubble at the edges. Remove the pan of chocolate from the water bath. Pour about one quarter of the hot cream into the center of the chocolate and stir with a rubber spatula in the center of the bowl until the cream is slowly incorporated into the chocolate and the mixture is glossy and thick. Run the spatula

around the outer edge of the bowl, folding lightly. It may look broken or separated at first, but the more cream you incorporate, little by little, the smoother it will get. Continue adding more cream, a little at a time. Once the hot cream has been completely incorporated, let the bowl stand until cooled slightly.

Meanwhile, whip the remaining 1½ cups cream to soft peaks. Add about ½ cup of the whipped cream to the chocolate mixture and fold until combined and lightened. Add the remaining whipped cream to the chocolate and fold gently until just incorporated and no streaks of cream are visible.

Pour the mousse into glasses or a container and chill for at least 2 hours and up to 1 day before serving.

Honey Roasted Plum MOUSSE

In the heat of July, my dad would buy a bag of plums at the farmer's market and we'd sit outside and eat them, plum juice dripping down our chins, spitting the pits off the porch. Plums are the sweetest and juiciest of the summer fruits. Roasting them removes excess moisture while intensifying that humble plum flavor. This mousse has a light texture, as it has no yolks and is stabilized by an Italian meringue. Using only egg whites lets the plum flavor shine through. **MAKES ABOUT 6 CUPS; SERVES 8**

3 red plums, halved and pitted

2 tablespoons honey (40 g)

3 sprigs fresh thyme

1 tablespoon plum liqueur or plum brandy (12 g)

3 large egg whites

⅔ cup sugar (130 g)

Pinch of cream of tartar

2 tablespoons water (30 g)

½ cup heavy cream (120 g)

Preheat the oven to 300°F.

Put the plum halves in a shallow baking dish, cut side up. Drizzle the honey over them and lay the thyme sprigs on top. Roast for about 30 minutes, until the fruit is very soft and beginning to break down.

Discard the thyme sprigs. Transfer the plums and any liquid they have released to a blender or food processor and purée them until very smooth. Pour the mixture through a fine-mesh strainer, pressing on the solids with a rubber spatula; discard the solids. Measure 1 cup purée (190 g) for the mousse, stir in the liqueur, and reserve any remaining purée for another use.

Put the egg whites and 1 tablespoon of the sugar into the bowl of a standing mixer. Add the cream of tartar and whisk to combine. Attach the bowl to the mixer with the whisk attachment and turn it on to low.

Put the remaining sugar in a small saucepan and add the water. Use a clean finger to stir the sugar until evenly moistened and place over medium heat. When the sugar is melted and begins to bubble, with a very clean pastry brush, brush down the sides of the pan with cool water to dissolve any sugar crystals.

When the sugar reaches a rolling boil, increase the mixer speed to medium. Continue cooking the sugar, brushing the pan sides if any crystals form, until it reaches 250°F (firm-ball stage). Increase the mixer speed to medium-high. The whites should be fluffy and shiny but still soft. Carefully pour the hot sugar syrup in a slow, steady stream into the mixer—pour it directly onto the whites between the mixer bowl edge and the outer reach of the whisk. Increase the mixer speed to high and whip the meringue for about 6 minutes, until cool to the touch. If the meringue level begins to recede in the mixing bowl, stop whipping immediately.

Meanwhile, in another bowl, whip the cream with a whisk until medium-firm peaks form.

Put the meringue into a large mixing bowl and, with a large rubber spatula, gently fold in the plum purée until streaky. Add about a third of the whipped cream to the mixture and fold until combined but still streaky. Add another third of the cream and fold; add the remaining cream and fold gently until no streaks remain.

Pour the mixture into a container or serving glasses and chill until set, at least 2 hours, but preferably overnight. This is best served within a day or two of making.

Frozen Green Tea-Lime MOUSSE

In Japan, I fell in love with matcha (green tea powder). Its pungent yet herbal qualities are both soothing and stimulating. I've used it in pastries, macarons, and with chocolate, but I like the flavor it brings to frozen desserts the best. Here the citrusy tang of green tea cuts through the richness of the cream. **SERVES 12**

1½ cups heavy cream (360 g)

3 tablespoons matcha (green tea powder), plus more for serving (27 g)

2 large egg yolks

1 large egg

½ cup sugar (100 g)

Grated zest of 1 lime

Juice of ½ lime

Candied Citrus Peel (page 332) made with kumquat halves, drained, for serving

---

Spray the cups of a 12-portion standard muffin tin lightly with cooking spray and line each cup with an individual piece of plastic wrap. Use your fingers to smooth out any wrinkles in the plastic.

In a small saucepan, cook ½ cup of the cream over medium heat for about 2 minutes, until steaming and hot but not boiling. Whisk in the matcha powder until well combined and let stand until cool. Pour the mixture into a medium bowl, add the remaining 1 cup cream, and refrigerate until very cold.

Meanwhile, fill a medium saucepan one-third full of water and bring to a simmer over medium heat. Put the egg yolks, whole egg, and sugar into a standing mixer bowl and set it over the simmering water, making sure the bowl does not touch the water. Whisk constantly until the sugar is dissolved and the mixture is very hot to the touch (180°F). Attach the bowl and whisk to the mixer and whip on medium-high speed until the eggs are thickened, hold the trail of the whisk, and the mixture is cool to the touch. If the volume of the mixture begins to recede in the bowl, immediately stop whipping. Add the lime zest and juice and whip until combined.

Pour the chilled matcha mixture through a fine-mesh strainer into a large bowl and discard any solids. Whip the green tea cream with a whisk until soft peaks form. Add about a third of the egg mixture to the whipped cream and fold several times until streaky. Add another third of the eggs to the cream and fold; add the remaining egg foam and fold until no streaks remain, but do not overmix.

Divide the mixture evenly among the lined cups of the muffin tin. Lay a piece of plastic wrap on top of the pan and wrap well. Freeze the mousse for at least 2 hours, but preferably overnight.

To unmold, remove the pan from the freezer and let stand for 10 minutes. Peel off the top layer of plastic and carefully pull one of the parfaits, using the plastic piece as a guide, out of the pan and invert it onto a small serving plate.

Garnish the parfaits with a light dusting of matcha powder and candied kumquat halves. Serve immediately.

Banana-Rum MOUSSE

I love the flavor of caramelized bananas and dark rum together, usually over ice cream. This recipe brings all these flavors together in one bite. Serve this rich dessert chilled or frozen, topped with chocolate shavings or salted peanuts, or use it to fill cakes or to add a creamy banana filling to a tart or plated dessert.

MAKES ABOUT 4 CUPS; SERVES 6

FOR THE BANANAS

¼ cup sugar (50 g)

¼ teaspoon kosher salt (1 g)

1 tablespoon unsalted butter (14 g)

2 ripe bananas, sliced ¼ inch thick

2 tablespoons spiced dark rum (30 g)

FOR THE MOUSSE

1 cup heavy cream (240 g)

2 large egg yolks

1 large egg

¼ cup sugar (50 g)

To prepare the bananas, put the sugar and salt in a dry skillet over medium-high heat; do not stir. Cook until the sugar is melted, begins to brown, and gives off white smoke. Roll the pan to cook the sugar evenly to a deep, dark honey color. Carefully add the butter and swirl to mix.

Remove the pan from the heat, add the bananas, and return the pan to medium-low heat. Continue cooking, tossing the bananas, for about 1 minute, until very soft. Pull the pan off the heat, add the rum, and swirl the pan. Return the pan to the heat, tip it slightly, and ignite the alcohol while swirling the pan. (If cooking on an electric stovetop, ignite the rum with a long match.) Once the flame is extinguished, transfer the mixture to a blender and purée until smooth; pour it into a bowl and set it aside to cool. Press the purée through a fine-mesh strainer into a large clean mixing bowl to remove any lumps.

To prepare the mousse, with an electric mixer or whisk in a large bowl, whip the cream until medium-firm peaks form. Refrigerate until ready to use.

Fill a saucepan one-third full with water and bring to a simmer over medium heat. Put the egg yolks, whole egg, and sugar into a standing mixer bowl and whisk to combine. Set the pan over the simmering water, making sure the bowl does not touch the water, and whisk until very hot to the touch and the sugar is dissolved. Attach the bowl and whisk to the mixer and whip on medium-high speed until the eggs are thickened, hold the trail of the whisk, and the mixture is cool to the touch.

Add the cooled egg mixture to the banana purée and fold gently until no streaks remain. Add about half of the whipped cream to the banana mixture and fold gently until just combined; add the remaining whipped cream and fold until evenly mixed with no white streaks of cream visible.

Divide the mixture among 6 small dessert glasses or bowls and chill until firm, about 2 hours, before serving. Or, put the mixture into a pastry bag fitted with a plain tip and use it to fill cakes, hollowed-out cupcakes, or prebaked tart shells before chilling to set.

Lemongrass-Lime SEMIFREDDO
with Chocolate "Shell"

LEMONGRASS-LIME SEMIFREDDO *with chocolate "shell"*

When I was a kid, there were no sugary breakfast cereals to be found in our house. I had no idea what I had been missing until I went off to college and discovered Fruit Loops and Fruity Pebbles in the cafeteria and pigged out on them every morning. Later, in the pastry kitchen, when I first tasted lemongrass, I could not put my finger on what it reminded me of until one day it dawned on me—the citrusy tang of lemongrass tastes amazingly like the milk left in the bowl after half a box of Fruit Loops. No wonder I love this flavor so much.

Drizzle the self-hardening chocolate glaze over this frozen treat and you'll be transported back to childhood, only with a much more sophisticated and intense flavor. The chocolate "shell" glaze is great for any ice cream—it will harden but not so firmly that it cracks off while you eat your treat. **MAKES ABOUT 5 CUPS; SERVES 8 OR MAKES 8 POPSICLES**

FOR THE SEMIFREDDO

1¾ cups heavy cream, plus more as needed (420 g)

3 large stalks lemongrass, smashed with a knife handle and coarsely chopped

Grated zest of 3 limes, plus more for garnish

½ vanilla bean, split and scraped

3 large egg yolks

1 large egg

½ cup sugar (100 g)

¼ cup fresh lime juice (from about 2 large limes) (60 g)

FOR THE CHOCOLATE SHELL

1 pound bittersweet chocolate, finely chopped (454 g)

½ cup vegetable oil (96 g)

1 teaspoon pure lime oil (optional; do not use extract, which will cause the chocolate to seize)

To make the semifreddo, prepare the container you want to freeze it in (see Note on page 101).

In a small saucepan, bring ¾ cup of the cream, the lemongrass, two thirds of the lime zest, and the vanilla seeds and bean to a boil over medium heat. Remove from the heat, cover, and let stand for 10 minutes. Add the remaining 1 cup cream and let stand until room temperature. Chill in the refrigerator for at least 2 hours but preferably overnight.

Pour the mixture through a fine-mesh strainer into a measuring cup, pressing on the solids with a rubber spatula; discard the solids. Add enough fresh cream to bring the total amount back to 1¾ cups. Chill until very cold.

Fill a saucepan one-third full with water and bring to a simmer over medium heat. Put the egg yolks, whole egg, and sugar into a standing mixer bowl and whisk to combine (1). Set the pan over the simmering water, making sure the bowl does not touch the water, and whisk until very hot to the touch and the sugar is dissolved (2). Attach the bowl to the mixer with the whisk and whip on high speed until the mixture has expanded in volume and cooled (3). Feel the outside of the mixer bowl—it should be roughly body temperature. Transfer the egg foam to a large mixing bowl (4) and clean the mixer bowl. Gently fold in the lime juice (5).

recipe continues

Remove the infused cream from the refrigerator, pour it into the standing mixer bowl, and whip on medium speed until very soft peaks form. Fold in the remaining lime zest, and continue whipping until medium-firm peaks form. Working in 3 batches, gently fold the whipped cream into the whipped egg mixture until just combined (6, 7); do not overmix. Pipe or pour the mixture into your chosen container(s) (8) and freeze for at least 2 hours or overnight.

About an hour before serving, make the chocolate shell. Fill a saucepan half full of water and bring to a simmer over medium heat. Put the chocolate, vegetable oil, and lime oil, if using, into a heatproof bowl, set it over the simmering water, making sure the bowl does not touch the water, and turn off the heat. Let stand for about 5 minutes; stir until very smooth. Remove the bowl from the water bath, wipe the moisture from the bottom of the bowl with a towel, and pour the chocolate into a tall, narrow pitcher or measuring cup. Let stand until room temperature.

To serve, unmold and unwrap the semifreddo or Popsicles. Put slices or individual portions of the semifreddo on serving plates and drizzle the chocolate over the top (9). Or dip the Popsicles into the chocolate to coat, allowing the excess to drip off. Sprinkle lime zest on the chocolate before it hardens (10). Serve immediately.

Note: The semifreddo can be frozen in muffin tins, a loaf pan, or Popsicle molds. Cut twelve 4-inch square pieces of plastic wrap; spray 12 standard muffin tin compartments lightly with cooking spray and evenly coat each compartment using a paper towel. Line each compartment with plastic, being sure the plastic is smooth inside each one. Or grease and plastic-line a 4½ × 8½-inch loaf pan. Fill the compartments or pan with the mixture before freezing and cover with plastic wrap. Use the plastic to remove the portions from the tin or pan. Or fill a Popsicle mold, freeze, and run the mold under slightly warm water to unmold them before dipping.

ALMOND-AMARETTO SEMIFREDDO
with Candied Almonds

Growing up in an Italian family, amaretto was a staple at dessert time, as it is across Italy as an aperitif or digestif. I remember my grandfather always having a nip of amaretto with his pignoli cookies after dinner. Even though I prefer brown spirits with a bit more of a kick (hello, bourbon!), I do like to cook with amaretto. Made with apricot kernels and botanicals, it's a great match for almonds. **SERVES ABOUT 12**

FOR THE CANDIED ALMONDS

½ cup sliced almonds (50 g)

¼ cup Amaretto di Saronno (60 g)

¼ cup sugar (50 g)

FOR THE SEMIFREDDO

3 large egg yolks

1 large egg

½ cup sugar (100 g)

½ teaspoon kosher salt (2 g)

½ teaspoon almond extract (2 g)

2 cups heavy cream (480 g)

Preheat the oven to 325°F. Line a baking sheet with a silicone baking mat or parchment paper.

To make the candied almonds, put the nuts in a small bowl and pour the amaretto over them. Let stand for at least 15 minutes. Drain the nuts well in a small strainer, reserving the liqueur for the semifreddo. Put the nuts in a medium bowl and sprinkle the sugar over them; toss until they are evenly coated. Spread the nuts out in a single layer on the baking sheet. Toast in the oven, gently stirring them once halfway through baking, for 12 to 15 minutes, until the sugar begins to crystallize around the edges of the nuts. The nuts should not be brown. Remove the almonds from the oven and cool on the pan.

To make the semifreddo, lightly grease a 4½ × 8½-inch loaf pan and line it with plastic wrap.

Fill a medium saucepan one-third full of water and bring to a simmer over medium-low heat. Whisk the egg yolks, whole egg, sugar, and salt together in a standing mixer bowl and set it over the simmering water, making sure the bowl does not touch the water. Whisk constantly until the mixture is hot to the touch and the sugar is dissolved (180°F). Attach the bowl to the mixer with the whisk and whip on medium speed until the eggs have gained volume and are cool to the touch. Add the amaretto used to soak the almonds and the almond extract and whip well. Transfer the mixture to a large bowl.

Meanwhile, in another bowl, with a whisk, whip the cream until soft peaks form. Add about a third of the whipped cream to the whipped egg mixture and fold until streaky. Add another third of the cream, fold to combine, and then add the remaining cream and fold until just combined and no white streaks remain. Pour the mixture into the lined loaf pan, smooth the top, cover with plastic wrap, and freeze for at least 4 hours and preferably overnight.

Remove the semifreddo from the freezer, invert it onto a plate or sheet pan, and unwrap it. Press the sugared almonds into the sides, top, and ends of the frozen loaf, covering it completely in a single, even layer. Cover lightly with plastic wrap and refreeze until ready to serve.

To serve, let the semifreddo stand at room temperature for 10 minutes. Slice into ½-inch-thick slices with a hot knife and serve.

CHOCOLATE SOUFFLÉS *with Raspberries*

I've made chocolate soufflés every which way under the sun—thousands of them.

As a young pastry cook, we had requests for soufflés from time to time in the restaurant. It was always a nail biter, hoping my soufflé would rise; if it didn't, the customer would have to wait another 15 minutes, which was unacceptable. I've had plenty of failures along the way, some resulting in a tongue lashing from my chefs and upset customers.

This technique, which I learned at the Valrhona School in France, is the most foolproof way to get a beautiful, rich, decadent, and luxurious soufflé. After making it for many years, I know this recipe works every time and will make you a rock star at your dinner party. **SERVES 4**

Butter, for greasing the ramekins

3 tablespoons granulated sugar, plus more for the ramekins (36 g)

½ cup fresh raspberries (70 g)

4½ ounces bittersweet chocolate (70% cacao), chopped (128 g)

1 ounce unsweetened chocolate, chopped (30 g)

4 large egg whites

Pinch of cream of tartar

⅔ cup whole milk (160 g)

1 tablespoon cornstarch (8 g)

2 large egg yolks

Confectioners' sugar (optional)

Position a rack in the lower third of the oven. Preheat the oven to 375°F. Butter four 6-ounce ramekins and coat them in granulated sugar, knocking out the excess. Put 4 or 5 raspberries into the bottom of each ramekin, press on them lightly to collapse the cavity in each berry, and set the dishes in a large roasting pan.

Fill a saucepan half full of water and bring to a simmer over medium heat. Put both chocolates into a heatproof bowl, set it over the simmering water, making sure the bowl does not touch the water, and stir until just melted. Remove from the heat and let stand until just warm.

Put the egg whites, 1 tablespoon of the granulated sugar, and the cream of tartar into a standing mixer bowl fitted with the whisk attachment and turn the speed on to low.

In a medium saucepan, whisk the milk and cornstarch together over medium-low heat. Whisk until the mixture comes to a boil. While stirring with a small rubber spatula, slowly pour the hot liquid into the center of the chocolate, a little at a time, stirring in the center of the bowl until the milk is incorporated before adding more (1). Don't be alarmed if the chocolate clumps a bit or looks like it is separating.

Increase the mixer speed to medium-high and sprinkle in another tablespoon of the granulated sugar.

recipe continues

Add the egg yolks to the chocolate mixture (2) and stir from the center out until combined and completely smooth and emulsified.

Slowly sprinkle the remaining tablespoon granulated sugar into the whipping whites and whip until they hold soft, fluffy peaks (3). Add about a quarter of the whites to the chocolate mixture (4) and stir gently until mixed well. (You lose the air in these whites, but it is necessary to bring the textures together.) Add the remaining whites to the bowl and fold, turning the bowl (5), until just combined and no egg white streaks remain.

Ladle the batter evenly into the prepared ramekins (6). Run your thumb around the top rim of each dish to pull the batter away from the rim and promote even baking (7). Fill the roasting pan with hot water until it reaches halfway up the sides of the ramekins (8).

Bake for 20 to 25 minutes, until the soufflés are risen and set. The top and sides should look dry, but the soufflé should still be wet in the center. Remove from the oven, carefully lift the soufflés out of the water bath, wipe the ramekin bottoms dry with a towel, sprinkle with confectioners' sugar, if desired, and serve immediately.

Blackberry SOUFFLÉS

This is another showstopping dessert featuring my favorite berry, which is not too sweet and has an amazing color. You can have all of the ingredients ready to go and put these together while your guests are finishing up dinner. By the time the coffee is ready, it will be time for you to show off. **SERVES 6**

Butter, for greasing the ramekins

¾ cup sugar, plus more for ramekins (150 g)

18 fresh blackberries, halved lengthwise (125 g)

1½ cups Blackberry Pastry Cream (360 g)
    (page 49)

2 tablespoons Chambord or blackberry liqueur
    (30 g)

1 tablespoon cornstarch (9 g)

Grated zest and juice of 1 lime

5 large egg whites

2 tablespoons water (30 g)

Blackberry-Vanilla Cream Sauce (page 30),
    for serving

Position a rack in the lower third of the oven. Preheat the oven to 375°F. Butter six 6-ounce ramekins and coat them with sugar, knocking out the excess. Put 6 blackberry halves, cut side down, into the bottom of each ramekin and set the dishes in a large roasting pan.

In a large mixing bowl, whisk the pastry cream, Chambord, cornstarch, and lime zest and juice together until very smooth.

Put the egg whites and 1 tablespoon of the sugar into the bowl of a standing mixer fitted with the whisk attachment and turn on to low speed.

Put the remaining 11 tablespoons sugar and the water into a small saucepan. Stir with a clean finger to evenly moisten the sugar; wet your finger and wipe down the sides of the pan and place the pot over medium heat. When the sugar is dissolved and the mixture is beginning to bubble, wash down the sides of the pan with a clean pastry brush dipped in cold water to dissolve any sugar crystals on the sides of the pan.

When the sugar mixture comes to a rolling boil, increase the mixer speed to medium. Continue cooking the sugar until it reaches 250°F (firm-ball stage). Increase the mixer speed to medium-high. The whites should be fluffy and shiny but still soft. With the motor running, carefully pour in the hot sugar syrup in a slow, steady stream—pour it directly onto the whites between the mixer bowl edge and the outer reach of the whisk so it doesn't splatter or create lumps. Increase the mixer speed to high and whip the meringue for 6 to 8 minutes, until cool to the touch. If the meringue level begins to recede in the mixing bowl, stop whipping immediately.

Put about a quarter of the meringue into the pastry cream mixture and stir gently with a large rubber spatula until combined and lightened. Add the remaining meringue to the soufflé base and fold gently, turning the bowl as you go, until just combined, with no streaks of egg white remaining.

Using a large spoon, divide the mixture evenly among the ramekins until slightly overfilled. Use a flat icing spatula to level off the top of each ramekin so they rise evenly. Run your thumb around the top rim of each dish to pull the batter away from the rim and promote even baking. Fill the roasting pan with hot water until it reaches halfway up the sides of the ramekins.

Bake for 25 to 30 minutes, until risen and the soufflé top and sides are dry and turning light golden on top. Remove from the oven, carefully lift the soufflés out of the water bath, wipe the ramekin bottoms dry with a towel, and transfer them to serving plates.

To serve, at the table, poke a small hole in the top of each soufflé with a knife and pour in enough blackberry-vanilla cream sauce until it begins to push the whole soufflé upward.

and Stormy SOUFFLÉS

One of my favorite postshift hangouts was Painkiller NYC, where my buddy Richie Boccato made a mean Dark and Stormy at his tiki cocktail haven. Sadly, the bar is long gone; I raise my glass to Richie and the best Dark and Stormy anywhere. It is a favorite cocktail of mine, so I thought the combination of rum, lime, and lots of ginger would be really refreshing in a frozen dessert. This is a great summertime treat—light and airy but with a nice boozy kick. What really makes this is the fresh ginger juice. Grate peeled fresh ginger into a small fine-mesh strainer set over a bowl. Once you have a fair amount of pulp, squeeze the juice out of it. You'll need a fairly large piece of fresh ginger, about 12 ounces (335 g) to get enough juice.

FROZEN DARK AND STORMY SOUFFLÉS

SERVES 6

---

5 large egg whites	6 tablespoons dark rum (not spiced) (90 g)
1⅔ cups sugar (330 g)	6 tablespoons strained fresh ginger juice (90 g)
Pinch of cream of tartar	Grated zest of 2 limes
2 tablespoons water (30 g)	¼ cup fresh lime juice (60 g)
1¾ cups heavy cream (420 g)	

Cut six 3 × 22-inch strips of parchment or wax paper. Wrap six 6-ounce ramekins tightly with the strips, creating a collar and using tape to secure it to the ramekin (1). Set them on a small baking sheet.

Put the egg whites, 2 tablespoons of the sugar, and the cream of tartar into a standing mixer fitted with the whisk attachment and turn on to low speed.

Put the remaining sugar and the water into a small saucepan. Stir with a clean finger to evenly moisten the sugar; wet your finger and wipe down the sides of the pan and place the pot over medium heat. When the sugar is dissolved and the mixture is beginning to bubble, wash down the sides of the pan with a clean pastry brush dipped in cold water to dissolve any sugar crystals on the sides of the pan.

When the sugar mixture comes to a rolling boil, increase the mixer speed to medium. Continue cooking the sugar for about 10 minutes until it reaches 250°F (firm-ball stage). Increase the mixer speed to medium-high. The whites should be fluffy and shiny but still soft. With the motor running, carefully pour in the hot sugar syrup in a slow, steady stream—pour it directly onto the whites between the mixer bowl edge and the outer reach of the whisk so it doesn't splatter or create lumps (2). Increase the mixer speed to high and whip the meringue for 6 to 8 minutes, until cool to the touch. If the meringue level begins to recede in the mixing bowl, stop whipping immediately.

In another large mixing bowl, with a whisk, whip the cream until it holds firm peaks.

In a small bowl, whisk the rum, ginger juice, and lime zest and juice together. Once the whites are cool and glossy, using a large rubber spatula, carefully fold the liquid into them until just combined.

Add about a third of the whites mixture to the whipped cream and fold until streaky. Add another third and fold again. Add the remaining whites to the cream and fold until just combined and no streaks remain. Using a folding motion, gently pull a whisk through the mixture to make sure it is homogenous (3). Using a pastry bag (4) or spoon, fill each prepared mold to the edge of the paper (5) and smooth the top, if necessary (6). Freeze the soufflés on the pan in the freezer overnight.

The following day, remove the paper collars and clean the sides of the molds with a warm, damp towel if necessary. Let the soufflés stand at room temperature for about 15 minutes before serving.

Marshmallows

These are a great way to end a meal—coffee and dessert in one bite. For marshmallows to be light and airy, they require a sturdy Italian meringue, with added gelatin, which sets the foamed whites and gives them that soft chew. These are also great as a gift or cut and sandwiched between soft chocolate cookies for a killer whoopie pie.

ESPRESSO

BERRY

ESPRESSO MARSHMALLOWS

MAKES ABOUT 4 DOZEN 1½-INCH SQUARE MARSHMALLOWS

7 tablespoons water (105 g)

4 teaspoons unflavored gelatin (12 g)

1 cup plus 2 tablespoons granulated sugar (224 g)

2 tablespoons light corn syrup (34 g)

5 large egg whites

Pinch of cream of tartar

¼ cup instant espresso powder (24 g)

Cornstarch, for dusting

Confectioners' sugar, for dusting

Moisten the inside of a 9 × 13-inch sheet pan with water. Line the pan with a single layer of plastic wrap and use a dry cloth to press and smooth the plastic on the surface to adhere the plastic to the pan.

Pour ¼ cup of the water into a small microwave-safe bowl and evenly sprinkle the gelatin over it. Set the bowl aside for about 10 minutes to allow the gelatin to soften and absorb the water.

Put 1 cup of the granulated sugar, the remaining 3 tablespoons water, and the corn syrup into a small saucepan. Stir with a clean finger to evenly moisten the sugar; wet your finger and wipe down the sides of the pan and put the pan over medium heat. When the sugar is dissolved and the mixture is beginning to bubble, wash down the sides of the pan with a clean pastry brush dipped in cold water to dissolve any sugar crystals on the sides of the pan.

Meanwhile, combine the egg whites, cream of tartar, and remaining 2 tablespoons granulated sugar in the bowl of a standing mixer fitted with the whisk attachment. Turn the mixer on to low speed. When the sugar mixture comes to a rolling boil, increase the mixer speed to medium. Continue cooking the sugar until it reaches 311°F (hard-crack stage).

Meanwhile, put the softened gelatin in the microwave and heat for about 20 seconds, until the gelatin is melted and liquefied. Alternatively, you can set the bowl of gelatin over a small saucepan of gently simmering water until it liquefies.

Remove the sugar from the heat, add the melted gelatin, and stir with a wooden spoon until completely combined. Increase the mixer speed to high and carefully pour in the hot sugar syrup in a slow steady stream—pour it directly onto the whites between the mixer bowl edge and the outer reach of the whisk. Whip the meringue on high speed for about 6 minutes, until the mixture is cool to the touch.

Reduce the mixer speed to medium and very slowly sprinkle the espresso powder onto the surface of the meringue; whip until incorporated. Remove the mixer bowl and whisk and, using a large rubber spatula, fold the mixture to make sure the espresso is completely dissolved and evenly distributed. Pour the mixture onto the plastic-lined sheet pan.

With a large offset spatula, gently spread the marshmallow evenly in the pan. Let the marshmallow stand to set for 30 minutes. Put some cornstarch into a fine-mesh strainer and lightly dust the surface of the marshmallow with cornstarch (1). Lay a clean piece of plastic wrap on the surface and invert the pan onto the counter. Using the plastic, lower the inverted marshmallows back into the pan (2) and peel off the bottom layer of plastic (3). Let stand for 30 minutes to dry; then dust the surface again with cornstarch. Wrap the pan tightly and let stand at room temperature overnight.

Berry Marshmallows

Freeze-dried fruits, which you can now find at most supermarkets, have super-concentrated flavor even though they are as light as air. I grind them into a powder and use them to flavor desserts.

To make Berry Marshmallows, put 2 ounces (57 g) of freeze-dried raspberries into a clean spice grinder and grind into a fine powder. Sift the powder twice through a fine-mesh strainer. Measure 5 tablespoons (25 g) of the powder and replace the espresso powder with the raspberry powder, folding it into the marshmallows as instructed.

The next day, dust a work surface with sifted confectioners' sugar. Unwrap the marshmallows and invert them onto the dusted surface; peel off the plastic. Cut the marshmallows into squares or rectangles and lightly dust the cut edges with confectioners' sugar. They can be served immediately or stored in an airtight container at room temperature for up to 3 days.

Vanilla Bean Marshmallows

For classic marshmallows flecked with vanilla seeds, scrape the seeds from 1 large vanilla bean and add them to the sugar and water before cooking. Omit the espresso powder. Or just add the vanilla seeds to the sugar syrup when making espresso marshmallows if you're one of those people who adds vanilla syrup to your latte at the coffee shop.

Cream Puffs and

Éclairs

Whenever we popped into a bakery when I was a kid, my dad had a chocolate éclair—it is his absolute favorite pastry. There's something really satisfying about the crisp golden brown exterior filled with gooey pastry cream. The mark of a good bakery is cream puffs and éclairs that have a crisp crust and are not soggy. The way to achieve that is to make sure the paste has dried out enough before the eggs are added and then bake the puffs long enough. I like to use bread flour for my cream puff shells, as the extra gluten gives the puffs added crispness. You should also try to wait to fill them until just before serving so that the moisture in the filling doesn't soften the puff too much.

CREAM PUFFS *and* ÉCLAIRS

MAKES ABOUT 1½ DOZEN CREAM PUFFS OR 1 DOZEN 4-INCH ÉCLAIRS

½ cup plus 2 teaspoons whole milk (125 g)

½ cup plus 2 teaspoons water (125 g)

8 tablespoons (1 stick) unsalted butter (113 g)

1 teaspoon sugar (4 g)

1 teaspoon kosher salt (4 g)

1¼ cups bread flour (165 g)

4 to 5 large eggs

Vegetable oil cooking spray

2 cups pastry cream or flavored whipped cream (see pages 41–49), for filling

Shiny Chocolate Glaze (page 328), for dipping

Preheat the oven to 375°F. Line 2 baking sheets with silicone baking mats or parchment paper.

In a large saucepan, slowly bring the milk, water, butter, sugar, and salt to a simmer over medium-low heat. Remove from the heat, add the flour all at once (1), and stir with a wooden spoon until combined and evenly moistened.

Return the pan to medium-low heat and stir continuously for 3 to 4 minutes to dry out the

mixture. The dough should pull away from the sides of the pan, and a skin should begin to form in the base of the pan (2). Transfer the dough to a standing mixer bowl and use the spoon to spread the dough out in a thin layer against the sides of the bowl (3). Let stand for at least 15 minutes, until cool.

Attach the paddle to the bowl and turn the mixer on to low speed. Add 2 of the eggs and mix until completely incorporated. Stop the mixer and scrape down the bowl. Turn the mixer back on to low and

add another egg; mix until incorporated. After 3 eggs, the dough should hold a peak when you pull the paddle out of the dough but should immediately fold over onto itself. If too firm, add the fourth egg and mix well. The dough should now be smooth, elastic, and firm enough to pipe and hold its shape but not runny (4). You can test it by putting a heaping tablespoon on a plate. The dough should collapse slightly but still hold a rounded shape. If the dough is still too firm, beat another egg in a small bowl until combined and add about half of it to the dough; mix on low speed until incorporated and check the consistency. If the dough is still too firm, add the remaining ½ egg and mix well; if it seems runny, refrigerate the dough for 15 to 20 minutes before piping.

For cream puffs, transfer the dough to a piping bag fitted with a ⅝-inch plain tip (Ateco #807) (5). For éclairs, use a ⁷/₁₆-inch star tip (Ateco #825).

To pipe cream puffs, hold the piping bag at a 45-degree angle with the tip nearly touching the pan. Squeeze the bag and pipe balls of dough 1 to 1½ inches in diameter (Ping-Pong-ball sized), pulling the tip up and counterclockwise when the puffs are large enough (6).

To pipe éclairs, hold the piping bag at a 90-degree angle away from you and start squeezing the bag. When the dough starts to flow, pull the bag up and over the point where you started (as if creating an S) toward you and pipe 3½- to 4-inch long cylinders. When long enough, stop squeezing and lift the bag straight up and over the dough, which will leave a point at the closest end (7).

recipe continues

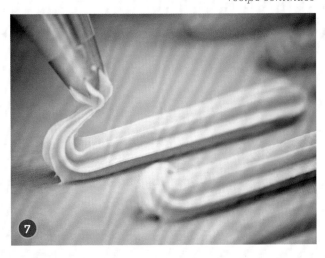

With a wet finger, press the points into the dough where you stopped piping (8); the surface of the puffs should be very smooth, and the éclairs should have rounded ends with no point. Use a wet finger to mold any misshapen éclairs (9). Spray a light coating of cooking spray over the surface of the puffs or éclairs. Put the pans in the oven, immediately reduce the temperature to 325°F, and bake for 30 minutes. Rotate the pans and continue baking for 25 to 30 minutes, until deep golden brown and the puffs or éclairs feel hollow.

Cool the cream puffs or éclairs completely on the pans before filling or freezing them.

To fill cream puffs, use a small knife to poke a small hole (the smaller the better) in the bottom of each puff. Attach a small plain tip to a pastry bag, fill it with pastry cream or flavored whipped cream, and insert the tip into the hole in the puff. Squeeze the pastry bag gently until the puff feels heavy and you see cream beginning to leak out of the hole around the tip. Place the filled puffs upright on a serving plate or tray, cover, and refrigerate for no more than 4 hours, until ready to glaze or serve.

To fill éclairs, poke a small hole in one end and fill as directed above.

To glaze éclairs, see the instructions opposite for Coffee-Cardamom Éclairs.

Note: *Cream puffs can either be glazed by dipping them halfway in room-temperature Shiny Chocolate Glaze (page 328), letting the excess drip off before setting them upright, or dipped in liquid caramel deep enough to just cover the bottoms, allowing the excess to drip off, and setting them upright on a silicone-mat-lined baking sheet.*

Coffee-Cardamom Éclairs

Since I'm such an espresso junkie, downing 4 or 5 every day, this could be one of my favorite desserts ever.

MAKES ABOUT 1 DOZEN 4-INCH ÉCLAIRS

---

pâte à choux (page 120),
    baked into éclairs

2 cups Coffee-Cardamom
    Pastry Cream (page 46)

1 recipe Shiny Chocolate
    Glaze (page 328)

Fill the éclair shells with the pastry cream as directed opposite. To glaze, the glaze must be very cool and thick. Dip a spoon into it and hold it upright—the glaze should hold fast and not run. If it drips, let the glaze stand for a few more minutes. To glaze the éclairs, grasp the éclair parallel to the glaze. Holding on to the sides with your fingers just below the halfway point, dip the top third of the éclair into the chocolate, and hold it over the bowl so that excess glaze drips off. You can rotate the éclair slightly in your hand to help get excess glaze off the top. Set the éclairs upright on a tray. Once the glaze has set, cover and refrigerate the éclairs for up to 1 day until ready to serve.

CHIPOTLE CHURROS *with Dulce de Leche Cream*

In the subways of New York, there are women with big baskets of 3-foot-long churros, and I always wonder how in the heck they make them. Surely they don't have deep fryers that big! It has me stumped. I do love them, though. One of the more creative ways to cook pâte à choux is to make churros, where the paste is piped directly into hot oil and fried. I decided to one-up this classic dessert by adding another common Mexican ingredient—chipotle chile. The result is crispy, sweet, salty, spicy, and addictive.

MAKES ABOUT 1 DOZEN CHURROS

FOR THE CHURROS

1 cup water (240 g)

8 tablespoons (1 stick) unsalted butter (113 g)

1 tablespoon adobo sauce from canned chipotle peppers in adobo (15 g)

½ cup sugar (100 g)

1 teaspoon kosher salt (4 g)

1 cup bread flour (132 g)

3 large eggs

1 teaspoon ground cinnamon (2 g)

1 teaspoon chipotle chile powder (2 g)

Vegetable oil, for deep frying

FOR THE DULCE DE LECHE CREAM

⅓ cup Dulce de Leche (page 329) (100 g)

¾ cup heavy cream, whipped to soft peaks (180 g)

To make the churros, in a large saucepan, bring the water, butter, adobo, ½ teaspoon of the sugar, and ½ teaspoon of the salt to a boil over medium heat. Remove from the heat. With a wooden spoon, stir in the flour all at once and mix until combined.

Return the pan to medium-low heat and stir continuously for 3 to 4 minutes to dry out the mixture. Transfer the dough to a standing mixer bowl and use the spoon to spread the dough out in a thin layer against the sides of the bowl. Let stand for at least 15 minutes, until cool.

Attach the paddle to the bowl and turn the mixer on to low speed. Add 2 of the eggs and mix until completely incorporated. Stop the mixer and scrape down the bowl. Turn the mixer back on to low speed

and add the remaining egg; mix until incorporated and the dough is shiny and elastic, 2 to 3 minutes.

Fill a large, heavy saucepan with oil to a depth of 3 inches and heat to 360°F.

Line a baking sheet with paper towels and set aside. Mix the remaining sugar and salt with the cinnamon and chipotle powder and pour it onto a plate.

Transfer the dough to a piping bag fitted with a medium star tip (Ateco #822). Holding the piping bag in one hand, and a paring knife in the other, squeeze 6-inch-long strips of churro dough directly into the oil, cutting them cleanly from the tip with the knife. Fry, turning frequently, for about 5 minutes, until golden brown. Remove from the oil and drain briefly on the paper towel–lined baking sheet. While still warm, roll them in the cinnamon sugar until coated. Continue frying until the batter is used, monitoring the oil temperature and being sure it remains at 360°F during the frying process.

To make the dulce de leche cream, put the dulce de leche into a large mixing bowl. Add about a third of the whipped cream and fold lightly to combine. Add the remaining cream and fold gently just until the mixture is streaky. Use immediately, or refrigerate until ready to serve for up to 1 day.

Serve the churros with the dipping cream on the side.

BASIC CREPES

I love crepes for breakfast, as a snack, and, of course, for dessert. They are a versatile, classic pastry that can be either savory or sweet. Once you master the basic recipe, you can add flavorings like spices or citrus to make these your own. For some reason the first few crepes in a batch are never perfect. Don't worry; toss them in sugar and roll them up for snacks. **MAKES ABOUT 12 CREPES**

3 tablespoons sugar (36 g)

Grated zest of ½ orange

1 cup all-purpose flour (125 g)

1 cup milk, at room temperature (240 g)

3 large eggs, at room temperature

½ teaspoon kosher salt (2 g)

2 tablespoons (¼ stick) unsalted butter, melted and cooled (28 g)

Vegetable oil cooking spray

Put the sugar into a small bowl and add the zest. Using your fingers, work the zest into the sugar until evenly combined. Whisk in the flour.

Put the milk, eggs, and salt into a blender and blend on low speed until smooth. With the motor running, slowly add the flour mixture a tablespoon at a time and mix until very smooth. While the motor is still running, slowly drizzle in the melted butter and blend for about 1 minute to emulsify the batter. Pour the mixture into a glass measuring cup with a spout, cover, and refrigerate for at least 2 hours and preferably overnight.

To make the crepes, spray an 8-inch nonstick skillet with cooking spray and heat the pan over medium heat. Stir the batter gently, being careful not to create bubbles.

Pull the pan off the burner, tilt it slightly, and while swirling the pan, slowly pour in enough batter to coat the base of the pan with a paper-thin layer of batter (use a 1-ounce ladle, which holds 2 tablespoons) (1, 2). Return the pan to the heat and cook, undisturbed, for about 1 minute, until the batter no longer looks wet in the pan and it begins to brown lightly around the edges. Use a small silicone spatula to lift one edge (3). Carefully grab the edges with your fingertips and flip the crepe (4). Cook for an additional minute on the other side. Transfer to a plate (5) and continue making crepes, wiping out the pan after every third or fourth crepe and respraying the pan lightly with cooking spray as needed.

Chocolate Browned Butter CREPES

Browned butter adds an unmistakable toasted, nutty flavor to anything it is added to. Called *beurre noisette* on many menus, browned butter pairs amazingly well with the bitter tones of dark chocolate. For this recipe good-quality cocoa powder is key; since it is the only type of chocolate used, Scharffen Berger or Valrhona would be a great choice here. **MAKES ABOUT 1½ DOZEN CREPES**

¾ cup all-purpose flour (74 g)

¼ cup sifted dark cocoa powder (20 g)

3 tablespoons sugar (36 g)

½ teaspoon kosher salt (2 g)

1 cup whole milk, at room temperature (240 g)

4 large eggs, at room temperature

¼ cup whiskey or bourbon (60 g)

¼ cup melted cool Browned Butter (opposite) (60 g)

½ cup heavy cream, at room temperature (120 g)

Whisk the flour, cocoa, sugar, and salt together. In a blender, mix the milk, eggs, and whiskey until smooth. With the motor running, slowly add the flour mixture a tablespoon at a time and mix until very smooth. While the motor is still running, slowly drizzle in the cool melted browned butter and cream and blend for about 1 minute to emulsify the batter.

Pour the mixture into a glass measuring cup with a spout, cover, and refrigerate for at least 2 hours and preferably overnight.

Cook the crepes as directed for Basic Crepes (page 127).

Chocolate Browned Butter Crepes with Caramel and Bananas

Spread 1 tablespoon Spreadable Caramel (page 151) evenly over each crepe and sprinkle a thin, even layer of finely grated bittersweet chocolate over it. Cover half of each crepe with very thinly sliced banana and then fold each crepe into quarters. Serve 3 per person.

Chocolate Browned Butter Crepes with Coffee-Cardamom Pastry Cream

Spread 3 tablespoons Coffee-Cardamom Pastry Cream (page 46) evenly over each crepe and top with some finely grated lemon zest and grated bittersweet chocolate. Fold each crepe into quarters and top with more grated chocolate before serving 1 to 2 per person.

BROWNED BUTTER

Butter is an emulsification of fat (cream) and water. If you melt it in a saucepan and keep cooking it, it will separate, as you've probably seen when melting it in quantity. If you continue cooking it, the fat will clump together in the bottom of the pan and the water will eventually evaporate, leaving the richer butterfat behind. If you continue cooking it even longer, the fats will begin to caramelize, giving it a delicious, nutty flavor. I've found that by agitating the butter while it cooks, the solids brown more evenly and the process happens a little more quickly. Always start with twice the amount of butter you need; the process will yield half the amount of browned butter than whole butter you started with. **MAKES ABOUT ¼ CUP**

Put 8 tablespoons (1 stick) unsalted butter (113 g) into a small saucepan over medium heat. Whisk constantly while the butter melts and begins to bubble. Continue whisking until the butter is a deep, nutty golden brown (like maple syrup), about 5 minutes. Line a fine-mesh strainer with cheesecloth and strain the butter; discard the solids. Cool to room temperature before using. Browned butter can be stored in the refrigerator for up to 2 weeks and used either in solid form, or melted in a small pan over low heat and cooled to room temperature.

Sesame CREPES

Two of my best friends are from Israel, and they introduced me to the cooking and ingredients of that region. One of the first things I fell in love with was halvah; sesame and honey work together to create a flavor that is comforting, homey, and unmistakable. The only thing that might improve these warm crepes would be a smear of fresh wildflower honey. **MAKES ABOUT 12 CREPES**

Basic Crepes batter (page 127)	¼ cup tahini (sesame paste) (40 g)
¼ cup whole milk (60 g)	1 tablespoon white sesame seeds (9 g)

Make the basic crepe batter as directed, adding the extra ¼ cup milk to the blender. After the flour has been added and mixed, add the tahini, mix well, and with the motor running, add the melted butter. Refrigerate the batter overnight.

When cooking the crepes, sprinkle ¼ teaspoon sesame seeds evenly over each one while the batter is still wet before you flip it. Continue cooking crepes until the batter is used up.

"No-tella" Cashew

Crepe Cake

"NO-TELLA" CASHEW CREPE CAKE

My heritage is half Italian, half French; this recipe reflects both. I love eating crepes smeared with Nutella on the street in Paris, but I also love the perfect crunchy-creamy cannoli from the amazing bakeries in Naples. This is my mash-up of the two that celebrates both countries. It also happens to be really easy to make once you master flipping crepes. This is really impressive for a holiday or celebration breakfast, too.

SERVES ABOUT 12

FOR THE "NO-TELLA" SPREAD

1 cup unsalted cashews, toasted until golden brown (see page 142), warm (150 g)

½ teaspoon kosher salt (2 g)

2 tablespoons vegetable oil (28 g)

4 ounces semisweet chocolate, chopped and melted (113 g)

FOR THE FILLING

¾ cup mascarpone cheese (165 g)

1 tablespoon honey (20 g)

Seeds from 1 vanilla bean

Grated zest of 1 lemon

1 teaspoon fresh lemon juice (5 g)

¼ teaspoon kosher salt (1 g)

¾ cup fresh ricotta cheese (185 g)

FOR THE CREPE CAKE

10 Chocolate Browned Butter Crepes or Basic Crepes (page 128 or 127)

Fresh raspberries, or coarsely crushed freeze-dried raspberries and toasted chopped cashew pieces (see page 142), for garnish

---

To make the "no-tella" spread, put the cashews and salt into a food processor and purée until the nuts start to clump together. Add the oil and purée until a paste forms. Add the melted chocolate and mix until homogenous. Transfer to a bowl and set aside at room temperature.

To make the filling, put the mascarpone, honey, vanilla seeds, lemon zest and juice, and salt into a bowl and stir until well mixed. With a rubber spatula, gently fold in the ricotta until just combined.

To assemble the crepe cake, put a crepe on a plate. With a small offset spatula, spread a heaping tablespoon of the cashew spread evenly over the entire surface (1, 2). With another small spatula or knife, spread 2 heaping tablespoons of the ricotta

filling over the entire surface (3, 4). Lay another crepe directly on top (5), spread a heaping tablespoon of the cashew spread and 2 tablespoons ricotta filling evenly over it. Continue layering the crepes and spreading cashew spread and filling over them (6), leaving one for the top of the cake. Place the last crepe on top and use a cake pan or baking sheet to press gently on the cake to compact it. Evenly spread the remaining cashew mixture over the top. Refrigerate the cake for at least 1 hour or until ready to serve, up to 3 days.

To serve, let the cake stand for at least 10 to 15 minutes before slicing. Garnish the cake with fresh raspberries or scatter crushed freeze-dried raspberries and cashew pieces over the top. Slice the cake with a warm, dry knife.

CHAPTER 3

CARAMEL

Working with sugar is magical. You can change its structure from grains in the sugar bowl to everything from gooey and chewy candy to firm, strong, and solid mortar. It is the "superglue" of the pastry kitchen, and when cooked to a deep brown caramel it can transform a simple apple tart into a rich, earthy tarte Tatin. The flavor of caramel that I prefer is not overly sweet but instead has a deep, rich, and somewhat bitter taste that hits your tongue in a different spot from the gooey-sweet caramel sauce sold in jars for pouring over ice cream. Imagine dropping some good balsamic vinegar on the center of your tongue; there is a little sweetness, but where you really taste the flavor is along the sides of your mouth in the back. This is the flavor dimension I work with when incorporating caramel into my desserts.

When you cook sugar, a few things happen. First, the sugar crystals melt, and the molecular structure changes. If you've ever made a simple syrup for iced tea or cocktails, just heating sugar in an equal amount of water until it melts suspends the sugar molecules in a liquid state. Plain sugar doesn't melt well in cold liquids—you need the addition of heat or extreme agitation. Then, if you keep boiling sugar, it continues to change molecular structure as it gets hotter and the moisture evaporates. Depending on how long you cooked it, once cool, it will transform into a soft candy like taffy or become crunchy and hard like a lollipop. That spectrum of textures is also what stabilizes meringues, batters, and icings.

Depending on the use, sugar can be cooked to stages that will solidify in different strengths. For example, "soft-ball stage," between 235°F and 240°F, is hot sugar syrup that will form a soft, squishy ball when dropped into cold water; it is used for making fudge and fondant. "Firm-ball stage," registered at 245°F to 250°F, is used for making caramels and other firmer, chewy candies. The cooked sugar stages continue up the temperature scale, depending on their use.

To make caramel, you keep on cooking the sugar and watch it begin to turn brown, when it is literally burning in the pan. The trick is to know when to stop the cooking process. Light, amber-colored caramel, to me, is really good for only one thing—to create "spun sugar" to garnish meringue and other desserts. If making a true dessert sauce, you cook the sugar until it is a deep amber-mahogany color before tossing in butter and fruits. To make garnishes or hard candies like nut brittles, I cook the sugar until it is a very dark brown, almost turning black.

Be aware that sugar cooked to any stage is *very* hot—hotter than boiling water. Boy, did I learn that the hard way in culinary school! Despite being warned repeatedly about the risk of burns the first time I made caramel, like an idiot, I stuck my finger into a pot of screaming-hot boiling sugar to taste it. I immediately felt the burn, so what did I do? Stuck my finger into my mouth to cool it. I ended up with a pair of nasty matching blisters, one on my finger and another on my tongue. Lesson learned. I recommend keeping a little ice water nearby as a precaution while you work with sugar. If it splashes or you spill some on yourself, quickly dipping the finger, hand, or arm into ice water will stop the burning and lessen the pain and severity of the injury. Don't be afraid of caramel, though. Just be cautious and focused while working with it and you will be fine.

There are basically two ways to caramelize sugar: a "dry" method in a skillet without water, and a "wet" method in a saucepan with water (and sometimes corn syrup added).

➡ *Tips for* SUCCESSFUL CARAMEL:

- Always make caramel in a very heavy stainless-steel skillet or saucepan. Caramelized sugar reaches extreme temperatures during the cooking process; heavier pans conduct heat more evenly.

- Never walk away from sugar cooking in a pan, especially when making a dry caramel. It can go from liquid to scorched in no time, and you'll have to start over. If this does happen, carefully add hot water to the pan—stand back and pour slowly since it will sputter and bubble—and bring it to a simmer. This will help melt the burned caramel and make the pan easier—and safer—to clean.

- Resist the urge to stir cooking sugar, especially at the beginning. Agitation can cause the sugar to recrystallize or seize in the pan, and you'll need to start over.

- No stovetop or oven heats things perfectly evenly, so as sugar caramelizes, swirl the pan to promote even cooking once you start to see the edges begin to brown.

- Most of my recipes call for very dark caramel, darker than you are likely used to. The color that you perceive in the pan as the sugar cooks is not a true representation of the actual caramel shade, which is usually lighter than you think. To get a good assessment of the caramel color, dip a whisk into it and hold the whisk (over the pan) up to the light or near a window. The color of the drips on the whisk indicates the true level of caramelization, so get into the habit of checking it with this technique. The darker the caramel, the more complex the flavor. If the caramel is too light, it will add only sweetness and little additional flavor.

- Another good way to monitor caramel is by watching for smoke. Usually when a caramel is ready, and dark enough, it will start to emit white smoke.

- If adding butter, cream, or other liquids to hot caramel, always reduce the heat and stand back— it will sputter and bubble up, especially if you add fat like butter or cream.

- *Never* add cold liquids or other ingredients to caramel. It will harden and need to be cooked until smooth again. Always warm cream prior to adding it to caramel. If there are pieces of hard sugar in your caramel after adding liquid, don't panic. Just cook it, stirring over low heat, until it is smooth again.

- Caramel waits for no one. Whatever role it is playing in the recipe, it needs to be used as soon as it is ready. Have all of your other ingredients or recipe components ready before you start cooking the sugar.

DRY CARAMEL

I usually use this method of making caramel only for finishing and garnishing desserts and "candying" other ingredients. You can smear this onto parchment paper, let it harden, and then break it into shards for garnishing ice cream or cake slices. Or dip fresh cherries on the stem or cape gooseberries into it, which become a minidessert all on their own. Stir hazelnuts or almonds into it, pour onto parchment, and grind it in a food processor; use it to fill cakes or sprinkle on cupcakes for crunch and flavor.

DRY CARAMEL TECHNIQUE: 1 *Sprinkle a thin, even layer of sugar into a skillet over medium-high heat.* **2** *Cook until sugar completely melts and begins to brown.* **3** *Sprinkle more sugar in a single layer and continue cooking.* **4** *As sugar caramelizes, tilt pan to evenly brown sugar.*

WET CARAMEL TECHNIQUE (OPPOSITE): 1 *Stir sugar and water with a finger until moistened.* **2** *Wet your finger and use to clean sides of pan.* **3** *When sugar is dissolved and boiling, brush sides of pan with a pastry brush dipped in water.* **4** *Gently swirl pan as sugar cooks for even browning.* **5** *Check color of caramel by dipping a whisk in and holding it up to light.* **6** *Dip pan in an ice bath to stop cooking process.*

WET CARAMEL

Most recipes that require caramelized sugar or sugar syrup will begin with wet caramel, where the sugar is heated with the water to start. It is a little easier to make than dry and is less temperamental. I use this method whenever the caramel is part of a recipe or when I'm making a sauce that I want to keep on hand to serve with cakes or tarts, for example. When making wet caramel, the amount of water you introduce at the beginning isn't important. Sugar will start to caramelize when there is only so much water left in the mixture; adding more at the start just means a longer cooking time for the level of caramel you need.

CARAMELIZED FRUIT

This dry caramel is a quick way to make an easy dessert sauce or topping or to prepare fruit for use in other desserts. Almost every fruit can be caramelized except for soft berries. This recipe produces not a crunchy, hard coating, but rather a deep rich caramel sauce that coats the fruit. Remember to keep the fruit slices uniform in size so the texture is similar in each bite. The firmer the fruit, such as apples or pears, the thinner the slices should be. Softer fruits like bananas or mangos should be cut at least ¼ inch thick, as they break down more easily. You don't want the fruit to break down but rather soften slightly in the caramel. **MAKES ABOUT 2 CUPS; SERVES 4**

¼ cup sugar (50 g)

¼ teaspoon kosher salt (1 g)

1 tablespoon unsalted butter (14 g)

CHOOSE ANY OF THE FOLLOWING

2 firm bananas, sliced ¼ inch thick

1 mango, peeled and sliced

¼ fresh pineapple, peeled, cored, and cut into chunks

1 crisp apple, such as Granny Smith, peeled, cored, and sliced

1 firm pear, peeled, cored, and sliced

1 ripe quince, peeled, cored, and sliced

Put the sugar and salt in a dry skillet over medium-high heat; do not stir. Cook for about 3 minutes, until the sugar is melted, begins to brown, and the sugar gives off white smoke. Once the sugar is liquefied, occasionally roll and tilt the pan to evenly cook the sugar to a deep, dark honey color. Add the butter and swirl to mix.

Remove the pan from the heat, add the fruit, and, using a fork, toss to coat evenly in the caramel. The fruit can be used immediately or can be poured out onto a parchment-lined sheet pan to cool. Use a fork to separate the pieces into 1 thin layer.

CRYSTALLIZED NUTS

CANDIED HAZELNUTS

TOASTING NUTS

Toasting nuts in the oven is key in coaxing the most possible flavor from them. I prefer to toast them until very dark brown, intensifying the flavor, but I always watch them closely. There is a fine line between well toasted and burned. To toast nuts, spread them out in an even layer on a baking sheet and roast in a 350°F oven, shaking the pan several times to turn the nuts, for 12 to 15 minutes, until deep golden brown, depending on the size and fat content. Cool completely before using.

CANDIED HAZELNUTS

Made using a wet caramel, these nuts add an amazing flavor to almost any sweet recipe. Use as a garnish or grind up to add to fillings or to top creamy desserts. This method works well for all hard nuts like walnuts, almonds, and pecans. **MAKES ABOUT 2 CUPS**

Vegetable oil cooking spray

½ cup sugar (100 g)

2 tablespoons water (30 g)

10 ounces blanched (peeled) hazelnuts, toasted (opposite) (300 g)

¼ teaspoon salt (1 g)

Line a baking sheet with parchment paper or a silicone baking mat. Spray 2 forks with cooking spray and set them aside.

Put the sugar and water into a medium saucepan and stir with your finger until the mixture is sandy and evenly moistened. Use a wet finger to wipe down the interior sides of the pan. Heat the sugar over medium heat until it is completely melted, washing down the sides of the pan with a brush dipped in cold water several times as the sugar melts. Once the mixture begins to boil, stop brushing down the sides.

Continue cooking the sugar, swirling the pan so it caramelizes evenly, until deep mahogany brown. Add the nuts and salt and stir lightly with a wooden spoon until the nuts are just coated; do not stir too much or the sugar will crystallize.

Pour the nuts out onto the lined pan and quickly use the forks to separate the nuts into a single layer. Cool completely before breaking any shards of sugar off the nuts and storing them in an airtight container for up to 3 days.

Note: *If the nuts get sticky after storing (which can happen in humid locations), spread them out on a lined baking sheet, put them in a 150°F oven for about 10 minutes, and then let cool.*

CRYSTALLIZED NUTS

Nuts that are added to cooked sugar before it caramelizes and stirred until the sugar recrystallizes, producing a thick, sugary white crunchy coating, are called *dragée (drah-ZHEY)* in French. This technique works well with softer, fattier nuts like peanuts, pine nuts, cashews, and pistachios. Hard nuts like almonds or hazelnuts work well also. These are great on their own packaged as a gift, baked into cookies or brownies, chopped and scattered over ice cream or sorbet, or tossed with popcorn. Consider yourself warned—they are addictive. **MAKES ABOUT 3 CUPS**

2 cups whole shelled nuts, such as almonds or pecans (290 g)

3 tablespoons confectioners' sugar (24 g)

1½ teaspoons kosher salt (6 g)

½ cup granulated sugar (100 g)

2 tablespoons water (30 g)

2 teaspoons light corn syrup (12 g)

Preheat the oven to 350°F.

Evenly spread the nuts on a baking sheet and toast, tossing the pan frequently, for 12 to 15 minutes, until golden. Remove from the oven, transfer to a large bowl, and let cool briefly.

While the nuts are still warm (but not hot) sprinkle the confectioners' sugar and salt over them (1) and toss them well in the bowl to completely coat them in sugar (2).

Put the granulated sugar, water, and corn syrup into a large saucepan and stir with your finger until the sugar is sandy and evenly moistened; wet your finger and wipe down the sides of the pan. Put the pan over medium heat and cook, brushing down the sides of the pan with a brush dipped in cold water, until the sugar is completely melted and begins to boil.

Cook until the temperature reaches 284°F (soft-crack stage).

Carefully pour the sugared nuts and any confectioners' sugar in the bowl into the pan (3), reduce the heat to low, and stir vigorously with a wooden spoon (4). The sugar will begin to melt but then start to crystallize on the nuts. Continue stirring until a hard white sugar coating appears evenly on the nuts. Transfer them to a large bowl and continue tossing them until the nuts cool and the sugar hardens. Do not stop agitating the nuts until they have cooled or they will clump together while the sugar hardens.

Pour the nuts out onto a silicone mat– or parchment-lined baking sheet (5) and cool completely before storing in an airtight container for up to 1 month.

Pistachio, Sunflower, and Sesame Brittle

PISTACHIO, SUNFLOWER, AND SESAME BRITTLE

I have always been a fan of brittle, but not when it is too thick or doesn't have enough nuts in it. The star is what you put in it; in this case earthy seeds take the place of traditional peanuts. East meets West. There is just enough caramel to hold everything together. **MAKES ABOUT 4 CUPS**

Vegetable oil cooking spray

1 cup sugar (200 g)

½ cup water (120 g)

½ cup light corn syrup (141 g)

½ teaspoon kosher salt (2 g)

½ cup raw shelled pistachios, coarsely chopped (70 g)

¼ cup unsalted shelled sunflower seeds (36 g)

¼ cup black sesame seeds (32 g)

1 tablespoon unsalted butter, softened (14 g)

1 teaspoon baking soda (6 g)

Line a baking sheet with a silicone baking mat or grease it lightly with vegetable oil.

In a heavy medium saucepan, stir the sugar, water, and corn syrup until combined. Using wet fingers, wash down the interior sides of the pan. Put the pan over medium-high heat and cook until the sugar is dissolved, washing down the sides of the pan with a brush dipped in cold water.

When the mixture begins to boil, add the salt and cook until the mixture reaches 320°F (hard-crack stage). The sugar should be light amber colored.

Remove from the heat and stir in the pistachios, sunflower seeds, and sesame seeds until coated. Quickly stir in the butter and baking soda. When the mixture foams up, pour it out onto the lined baking sheet and allow the mixture to spread out into a thin layer. If the mixture does not spread, use an offset spatula to push the mixture into the pan to a layer about ¼ inch thick.

Let the brittle cool to room temperature before breaking into pieces. Store in an airtight container for up to 2 weeks.

Caramel PUDDING

This pudding is a bit denser, creamier, and richer than a mousse, because it has no eggs but does include butter. It can be lightened by folding in some softly whipped cream, used as is for a cupcake or cake filling, or served along with sliced bananas and toasted walnuts. **MAKES ABOUT 1 QUART; SERVES 6**

FOR THE CARAMEL

½ cup sugar (100 g)

3 tablespoons light corn syrup (50 g)

½ teaspoon kosher salt (2 g)

1 vanilla bean, split and scraped

FOR THE PUDDING

2 cups half-and-half (480 g)

½ cup sugar (100 g)

¼ cup cornstarch (36 g)

2 tablespoons (¼ stick) unsalted butter, diced (28 g)

Prepare an ice bath in a large bowl.

To make the caramel, put the sugar, corn syrup, salt, and vanilla bean and seeds into a medium saucepan and stir with your finger until the sugar is sandy. Put the pan over medium heat and cook, without stirring, until the sugar is completely dissolved. Brush the sides of the pan with a clean pastry brush dipped in cold water. Continue cooking, swirling the pan for even heating, until the mixture turns a dark mahogany brown and gives off white smoke.

Meanwhile, to make the pudding, put the half-and-half into a medium saucepan and whisk the sugar and cornstarch into it until dissolved. Heat until warm over low heat while the caramel is cooking.

When the caramel is ready, reduce the heat to medium-low and slowly pour the warm cream into the caramel (be careful—it will bubble up) and whisk until the mixture is smooth and comes to a boil. Cook for a full 2 minutes at a slow boil. Remove from the heat and whisk in the butter until smooth.

Pour the mixture through a fine-mesh strainer into a bowl, pressing with a rubber spatula to remove any solids. Discard the vanilla bean or rinse and reserve for another use. Lay a sheet of plastic wrap directly on the surface of the pudding; chill the mixture in the ice bath until cool. Refrigerate for at least 2 hours before serving.

SPREADABLE CARAMEL

This caramel is thicker than commercial caramel sauce but not as firm as candy. It is great spread inside crepes, used as a filling for cakes, or drizzled over crisp, cold apple slices for a simple, quick dessert. You can even use it to flavor milk shakes. Make a batch and keep it on hand in the fridge for weeks; it adds a sweet but bitter, salty edge to anything it tops. **MAKES ABOUT 2½ CUPS**

---

1 cup heavy cream (240 g)

1 vanilla bean, split and scraped

½ teaspoon kosher salt (2 g)

1 cup sugar (200 g)

1 tablespoon light corn syrup (17 g)

3 tablespoons water (45 g)

4 tablespoons (½ stick) cold unsalted butter, diced (57 g)

In a saucepan, warm the cream, vanilla bean and seeds, and salt gently over medium-low heat. Do not boil.

Prepare an ice bath in a large bowl.

Put the sugar, corn syrup, and water into a large saucepan and stir with your finger until the mixture is sandy and evenly moistened. Use a wet finger to wipe down the sides of the pan. Put the pan over medium-high heat and cook until the sugar is completely melted and liquefied, brushing down the sides of the pan with a brush dipped in cold water several times. Once the sugar is melted and begins to boil, do not stir; if any sugar crystals appear on the pan, wash the sides down again with the brush.

Cook the sugar, swirling the pan for even cooking, until a deep mahogany brown. The sugar will give off white smoke when ready. Reduce the heat to low and carefully whisk in the warm cream, a little at a time, whisking well between additions. The sugar will bubble up, so be careful. Once all the cream has been added, whisk well to dissolve any sugar lumps that appear. Remove the pan from the heat and whisk the butter into the caramel, a little at a time, until very smooth.

Pour the caramel through a fine-mesh strainer into a clean bowl; discard the vanilla bean or rinse and reserve for another use. Set the bowl in the ice bath and stir occasionally until cold. Use immediately or transfer the caramel to an airtight container and refrigerate for up to 2 weeks.

Salted CARAMELS

Here is the best way to taste how the cooked sugar color affects the resulting caramel flavor. Don't be afraid to cook the sugar until it is very, very dark for the best results. These are much softer than most caramels you will eat, so if they are too gooey in the wrappers, refrigerate them. While some people like the texture of taffy, I prefer a softer caramel that is chewy but also unctuously velvety at the same time. These are rich, salty, and smoky, and just a little bite goes a long way. **MAKES ABOUT 60 CARAMELS**

Vegetable oil cooking spray

1 cup heavy cream (240 g)

⅓ cup light corn syrup (95 g)

¼ cup honey (74 g)

1 vanilla bean, split and scraped

Heaping ½ teaspoon gray sea salt or Maldon salt (3 g)

¾ cup sugar (175 g)

Line an 8-inch square cake pan with aluminum foil and spray it lightly with cooking spray.

In a small saucepan, bring the cream, corn syrup, honey, vanilla bean and seeds, and salt to a simmer over medium heat. Reduce the heat to very low and keep warm.

In a large saucepan, cook the sugar over medium heat until completely melted. If there are any sugar crystals on the edges of the pan, wash the sides down with a brush dipped in cold water. Continue cooking the sugar, swirling the pan as necessary for even cooking, until the sugar is deep mahogany brown. The pan will give off white smoke—if the smoke gets darker, it means the sugar is burning and has gone too far.

Reduce the heat to low; remove the vanilla bean from the warm cream and very slowly pour it into the sugar (the sugar will bubble up). Once the mixture has stopped bubbling, whisk the mixture well and return to medium heat. Continue cooking until the temperature reaches 245°F (firm-ball stage). Immediately pour the mixture into the foil-lined pan. Let it settle briefly and then tap the pan on the counter to release any bubbles.

Let the pan stand until the candy is completely cool, preferably overnight. Using the foil, lift the caramel out of the pan and set it on a cutting board. Using a sharp knife, cut the caramel into ½ × 1½-inch pieces and wrap them in wax paper. If the caramels are very soft, refrigerate them briefly until they hold their shape and are easy to work with. The caramels will keep in a cool spot or in the refrigerator for up to 1 month.

Earl Grey CRÈME CARAMEL

Crème caramel is the perfect marriage of sweet and bitter, custard and liquid caramel. You can flavor the custard just about any way you like—with fruit purées, spices, or in this case by steeping the liquid with tea leaves. Earl Grey tea is soothing, calming, and gentle and a natural pairing for custard. Plus the light hint of smoke in the tea works beautifully with caramelized sugar. For the silkiest crème caramel, it is best to make the custard and let it chill overnight. Once baked, these need another day for the caramel to dissolve before being served, so plan ahead. It's well worth the effort. **SERVES 8**

FOR THE CUSTARD

3 cups whole milk (720 g)

3 tablespoons honey (60 g)

2 tablespoons loose Earl Grey tea leaves (10 g)

⅓ cup sugar (65 g)

½ teaspoon kosher salt (2 g)

2 large egg yolks

4 large eggs

FOR THE CARAMEL

¾ cup sugar (150 g)

2 tablespoons light corn syrup (34 g)

2 tablespoons water (30 g)

⅛ teaspoon kosher salt

To make the custard, heat the milk and honey in a saucepan over medium heat until very hot but not boiling. Stir to dissolve the honey. Add the tea leaves, remove from the heat, and let stand for 10 minutes.

Pour the mixture through a fine-mesh strainer into a bowl, discarding the tea leaves, and cool the milk to room temperature.

In a medium bowl, whisk together the sugar and salt. Add the egg yolks and whole eggs and whisk vigorously until very smooth and lightened. Slowly whisk the cooled milk into the eggs until combined. Transfer to an airtight container and refrigerate overnight.

To make the caramel, set eight 4-ounce ramekins into a deep baking dish or roasting pan. Fill a bowl with cold water and set aside.

Put the sugar, corn syrup, water, and salt in a small saucepan and make a wet caramel as for Spreadable Caramel (page 151), cooking the mixture until the sugar is a deep golden brown. Dip the base of the saucepan in the cold water briefly to stop the cooking, which will ensure an even caramel in each ramekin (sugar will continue to caramelize in a hot pan even off the heat). Let the caramel stand for a minute and then carefully drizzle it evenly among the ramekins (1). If the sugar begins to harden, warm the pan gently over low heat until the caramel liquefies. Immediately pick up each ramekin and rotate the dish to coat the bottom with caramel. If the caramel hardens before it is spread, you can heat the ramekins in the microwave or in a low oven until the caramel liquefies again. Let stand until the caramel sets.

Preheat the oven to 300°F. Remove the custard from the refrigerator and let stand until room temperature.

Stir the custard gently without creating bubbles and divide it evenly among the caramel-lined ramekins in the baking dish (2). Carefully pour hot water into the dish to reach halfway up the sides of the ramekins. Bake in the center of the oven, without moving the pan, for 65 to 70 minutes, until the custards are just set but still very wobbly in the center.

Remove from the oven and let the crème caramels cool completely in the water bath. Transfer them to the refrigerator and chill overnight.

To unmold, dip each ramekin in hot water for about 10 seconds (3) and run the tip of a thin, sharp knife or a metal cake tester around the edge of each custard to release, pressing all the way down the sides if necessary to break the seal (4). Once the sides are loosened, invert a dessert plate onto the top and flip the ramekins over on the plate. Shake the plate and ramekin gently to release the custard and then remove the ramekin (5). Repeat with the remaining custards and serve immediately.

Individual Caramel Apple and Sweet Potato
BREAD PUDDINGS

Most of my career in the kitchen has been spent creating individual portions for restaurant menus. While some recipes can be expanded for a large dessert, I like this one best as an individual dessert, because it has a greater visual impact. As a kid in upstate New York, a favorite pastime was apple picking—we didn't have a lot of sweets in the house, so Mom made apple chips, applesauce, and sometimes pies. Pairing a good ripe, crisp apple with sweet potatoes and a maple-flavored, custardy bread pudding creates flavors that feel like home. **SERVES 8**

FOR THE CARAMEL

Vegetable oil cooking spray

¾ cup sugar (150 g)

½ teaspoon kosher salt (2 g)

3 tablespoons water (45 g)

1 tablespoon honey (20 g)

3 tablespoons unsalted butter, diced (42 g)

FOR THE PUDDING

1 medium sweet potato (about 12 ounces), peeled (340 g)

1 large Granny Smith apple, peeled and cored

2 tablespoons sugar (24 g)

1 tablespoon unsalted butter (14 g)

2 cups half-and-half (480 g)

2 large eggs

2 large egg yolks

¼ cup pure maple syrup (72 g)

1 teaspoon vanilla extract (5 g)

½ teaspoon kosher salt (2 g)

4 ounces day-old Brioche (page 292) or egg bread, cut into ½-inch cubes and lightly toasted (about 10 cups) (113 g)

Preheat the oven to 325°F. Spray eight 4-ounce ramekins with cooking spray and put them in a large baking dish.

To make the caramel, put the sugar, salt, and water in a small saucepan and make a wet caramel as for Spreadable Caramel (page 151), cooking the mixture until the sugar is a deep golden brown. Remove from the heat and add the honey and butter, stirring until well combined. Set aside to cool until warm but still pourable. Divide the warm caramel evenly among the ramekins (about 1 tablespoon in each), swirling each ramekin to completely coat the bottom of each.

To make the pudding, cut the sweet potato and apple into ½-inch cubes, keeping them separate. In a medium skillet, cook the sugar over medium heat, swirling the pan but not stirring, until it dissolves and turns golden brown. Add the butter and stir to combine and dissolve any sugar crystals. Add the sweet potato cubes and cook, stirring gently, for about 6 minutes, until just tender when pierced with a knife but still holding their shape. Add the apples, stir gently, and continue cooking for 4 minutes, until the apples soften slightly. Remove from the heat and let stand until cool. Put an even, single layer of potatoes and apples into each ramekin, covering the bottom. Reserve the remaining potatoes and apples.

Meanwhile, in another saucepan, heat the half-and-half over medium heat until hot and the edges are just beginning to bubble. Whisk the eggs, egg yolks, syrup, vanilla, and salt together in a mixing bowl. While whisking, pour about a third of the hot half-and-half mixture into the eggs and whisk well until very smooth and combined. Whisk in the remaining hot half-and-half mixture until combined. Let the custard stand until room temperature.

Put the brioche cubes and the reserved potatoes and apples into a mixing bowl and pour the custard over them. Toss lightly and let them stand for a few minutes to absorb the custard. Using a large spoon, pour enough custard into the bottom of each ramekin to cover the sweet potato and apple cubes. Divide the soaked bread cubes among the ramekins and evenly pour any custard left in the bowl over each.

Fill the baking dish with hot water until it comes halfway up the sides of the ramekins. Transfer the dish to the oven and bake for 40 to 45 minutes, until the custard is set and the top feels firm to the touch. Remove the pan from the oven and let the bread puddings cool completely in the water bath. Remove the puddings from the water bath and serve or refrigerate for up to 2 days before serving.

To serve, preheat the oven to 300°F.

Run a knife around the outer edges of the ramekins to loosen the puddings. Set the ramekins on a baking sheet and warm them in the oven for 10 minutes to loosen the caramel. Invert the bread puddings onto serving plates and serve warm.

Sticky Caramel DATE CAKE

This is a riff on the English sticky toffee cake, which usually I find sickeningly sweet. However, if you pay attention to the salt in the recipe and balance the bitter levels of the caramel with the other ingredients, you can achieve complex flavors instead of giving yourself a toothache. You'll still have a moist, sticky, date-flavored treat that completely satisfies. **SERVES 6 TO 8**

FOR THE CAKE

3 tablespoons cold unsalted butter, diced, plus more for the pan (42 g)

1 cup pitted dates (about 18), chopped (131 g)

1 cup water (240 g)

1 teaspoon baking soda (6 g)

½ cup sugar (100 g)

2 large eggs, at room temperature

Grated zest of ½ orange

¾ teaspoon vanilla extract (5 g)

¼ teaspoon orange extract or oil (1 g)

1 cup all-purpose flour (125 g)

1 teaspoon baking powder (4 g)

½ teaspoon kosher salt (2 g)

FOR THE CARAMEL SAUCE

1 cup heavy cream, at room temperature (240 g)

¼ cup sugar (50 g)

1 tablespoon light corn syrup (17 g)

1 tablespoon pure maple syrup (17 g)

1 tablespoon unsalted butter (14 g)

1 tablespoon fresh lemon juice (15g)

½ teaspoon kosher salt (2 g)

To make the cake, preheat the oven to 350°F. Butter an 8-inch square cake pan.

In a small saucepan, bring the dates and water to a boil over medium-high heat. Reduce the heat to medium-low and simmer for 5 minutes. Remove the pan from the heat, mash the dates into a paste with a potato masher or spoon, and stir in the baking soda. Let stand until cool.

Put the 3 tablespoons butter and the sugar into the bowl of a standing mixer and toss until the butter is coated in sugar. Attach the bowl and paddle to the mixer and beat the butter on medium-low speed until a thick paste forms with no visible butter lumps. Add the eggs, one at a time, mixing well between

additions. Add the orange zest and vanilla and orange extracts and mix well. Scrape down the bowl with a rubber spatula.

Sift the flour and baking powder together and sprinkle the salt over it. With the mixer on low, slowly add the dry ingredients and mix until just combined. Add the cooled date paste and mix well until combined.

Transfer the batter to the prepared pan and set the pan inside a larger cake pan or roasting pan. Fill the large pan with hot water until it reaches halfway up the sides of the cake pan. Cover the large pan tightly with aluminum foil. Bake the cake in the center of the oven until a cake tester comes out clean, about

30 minutes. Remove the pan and let the cake cool for 15 minutes in the water bath, covered.

Meanwhile, to make the caramel sauce, put half of the cream, the sugar, corn syrup, maple syrup, butter, lemon juice, and salt into a medium saucepan and stir well. Bring the mixture to a boil over medium-high heat. Whisk frequently for 20 to 30 minutes, until the mixture turns medium golden brown. Reduce the heat, carefully add the remaining cream, and whisk well to dissolve any lumps of sugar that form. Continue cooking over low heat for about 10 minutes, until deep golden brown. Remove from the heat.

Carefully lift the cake pan from the water bath, wipe the bottom of the pan, and use a knife to release the cake from the sides of the pan if necessary. Invert the cake onto a cutting board. Pour about half of the caramel sauce into the bottom of the pan. Using 2 large spatulas, return the cake to the pan, upside down, and pour the remaining sauce over the cake. Let the cake cool completely before serving or refrigerate for up to 3 days.

Remove the cake from the refrigerator at least 15 minutes before serving. Cut the cake into small squares or circles and transfer to small dessert plates. Drizzle a little of the caramel sauce from the pan over the top.

Note: *The cake is sturdy and can be cut into any size with cookie cutters. It can be part of a plated dessert with ice cream or stacked and served with more caramel sauce drizzled over it.*

Spiced Apple, Mango, and Banana TARTE TATIN

A traditional apple tarte Tatin is made all in one pan, usually a French copper-bottomed sauté pan. First you make caramel, add the apples to cook briefly, and then top the fruit with a sheet of puff pastry and bake it. Once it cools slightly, you invert it onto a serving plate. The flavors are amazing; I love the moist, fudgelike texture of the fruit paired with the crisp crust. But sometimes the dough gets soggy where it meets the fruit, so I bake an additional disk of pastry separately to serve it on. You get soft, rich fruit, warm caramel, and crunchy puff pastry all in one bite. I've rocked this dessert out further by adding some spices to the caramel and some tropical fruits to the mix. Apologies to my French chef colleagues; I like my version better.

SERVES 12

1½ pounds Puff Pastry (page 264) or store-bought, chilled

All-purpose flour, for rolling

½ cup plus 2 tablespoons sugar (124 g)

¼ teaspoon kosher salt (1 g)

2 tablespoons water (30 g)

½ teaspoon coriander seeds (1 g)

½ teaspoon allspice berries (2 g)

½ teaspoon white peppercorns (2 g)

5 tablespoons unsalted butter, diced (70 g)

8 Granny Smith apples, peeled and cored

1 large mango, peeled, pitted, and sliced crosswise into ½-inch-wide strips

2 firm bananas

Crème fraîche, whipped cream, or ice cream, for serving

Preheat the oven to 400°F. Line 2 baking sheets with silicone baking mats or parchment paper.

Cut the puff pastry in half. Lightly flour a work surface and roll one half to a rough circle at least 10 inches in diameter. Invert a 10-inch cake pan onto it. Using a sharp knife, use the cake pan as a template to cut a perfect circle. Transfer the dough round to a lined sheet pan, prick it all over the surface with a fork, and refrigerate it. Roll the second piece of puff pastry to at least a 10-inch-diameter rough circle, transfer it to the remaining sheet pan, and prick it with a fork. Lay a piece of parchment paper over it, top with an inverted cookie cooling rack, and transfer to the oven. Bake until light golden brown, about 20 minutes. Carefully remove the cooling rack

and peel off the top parchment layer. Bake for 5 to 10 minutes longer, until evenly deep golden brown. Remove from the oven and let the pastry cool on the pan.

Reduce the oven temperature to 375°F.

Meanwhile, put the sugar, salt, and water into a medium saucepan and stir it with your finger until the sugar is sandy. Wet 2 fingers and wipe down the sides of the pan. Put the pan over medium-high heat and cook until the sugar is dissolved and the mixture starts to boil. Brush the sides of the pan down with a clean pastry brush dipped in cold water. Add the coriander, allspice, and peppercorns

recipe continues

and cook, swirling the pan for even cooking, until deep mahogany brown. Reduce the heat to low and carefully add 2 tablespoons of the butter, stirring, until well combined. Remove the pan from the heat and pour the caramel through a fine-mesh strainer into an ovenproof 9-inch nonstick skillet. Swirl the pan to coat it evenly in caramel and let stand until just warm.

Halve the apples lengthwise and arrange the halves on top of the caramel, standing upright in a concentric circle around the outer edge of the skillet. Insert more halves into the center to pack the pan tightly. Fill the cores of the apples and any open spaces with mango pieces, packing them in. Dot the remaining 3 tablespoons butter over the fruit. Put the pan over medium heat and cook for 6 to 8 minutes, until the caramel is simmering and you can see liquid around the sides of the apples (1). Transfer the pan to the oven and bake for 15 minutes.

Remove the skillet from the oven. Slice the bananas diagonally, ¼ inch thick, and lay them evenly over the tops of the apples and into any crevices (2). Remove the puff pastry round from the refrigerator, lay it on top of the fruit (3), and carefully tuck the sides down into the pan (4). Return the skillet to the oven and bake for 25 to 30 minutes, until the puff pastry is deep golden brown (5).

Meanwhile, invert a 9-inch cake pan onto the crisp sheet of baked puff pastry and use a sharp knife to trim around the pan to cut out a perfect circle. Reserve the scraps for another use.

When the tart is finished baking, remove the skillet from the oven, carefully lay the crisp puff disk on top of the tart, and press it gently into the pan without breaking it. Cool the tart completely in the pan. Do not try to unmold while it is still warm; the fruit needs time to set.

Run a small rubber spatula around the edges of the pan to loosen any sides that are stuck to it. Invert a serving platter onto the skillet. Carefully flip the plate and pan over and let it stand a few minutes for the tart to release itself from the pan. Carefully lift off the skillet.

The tart can be served at room temperature with a dollop of crème fraîche or can be transferred carefully to a baking sheet and warmed in a 250°F oven for about 10 minutes before serving.

Note: *For the best results when coating ingredients with caramel, have them all warm before you add the caramel to them, including the mixing bowl you are using, so it will spread easily and not immediately clump.*

Smack CARAMEL CORN

Since I like a salty edge to my caramel, bumping it up with crisp bacon bits and bacon fat makes perfect sense. I'm a fan of the textures and flavors of Cracker Jack, so here's my own addictive version with a savory bent. Plus I no longer need the temporary tattoos from the box—I have my own now. **MAKES ABOUT 14 CUPS**

---

8 slices bacon

Vegetable oil cooking spray

1½ cups plain unsalted roasted peanuts (225 g)

½ cup slivered almonds, toasted (see page 142) (54 g)

1 cup granulated sugar (200 g)

¾ cup (packed) dark brown sugar (174 g)

¼ cup pure maple syrup (72 g)

¼ cup light corn syrup (72 g)

6 tablespoons (¾ stick) unsalted butter (84 g)

2 teaspoons kosher salt (8 g)

1 teaspoon baking soda (6 g)

12 cups popped popcorn

Preheat the oven to 200°F. Line 2 baking sheets with silicone baking mats or parchment paper.

In a large skillet, cook the bacon over medium heat, turning several times, for 6 to 8 minutes, until very crisp and the fat is rendered. Transfer the bacon to a paper-towel-lined plate to drain. Pour the bacon fat through a fine-mesh strainer into a heatproof bowl. Measure 3 tablespoons of the fat and reserve; discard the remaining fat or reserve for another use. Once the bacon has cooled, finely chop it and set it aside.

Spray a large stainless-steel bowl lightly with cooking spray, add the peanuts and almonds to it, and put the bowl in the oven to warm. Spray 2 large spoons or rubber spatulas with cooking spray and set them aside.

Put the granulated sugar, brown sugar, maple and corn syrups, butter, and reserved bacon fat into a saucepan and bring to a boil over medium-high heat. Swirl the pan gently to mix the ingredients, but do not stir. Cook, brushing the sides of the pan down with a pastry brush dipped in cold water, until the temperature on a candy thermometer reads 290°F.

Stir together the salt and baking soda, add them to the caramel, and remove the pan from the heat. Be careful—the caramel will foam up; stir it with a wooden spoon until the mixture stops foaming. Remove the bowl from the oven and add the nuts to the caramel, stirring to combine. Put the popcorn and chopped bacon into the warm bowl and pour the caramel mixture over it; using the greased spoons, toss the popcorn quickly and keep tossing for about 1 minute, until it is very evenly coated.

Pour the caramel popcorn out onto the lined pans and spread it out with the spoons into an even layer. Let the popcorn cool briefly and then carefully separate the kernels with your hands so there are no large clumps. Cool completely on the pans.

Store the caramel popcorn in an airtight container or plastic bag for up to 3 days.

BANANA FRITTERS *with Tahini Caramel Cream*

While I try not to eat too much fried food, these fried coconut-coated bananas are an exception. The poppy and sesame seeds add another layer of nutty crunch. Frying creates a crisp shell while maintaining the silky-velvet texture of the bananas. Baking just doesn't deliver the same magic here. These are terrific dipped in mango chutney or plain honey, but try the sesame paste and caramel cream recipe here. Salty, crunchy, sweet, nutty, and creamy, these fritters are over the top. **SERVES ABOUT 12**

FOR THE TAHINI CARAMEL CREAM

3 tablespoons tahini (sesame paste) (60 g)

¾ cup heavy cream, whipped to medium-firm peaks (180 g)

¼ cup Spreadable Caramel (page 151) (80 g)

FOR THE FRITTERS

Vegetable oil, for frying

1 cup sweetened shredded coconut, finely chopped (71 g)

2 tablespoons poppy seeds (20 g)

2 tablespoons white sesame seeds (18 g)

3 firm bananas

1 cup all-purpose flour (125 g)

2 tablespoons sugar (24 g)

½ teaspoon kosher salt, plus more for sprinkling (2 g)

½ teaspoon baking powder (3 g)

1 cup beer, preferably a light ale (240 g)

To make the tahini caramel cream, put the tahini into a large bowl, add about a quarter of the whipped cream, and stir well to combine and lighten it. With a large rubber spatula, gently fold the remaining whipped cream into the mixture just until combined. Add the caramel and gently fold just until streaky. Transfer to a serving bowl and refrigerate until ready to use.

To make the fritters, fill a heavy pot with vegetable oil to a depth of 3 inches and heat to 375°F.

Meanwhile, in a shallow dish, stir together the coconut, poppy seeds, and sesame seeds until combined. Slice each banana on a slight diagonal into 6 equal-sized pieces. In a mixing bowl, whisk together the flour, sugar, salt, and baking powder.

When the oil is hot, slowly whisk the beer into the flour mixture until just combined; do not overmix—there should be lumps in the batter. Using a fork and working with about 4 pieces at a time, dip the bananas in the batter, shaking off the excess. Drop into the coconut mixture and then gently roll the banana pieces in it with a fork to coat on all sides. Using a slotted spoon, lower the slices into the oil and fry, turning frequently, for about 1½ minutes, until golden brown.

Transfer to a paper-towel-lined plate to drain. Sprinkle salt over the fritters while they are still warm. Repeat with the remaining bananas, monitoring the oil temperature and adjusting the heat to maintain it.

Transfer the fritters to a serving platter and serve immediately with toothpicks for skewering and the tahini caramel cream for dipping.

Note: *These are a great dessert for a cocktail party when you want to serve a little sweet bite. You can mix fresh batter as the party progresses and fry them in batches. You'd be surprised at how well the salty-sweet, crunchy coating matches up with cocktails.*

CHAPTER 4

CAKES, CUPCAKES, BROWNIES,

and

MUFFINS

CAKES

I've always had some form of cake on the hundreds of dessert plates I've composed over the years, because, next to ice cream, it could be the dessert of choice in this country. Cake can be the star of the show or a component in an extravagant dessert. Sometimes you want a light egg foam or meringue-based cake to pair with a delicate ice cream or custard; other times you may crave a rich, dense butter cake for a special-occasion creation. Cakes can vary in texture and taste more than just about any other type of dessert.

I love rich, moist cakes. If I had to pick one as a favorite, I'd say devil's food, made with homemade mayonnaise—the leadoff cake recipe I picked for my first cookbook. Here you'll find some new and interesting-flavored cakes that are awesome layered with buttercream or mousse or served with pudding or ice cream.

There are two basic types of cakes: butter or oil cakes and egg foam or meringue cakes.

BUTTER *and* OIL CAKES

While these are both fat-based cakes, they yield two very different results. Butter cakes are rich and often dense, whereas oil cakes tend to be lighter and to stay moist longer. In either case, the butter or oil acts as a barrier to gluten, the protein in flour that gives cakes and breads their structure and texture. When liquid is introduced to flour, it activates the gluten, which begins to create the bonds that hold the structure of the cake in place. Butter or oil, though, coats the flour so that the gluten has a minimal chance of developing, which keeps the texture tender. Butter cakes always begin with beating the butter and sugar together; this aerates the butter, adding air bubbles, which—with the addition of whole eggs—makes a cake rise. Oil, however, cannot be aerated, so typically these types of cakes and muffins have added leavening agents like baking soda and baking powder. In either case, other liquids are usually added last to the batter; if the flour particles are coated in fat, they cannot absorb much liquid, keeping the finished cake soft and tender.

I use butter cakes mostly when making stand-alone desserts; they have more heft and structure and are filling and satisfying enough to need just a complementary icing or glaze. Oil cakes, on the other hand, are what I turn to for constructing multicomponent desserts; they can be layered with icings, fillings, pastry creams, or puddings and even soaked with flavored syrups before they are iced.

➡ *Tips for* CAKE BAKING:

- Cakes need constant, even heat to rise properly and bake evenly throughout. Check the temperature of your oven to make sure it is working properly (see page 16).

- Always use flat, sturdy stainless-steel baking pans. If all you have are your grandma's beaten-up tin cake pans, it's time for new ones.

- When filling multiple cake pans or cavities in a cupcake tin, make sure to fill all compartments evenly with batter so they bake at the same speed. For cakes, you may want to weigh the batter so you can divide it perfectly among pans. For muffins or cupcakes, use ice cream scoops to disperse the batter evenly.

- When spreading cake batters on a flat sheet pan, I like to run my thumb or the tip of a spatula around the edges before I put it in the oven to make releasing the baked cake from the pan a lot easier.

- Proper cake baking requires understanding when cakes are cooked through. Don't rely solely on a cake tester—learn to know by touch whether a cake is baked. It should spring back lightly and not leave an indentation when you press your finger lightly into the center. Cakes that are ready usually also begin to pull away from the sides of the pan.

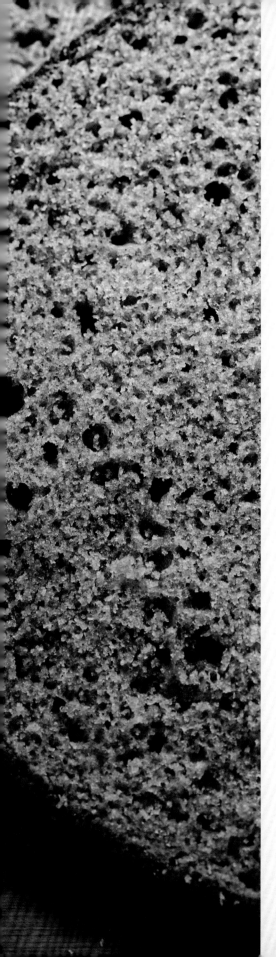

➡ *Tips for* SUCCESSFUL BUTTER *or* OIL CAKES:

- Most cake recipes call for the butter to be softened or at room temperature. I have found, though, that working with cold butter produces a better final texture. Modern kitchen mixers can overheat butter quickly simply by beating it too long; if the butter is too soft when you start mixing the batter, it essentially melts into the flour. Butter is an emulsion; if it gets too warm, the emulsion breaks, which can result in a greasy cake.

- However, eggs and liquids (milk, cream, buttermilk, etc.) should be at room temperature. Cold eggs can cause the fat to separate and break the emulsion of fat and water in the butter. If you have ever made a batter and seen the butter go from smooth and creamy to clumped and curdlike, cold liquids and/or eggs might have been the culprit. If this happens, the cake batter is not ruined, but the texture will be affected and may not be as tender and moist as you'd like.

- Toss the sugar and diced butter by hand to coat the butter, then attach the mixer bowl and paddle and beat them together until the mixture is sandy and somewhat smooth with no clumps of butter remaining. This takes about 5 minutes. Be sure to beat the butter and sugar long enough; it aerates the butter, which helps cakes rise.

- Always sift dry ingredients together, both to remove impurities or clumps and to pre-aerate the ingredients so they combine with the wet ingredients more evenly and lightly. Since I prefer to use kosher (coarse) salt in my recipes, which won't go through fine-mesh strainers, I typically sift all the other ingredients together and then sprinkle the salt evenly over the top before beginning to add them to the beaten butter.

- Once you've added the flour and dry ingredients, stop the mixer and scrape the bowl with a rubber spatula several times to promote even mixing.

- Do not overmix cake batter; once the dry ingredients are added, mix only until combined and moistened. Overbeating cake batter activates the gluten (protein) in the flour and will make the cake tough and chewy.

MERINGUE *or* EGG FOAM CAKES

These cakes are lighter, more flexible, and have many uses. Typically foam cakes are made from a moist batter with meringue or whipped whole-egg foam folded into it. Even lighter versions, like angel food or génoise (*zhen-WAHZ*), the classic French sponge cake, begin with fluffy meringue or foam that is very lightly combined with a mixture of dry ingredients. They are less dense and more malleable than butter or oil cakes.

Like a soufflé, the main structure that holds them together is made of aerated egg whites and yolks; they do not get their airiness from chemical leaveners. As with butter cakes, coating the flour particles in whipped egg (rather than fat) also minimizes the activation of gluten when other liquids are introduced, keeping these cakes tender.

Meringue and foam cakes generally contain less fat, which makes them prone to drying out more easily or being tough. Most foam cakes become a vehicle for other flavors: They are commonly rolled with a filling to make jelly rolls or bûche de Noël (Yule log cake) or baked in round cake pans, brushed with flavored syrups, and filled with buttercream or fruit fillings as a lighter option for a layer cake as dessert. Some foam-based cakes, however, do have oil, melted butter, or other fats added to give them richness and tenderness, while the egg foam still does the heavy lifting of raising the cake in the oven.

Sponge cakes are great to bake and save for future uses; they freeze very well. Just be sure, if you stack the cakes to freeze them, to put 2 pieces of parchment in between layers before wrapping them tightly with plastic wrap. Or freeze them separately on cardboard cake rounds. Allow frozen sponge cakes to thaw at room temperature before icing them. Do not reheat them to thaw them; it will make them tough and chewy.

➡️ *Tips for* BAKING MERINGUE *or* FOAM-BASED CAKES:

- The key to a great meringue sponge cake is to have everything ready to go before starting the recipe. Meringue waits for no one.

- Contrary to popular belief, don't whip the meringue too stiff. It makes it harder to fold in dry ingredients, and you end up with lumps of meringue within the batter, which will cause the cake to rise and bake unevenly. Plus, if you try to break down any lumps to smooth them out, you will deflate the batter and lose the air you whipped into it. For the best results, whip meringues to soft peaks (like softly whipped heavy cream).

- Egg foams should be whipped until they are firm enough to hold the trail of the whisk within the foam, called the *ribbon stage*. To check this, lift the whisk out of the bowl and drizzle the foam off the end of the whisk back and forth onto itself—the shape of the "ribbons" you created should hold and not sink back into the foam.

- Don't fold ingredients together within the mixer bowl. *Always* transfer the meringue to a larger, wider bowl so you can comfortably fold in the dry ingredients without crushing and compacting the meringue.

- Once the meringue is transferred to a large bowl, carefully scoop about a third of the sifted dry ingredients and "feather" (very lightly and evenly scatter with your fingertips) the mixture over the top of the whites. Fold gently, turning the bowl as you fold, until mostly combined; do not overmix. Feather the dry ingredients in two more batches, folding after each addition. After the last addition of dry ingredients to the top of the whites, slowly and steadily fold and turn the bowl, being careful not to deflate the meringue. Mix until the batter looks homogenous and no further. The more you practice this, the better you'll be at recognizing exactly when to stop folding.

  ◦ If you are baking in a sheet pan, pour all the batter out at once onto the prepared pan. Using a large offset spatula, gently press the mass in two or three strokes into the corners before evening the batter in the pan. (See the photos on page 199 for spreading batter in sheet pans.)

  ◦ To test whether you have spread the batter evenly, press a fingertip into all four corners and the center and observe the thickness of the batter on your finger. You want it as perfectly even as possible so that the cake bakes evenly from one side to the other. If the batter is not even, you can end up with crisp overbaked edges or sides instead of an even, tender cake throughout.

  ◦ To help with releasing the cake after baking, run a finger, thumb, or the angled tip of the spatula around the edges of the pan to separate the batter from the sides, creating a "moat" between the batter and the pan edge before it goes in the oven.

- Sponge cakes tend to bake very quickly, so keep an eye on them in the oven. If you test with a cake tester, and it comes out very dry, chances are the cake will overbake once removed from the oven due to the residual heat. If you are baking a very thin cake like a jelly roll, a few moist crumbs on the tester are preferable. If testing with your finger, the cake should be dry to the touch and spring back lightly when pressed.

- Immediately set the pan on a cooling rack and keep in mind that leaving a thin sponge cake in a hot sheet pan after it is removed from the oven can cause it to overbake while it cools and can make it tough and chewy. For the best result, foam-based thin sheet cakes should be loosened carefully from the edges of the pan the moment you take them out of the oven. Immediately slide the cake, along with the baking mat or parchment it is baked on, onto a work surface to cool out of the pan.

- If baking in a round, square, or rectangular pan, put about a third of the batter into the prepared pan, spread it to cover the base of the pan, and then gently tap the pan on a work surface two or three times to settle the batter into the corners. Add the rest of the batter and use a small offset spatula to smooth the top. To test for doneness, use a cake tester. For thicker cakes, there should be no crumbs stuck to it when you pierce the center, but make sure you don't overbake and dry out the cake. The cake should be just starting to pull away from the sides of the pan. Larger, thicker sponge cakes should cool for 10 minutes in the pan before you invert them onto a rack to cool completely.

Citrus Butter LOAF CAKE

This is the cake I like to have hanging around for a bite with morning coffee or an afternoon snack. It is dense, rich, and better than any store-bought pound cake. It is also great if you toast up a slice in a pan and serve it with fresh, lightly stewed, or caramelized fruit. **MAKES ONE 4½ × 8½-INCH LOAF CAKE (OR ONE 9-INCH ROUND CAKE); SERVES 8 TO 10**

½ pound (2 sticks) cold unsalted butter, diced, plus more for the pan (226 g)

2 cups all-purpose flour, plus more for the pan (250 g)

1½ cups sugar (300 g)

Grated zest of 2 lemons

Grated zest of 1 orange

5 large eggs, at room temperature

3 tablespoons buttermilk, at room temperature (45 g)

3 tablespoons fresh lemon juice (45 g)

3 tablespoons fresh orange juice (45 g)

1½ teaspoons baking powder (6 g)

1 teaspoon kosher salt (4 g)

FOR THE GLAZE

2 tablespoons buttermilk (30 g)

1 tablespoon honey (20 g)

Preheat the oven to 375°F. Butter and flour a 4½ × 8½-inch loaf pan.

In the bowl of a standing mixer, toss the butter, sugar, lemon zest, and orange zest together (1) until the butter is coated (2). Attach the bowl to the mixer with the paddle and beat on medium speed until it is homogenous and no lumps of butter remain, 5 minutes (3). Add the eggs, one at a time, scraping down the bowl with a rubber spatula between additions (4).

Meanwhile, stir together the buttermilk, lemon juice, and orange juice. Sift together the 2 cups (250 g) flour and the baking powder in a bowl and sprinkle the salt over the top.

With the mixer on low speed, alternately add the dry and wet ingredients to the butter mixture in 3 additions, beginning and ending with the dry (5).

Stop the mixer to scrape down the bowl several times and mix just until smooth. Pour the batter into the prepared pan, smooth the top with a spatula (6), and bake for 15 minutes. (For a 9-inch cake, bake at 375°F for 40 minutes, brush with glaze, and bake for an additional 5 minutes.)

Reduce the oven temperature to 325°F and continue baking for 35 to 40 minutes, rotating the pan halfway through, until the cake is golden brown and a tester inserted into the thickest part comes out clean. Leave the oven on.

Meanwhile, to make the glaze, in a small bowl, stir together the buttermilk and honey until combined. When the cake is done, brush the glaze evenly over the surface and return the cake to the oven; bake for 5 minutes longer. Cool the cake completely in the pan on a rack before inverting and slicing to serve.

Root CAKE

This cake is based on a carrot cake recipe that one of my cooks at Jean-Georges, Renata Ameni-Belknap, shared with me when I needed a Brazil-inspired dessert for a culinary event. It uses an unusual technique—the batter is made in a blender—that produces an amazingly moist cake. I add even more root vegetables to the recipe, giving it a robust, earthy flavor and richness. I also add some sambuca to the traditional chocolate glaze; the slight anise/licorice flavor is a great match for parsnips and carrots. **MAKES ONE 9 × 13-INCH CAKE; SERVES 10 TO 12**

FOR THE CAKE

¾ cup vegetable oil, plus more for the pan (144 g)

2 cups all-purpose flour, plus more for the pan (250 g)

8 ounces peeled and coarsely chopped parsnips (about 2 packed cups, from about 1 large) (227 g)

1 cup whole milk (240 g)

4 large eggs

12 ounces peeled and coarsely chopped carrots (about 2½ packed cups, from about 3 medium) (340 g)

1¾ cups sugar (350 g)

1½ teaspoons kosher salt (6 g)

1 teaspoon ground star anise (3 g)

1 teaspoon ground ginger (3 g)

¼ teaspoon ground white pepper (1 g)

½ teaspoon almond extract (3 g)

1 tablespoon baking powder (12 g)

FOR THE CHOCOLATE GLAZE

3½ ounces bittersweet chocolate, chopped (100 g)

1 cup whole milk (240 g)

1 tablespoon unsalted butter (14 g)

2 teaspoons honey (12 g)

2 tablespoons sambuca or other anise-flavored liqueur (30 g)

Preheat the oven to 350°F. Grease and flour a 9 × 13-inch cake pan.

For the cake, in a medium saucepan, bring the parsnips and milk to a simmer over medium heat. Cook until tender, about 5 minutes. Remove from the heat, cover the pan, and let stand until cool. Drain the cooled parsnips, discard the milk, and transfer them to a blender. Add 2 of the eggs and blend until very smooth. Pour the mixture into a large mixing bowl.

Add the carrots, remaining 2 eggs, sugar, ¾ cup oil, salt, ground spices, and almond extract to the blender and blend on high speed until very smooth. Pour the carrot mixture into the puréed parsnips and stir well until combined.

Sift together the 2 cups flour and the baking powder into a bowl. Add the dry ingredients to the wet and, using a large rubber spatula, fold together until well incorporated. Pour the batter into the pan and bake for 45 to 50 minutes, rotating the pan halfway through, until golden brown and a tester inserted into the center comes out clean.

Meanwhile, when the cake is almost done, make the glaze. In a medium saucepan, combine the chocolate, milk, butter, and honey over medium heat. Stir continuously until the chocolate is melted and the mixture is smooth. Bring the glaze to a boil, reduce the heat to a simmer, and cook, stirring constantly to prevent scorching, for 5 minutes. Remove from the heat and stir in the sambuca; let stand until just warm and still pourable.

Pour the glaze over the surface of the warm cake in the pan. Let stand until room temperature and up to 1 day before cutting. Refrigerate any leftovers for up to 3 days.

Banana-Walnut SHEET CAKE

Bananas and walnuts are a classic combination and one of my favorites. Ground cardamom and ginger enhance the banana flavor while yogurt imparts some sourness to cut the sweetness and adds moisture to the cake. This is great for stacking and layering or just cutting into squares for an afternoon snack.

MAKES ONE 11 × 17-INCH CAKE; SERVES ABOUT 20

8 tablespoons (1 stick) cold unsalted butter, diced, plus more for the pan (113 g)

1 cup sugar (200 g)

2 large eggs, at room temperature

1 cup mashed banana (from about 3 whole) (250 g)

¼ cup whole-milk yogurt, at room temperature (60 g)

2 teaspoons vanilla extract (10 g)

2 cups all-purpose flour (250 g)

1 teaspoon baking powder (4 g)

½ teaspoon baking soda (3 g)

2 teaspoons ground cardamom (4 g)

1 teaspoon ground ginger (2 g)

1 teaspoon kosher salt (4 g)

1 cup walnut pieces, toasted (see page 142) and coarsely chopped (119 g)

Preheat the oven to 375°F. Line a 11 × 17-inch sheet pan with 1-inch-high sides with a silicone baking mat or parchment paper. Butter the sides of the pan.

Put the butter and the sugar into a standing mixer bowl and toss with your fingers to coat the butter. Attach the bowl and paddle to the mixer and beat the butter and sugar on medium-low speed for about 5 minutes, until a light paste forms, with no visible butter lumps. Add the eggs one at a time, scraping down the bowl with a rubber spatula between additions. Stir the mashed banana, yogurt, and vanilla together and, with the motor running on low speed, slowly add to the butter mixture; mix until combined.

Meanwhile, sift together the flour, baking powder, baking soda, cardamom, and ginger into a bowl; sprinkle the salt evenly over the top. With the mixer on low speed, slowly add the dry ingredients in

3 additions, scraping down the bowl as necessary and mixing until just combined.

Spread the batter evenly into the sheet pan and smooth the top with a large offset spatula. Evenly scatter the walnuts over the top of the cake. Run the tip of the spatula or your finger around the edges of the pan to push the batter away from the edge about ½ inch to prevent the cake from sticking to the sides of the pan. Bake for 18 to 20 minutes, until light golden brown and firm and springy to the touch.

Use a small knife to release any sides of the cake that are stuck to the pan. Use a large spatula to lift a corner of the cake off the pan and very carefully pull the cake (along with the baking mat or parchment) onto a large rack to cool completely.

Peanut Butter–Banana Layer Cake

Trim the Banana-Walnut Sheet Cake edges with a large serrated knife (1) and evenly split the cake horizontally. Invert the cake and remove the paper (2). Spread about 1 cup of Peanut Butter Pastry Cream (page 47) evenly over the bottom half of the cake (3) and cover with banana slices (4). Position the other cake half on top (5), cover the sides with about 1 cup more of pastry cream (6), and press chopped roasted unsalted peanuts into the sides. Keep refrigerated until ready to serve.

Chocolate-Sesame Seed CAKE

Similar to devil's food cake, this rich, moist cake is great with just a simple ganache glaze or buttercream coating. Sesame has such an unusual and interesting taste; its flavor is strong enough to pair with chocolate yet mild enough to work with grapefruit. Grapefruit and chocolate may seem like an odd couple, but the astringent yet floral nature of this fruit pairs well with the roasted, bitter flavors of chocolate. I especially like this cake with a rough, spiky layer of Miso Buttercream (page 321) and more black and white sesame seeds sprinkled over the top. **MAKES ONE 9-INCH CAKE; SERVES 10 TO 12**

¾ cup (1½ sticks) cold unsalted butter, diced, plus more for the pan (170 g)

⅓ cup dark cocoa powder, plus more for the pan (35 g)

¾ cup sugar (150 g)

2 large eggs, at room temperature

1 cup all-purpose flour (125 g)

¾ cup cake flour (83 g)

1 tablespoon baking powder (12 g)

¾ teaspoon baking soda (4 g)

¾ teaspoon kosher salt (3 g)

Grated zest of 1 ruby grapefruit

½ teaspoon lemon extract (2 g)

½ teaspoon vanilla extract (2 g)

¼ cup fresh ruby grapefruit juice (60 g)

¼ cup buttermilk, at room temperature (57 g)

¼ cup sesame seeds, toasted (see page 142) (35 g)

Preheat the oven to 375°F. Grease a 9-inch round cake pan and dust lightly with cocoa powder, tapping out the excess.

Put the ¾ cup butter and the sugar into a standing mixer bowl and toss together to coat the butter. Attach the paddle and bowl to the mixer and beat the butter and sugar on low speed until a light paste forms, about 5 minutes. Add the eggs, one at a time, mixing well and scraping down the bowl with a rubber spatula between additions.

Meanwhile, sift together the all-purpose flour, cake flour, ⅓ cup cocoa powder, baking powder, and baking soda into a bowl; sprinkle the salt evenly over the top. Stir the zest and extracts into the grapefruit juice. On low speed, add the dry ingredients to the butter in 3 additions, beginning and ending with the dry and alternating with the buttermilk and grapefruit juice. Stop the mixer several times and scrape down the bowl. Mix until just combined; add the sesame seeds and mix briefly to distribute them.

Transfer the batter to the prepared pan, smooth the top with a spatula, and tap the pan several times on the counter to settle the batter and release any air bubbles. Bake in the center of the oven for about 40 minutes, until the sides begin to pull away from the pan, the top is firm to the touch, and a cake tester inserted into the center comes out clean.

Cool the cake in the pan for 10 minutes before inverting onto a rack to cool completely.

Brown Sugar–Molasses CAKE

I don't think molasses gets enough credit. It has such an interesting taste—sweet, sour, and tart all at once but with a savory note as well. Its texture and deep flavor give cakes richness and moisture without making them too sweet. The warm flavors of Chinese five-spice powder play off the rich caramelized sugar notes of the molasses. A little orange juice and zest add a burst of acidic freshness. This is a sturdy cake that's great to split and layer with buttercream like Coffee Buttercream or Salted Dulce de Leche Buttercream (page 320).

MAKES TWO 9-INCH CAKES; SERVES 12 TO 16

½ pound (2 sticks) cold unsalted butter, diced, plus more for the pan (226 g)

2¾ cups all-purpose flour, plus more for the pan (345 g)

1½ cups (packed) light brown sugar (348g)

¼ cup molasses (100 g)

8 large egg yolks, at room temperature

2 teaspoons Chinese five-spice powder (4 g)

1 teaspoon baking soda (6 g)

¾ teaspoon baking powder (3g)

1 teaspoon kosher salt (4 g)

1 cup Greek yogurt, at room temperature (234 g)

Grated zest and juice of 1 large navel orange

Preheat the oven to 375°F. Grease and flour two 9-inch round cake pans.

Put the ½ pound butter and the brown sugar in a standing mixer bowl and toss well with your fingers until the butter is coated. Attach the bowl and paddle to the mixer and beat the butter and brown sugar on low speed for about 5 minutes, until a light paste forms. Add the molasses and mix to combine; add the egg yolks, one at a time, scraping down the bowl between additions.

Meanwhile, sift together the 2¾ cups flour, five-spice powder, baking soda, and baking powder; sprinkle the salt evenly over the top. With the mixer on low speed, gradually add about half of the dry ingredients and mix just until combined. With a rubber spatula, scrape down the bowl, add the yogurt and orange zest and juice, and mix again on low speed until just combined. Slowly add the remaining dry ingredients, stopping to scrape down the bowl as needed, until just combined.

Divide the batter evenly between the prepared pans and smooth the tops with an offset spatula. Bake in the center of the oven for about 30 minutes, rotating the pans halfway through, until lightly browned, the cakes begin to pull from the sides of the pan and are springy to the touch, and a tester inserted in the center comes out clean.

Cool the cakes in the pan for 10 minutes and then invert them onto a rack to cool completely.

CRUMB CAKE

During my tenure as pastry chef at four-star Restaurant Daniel, I had a group of very special interns every Saturday, who were lovingly referred to as "Johnny's Angels." One of the angels was Martha Magliula, who is an avid home baker extraordinaire. Every Saturday she would bring two coffee cakes—one for the team and one just for me. I had to ration it to get me through until the next Saturday. When I decided to do a cookbook focused on home bakers, I knew I just had to feature her incredible coffee cake, which doesn't skimp on the crumble topping. **MAKES ONE 9 × 13-INCH CAKE; SERVES 12 TO 16**

FOR THE CAKE

Vegetable oil cooking spray

2 cups all-purpose flour, plus more for the pan (250 g)

5⅓ tablespoons (⅓ cup) unsalted butter, at room temperature (75 g)

½ cup granulated sugar (100 g)

1 large egg, at room temperature

¼ cup sour cream, at room temperature (60 g)

⅔ cup whole milk, at room temperature (160 g)

1 tablespoon vanilla extract (15 g)

1 tablespoon baking powder (12 g)

Pinch of kosher salt

FOR THE CRUMB TOPPING

2¼ cups all-purpose flour (280 g)

1¼ cups (packed) light brown sugar (290 g)

1 tablespoon ground cinnamon (6 g)

½ pound (2 sticks) unsalted butter, melted (226 g)

Confectioners' sugar, for dusting

To make the cake, preheat the oven to 350°F. Spray a 9 × 13-inch glass baking dish with cooking spray, dust it with flour, and tap out the excess.

Beat the butter and granulated sugar in a standing mixer fitted with the paddle on medium speed until lightened. Add the egg and sour cream and mix well.

Meanwhile, stir the milk and vanilla together. Sift together the 2 cups flour and the baking powder into a small bowl and sprinkle the salt on top.

With the mixer on low speed, alternately add the dry and wet ingredients to the bowl, beginning and ending with the dry. Stop the mixer several times to scrape down the bowl with a rubber spatula; mix until just combined. Transfer the batter to the baking dish and spread it evenly with an offset spatula.

To make the topping, whisk the flour, brown sugar, and cinnamon together in a bowl until well mixed. Add the melted butter and stir until the dry ingredients are thoroughly moistened. Using your hands, gently roll the mixture together between your palms and fingers until very small balls form; scatter the topping evenly over the cake batter in the pan right from your hands as you roll.

Bake the cake on the center rack of the oven for about 30 minutes, until the center is firm to the touch and springs back lightly. If the cake is not baked through, reduce the temperature to 325°F and continue baking in 5-minute increments until the cake is set in the center but the topping does not get too brown.

Dust the surface of the cake lightly with confectioners' sugar and cool completely on a rack. Once cool, dust the surface generously with confectioners' sugar before cutting and serving.

Jamaican CHRISTMAS CAKE

When my best friend, Bradford Thompson, married a native Jamaican, Kerry-Ann, I was exposed to the flavors of her incredible country. He shared one of their traditional holiday dessert recipes with me—this moist, dense cake studded with liquor-soaked fruit that I have grown to love. This is no doorstop fruitcake; it is a rich butter cake that can sit, wrapped tightly, for weeks on the kitchen counter, getting better by the day. You can soak the fruit at any time of the year, store it in the fridge in an airtight jar, and pull some out when you want to bake the cake. As you use it, add more dried fruit to the jar, any combination you like, and cover it with more liquor; it keeps for ages. **MAKES ONE 9-INCH CAKE; SERVES ABOUT 12**

FOR THE SOAKED FRUIT

8 ounces golden raisins (227 g)

8 ounces dark raisins (227 g)

4 ounces currants (113 g)

4 ounces pitted prunes (113 g)

4 ounces dried cherries (113 g)

2 ounces Candied Citrus Peel (page 332) or store-bought (57g)

2 cups white rum, plus more as needed (448 g)

1 cup dry red wine, plus more as needed (224 g)

FOR THE CAKE

1½ pounds drained soaked fruit (680 g)

¼ cup granulated sugar (50 g)

¼ cup water (60 g)

½ pound plus 2 tablespoons (2¼ sticks) unsalted butter, softened, plus more for the pan (250 g)

Demerara sugar, for coating the pan

1⅓ cups (packed) light brown sugar (307 g)

6 large eggs, at room temperature

1 teaspoon vanilla extract (5g)

2 cups all-purpose flour (250 g)

1 teaspoon baking powder (4 g)

¼ teaspoon ground cinnamon

¼ teaspoon freshly grated nutmeg

½ teaspoon kosher salt (2 g)

1½ cups finely ground dry Brioche (page 292) or challah crumbs (150 g)

To soak the fruit, put the golden and dark raisins, currants, prunes, cherries, and citrus peel into a 1½-quart jar with a lid, add the rum and wine, and stir to mix well. Add more rum and wine, if needed, to cover the fruit completely. Macerate the fruit for at least one full day before using; the longer it soaks, the better. Store in the refrigerator.

When ready to make the cake, remove the fruit from the jar with a slotted spoon and let it drain in a strainer set over a bowl to catch any liquid. Weigh out 1½ pounds (680 g) of the fruit and pour any liquid that drains off back into the jar of macerating fruit. Finely chop the fruit with a sharp knife and return the fruit to the strainer set over a bowl to continue draining while you make the batter.

To make the cake, put the granulated sugar into a small skillet over medium-high heat. Cook, swirling

recipe continues

the pan occasionally, for about 3 minutes, until the sugar turns a deep golden brown. Reduce the heat to low and carefully pour in the water. Simmer the mixture briefly to dissolve the sugar completely. Remove the mixture from the heat and pour it into a small bowl; cool to room temperature.

Preheat the oven to 300°F. Grease a 9-inch cake pan with butter and dust it with Demerara sugar, tapping out the excess.

In the bowl of a standing mixer fitted with the paddle, beat the ½ pound plus 2 tablespoons butter and the brown sugar for about 3 minutes, until pale and fluffy. With the mixer on low, add the eggs, one at a time, stopping the mixer and scraping down the bowl with a rubber spatula between additions. Add the vanilla and cooled caramel and mix well.

Meanwhile, in a separate bowl, sift the flour, baking powder, cinnamon, and nutmeg together; sprinkle the salt evenly over the top. With the mixer on low,

slowly add the dry ingredients to the butter and mix just until incorporated, about 1 minute. Add the bread crumbs and mix until combined.

Press on the chopped fruit in the strainer with a rubber spatula to remove as much liquid as possible. Remove the bowl from the mixer and, with the spatula, fold the chopped fruit into the cake batter until evenly distributed. Pour the batter into the pan and spread it evenly to smooth the top. Set the pan in a larger, deep baking dish or pan and fill it with enough hot water to come halfway up the sides of the cake pan. Transfer the pan to the oven and bake for about 90 minutes, until a cake tester inserted in the center of the cake comes out clean.

Let the cake cool completely in the pan in the water bath before inverting onto a serving platter.

Note: *This cake tastes better as it sits, so try to make it well in advance of serving. To store it, keep it wrapped very tightly in plastic wrap at room temperature.*

Pineapple-Cornmeal UPSIDE-DOWN CAKES

I love the texture combination of soft pineapple and crunchy cornmeal. These individual butter cakes are made in a nonstick muffin tin, which helps caramelize the pineapple. They will remind you of that overly sweet upside-down cake your mother used to make, only without the maraschino cherries and toothache afterward. This cake batter can be made a day or two ahead and has better flavor if chilled overnight.

SERVES 8

8 tablespoons (1 stick) unsalted butter, plus more for the pan (113 g)

1⅓ cups confectioners' sugar (160 g)

⅓ cup cake flour (43 g)

¼ cup plus 3 tablespoons fine cornmeal (78 g)

¼ teaspoon baking powder (1 g)

4 large egg whites

Grated zest of ½ orange

2 tablespoons sour cream, at room temperature (30 g)

Demerara sugar, for the pan

½ fresh pineapple, peeled, cored, and very thinly sliced (⅛ inch thick) crosswise

Put the 8 tablespoons butter into a small saucepan and melt it over medium heat. When the butter starts to boil, whisk it constantly for about 5 minutes, until it turns deep golden brown. Pour the hot butter into a bowl and let stand for a few minutes until cool. Use a tablespoon measure to transfer 6 tablespoons of the browned butter to a small bowl, skimming it from the top and leaving the sediment behind.

Put the confectioners' sugar, flour, cornmeal, and baking powder into a standing mixer with the paddle and mix on low speed until combined. Add the egg whites and mix on low speed until combined. Stop the mixer and scrape down the bowl with a rubber spatula. Add the orange zest and sour cream and mix well. With the mixer on low speed, slowly drizzle in the melted browned butter and mix well. Transfer to a container and refrigerate overnight.

To make the cakes, preheat the oven to 350°F. Generously butter 8 cups of a 12-portion nonstick muffin tin. Sprinkle Demerara sugar over the muffin cups and rotate the pan, knocking out excess sugar.

Arrange the pineapple slices in the buttered muffin cups, cutting the pieces as needed to fit and making sure there is a solid layer of pineapple against the sides and bottom of the pan. Stir the cake batter and divide it among the muffin cups. Bake in the center of the oven for about 25 minutes, rotating the pan halfway through, until the cakes are light golden on top and a cake tester comes out clean.

Cool the cakes in the pan on a rack for 10 minutes. Using a small offset spatula, carefully release the pineapple from the sides of the muffin tin, being careful not to tear the pineapple. Put a rack over the pan and invert the cakes. Let stand until cool. Serve at room temperature or slightly warm.

Banana CUPCAKES

I love, love, love bananas in dessert, especially when paired with caramel. Here's an amazingly moist banana cake stuffed with caramelized bananas and topped with rich vanilla-mascarpone icing. If you're gonna make cupcakes, might as well kick some butt with them. **MAKES 12 CUPCAKES**

FOR THE CUPCAKES

6 tablespoons (¾ stick) cold unsalted butter, diced (84 g)

¾ cup granulated sugar (150 g)

¾ cup plus 1 tablespoon all-purpose flour (102 g)

¾ teaspoon baking powder (3 g)

½ teaspoon baking soda (3 g)

½ teaspoon kosher salt (2 g)

2 very ripe bananas, mashed

¼ cup sour cream, at room temperature (61 g)

1 teaspoon vanilla extract (5 g)

2 large eggs, at room temperature

FOR THE FILLING

¼ cup granulated sugar (50 g)

4 tablespoons (½ stick) unsalted butter (57 g)

1½ bananas, sliced

FOR THE ICING

1 cup mascarpone cheese, at room temperature (231 g)

1 cup crème fraîche, at room temperature (231 g)

¾ cup heavy cream, at room temperature (180 g)

Seeds from 1 vanilla bean

¼ cup confectioners' sugar (30 g)

Chopped walnuts, for garnish (optional)

To make the cupcakes, preheat the oven to 350°F. Line a 12-portion standard muffin tin with paper muffin liners.

In the bowl of a standing mixer, toss the butter with the granulated sugar until coated. Attach the bowl and paddle to the mixer and beat the butter and sugar together on medium speed for about 5 minutes, until a thick paste forms and no lumps of butter remain.

Meanwhile, in a separate bowl, sift together the flour, baking powder, and baking soda and sprinkle the salt over the top. Stir the mashed bananas, sour cream, and vanilla together.

Add the eggs to the mixer, one at a time, mixing well between additions. Stop the mixer and scrape down the bowl with a rubber spatula. With the mixer on low speed, add the dry ingredients to the batter and mix until just combined. Scrape down the bowl several times. Add the banana mixture and mix just until combined.

Evenly divide the batter among the liners and bake until a cake tester inserted in the center of a cupcake comes out clean, 12 to 15 minutes. Transfer the cupcakes to a rack and cool completely.

Using an apple corer or ¾-inch plain cutter, hollow out the center of each cupcake, cutting about three quarters of the way down, keeping the structure intact.

To make the filling, sprinkle the granulated sugar evenly over the surface of a medium skillet and place it over medium-high heat. Cook, without stirring, for about 3 minutes, until the sugar melts completely and begins to caramelize. When the edges begin to turn brown, swirl the pan gently to cook the sugar evenly. Once the sugar is golden brown, add the butter and swirl the pan until completely melted. Gently stir in the bananas, reduce the heat to medium-low, and cook for 1 to 2 minutes, until the bananas begin to soften and break down. Cool the banana mixture completely, coarsely mash it with a fork, and transfer it to a pastry bag with no tip. Fill the holes in the cupcakes with the banana filling.

To make the icing, put the mascarpone, crème fraîche, cream, vanilla seeds, and confectioners' sugar into a standing mixer bowl and whip with the whisk attachment until stiff peaks form. Transfer to a piping bag fitted with a plain or star tip and pipe the icing onto the tops of the cupcakes. Sprinkle chopped walnuts over the tops of the cupcakes if desired.

Almond-

Orange Cupcakes

with Rose Meringue

ALMOND-ORANGE CUPCAKES *with rose meringue*

When I first served this delicious almond cupcake filled with tart orange curd, there were candied kumquats, crystallized rose petals, and pomegranate seeds garnishing the rose-flavored Italian meringue icing. Over the top? Perhaps, but the intense almond, orange, and rose flavors together are amazing. For optimum flavor, make the orange curd a day ahead and chill it overnight. **MAKES 12 CUPCAKES**

FOR THE CUPCAKES

10 tablespoons (1¼ sticks) cold unsalted butter, diced (140 g)

½ cup sugar (100 g)

⅔ cup almond flour (60 g)

2 large eggs, at room temperature

½ teaspoon almond extract (3 g)

1 cup all-purpose flour (125 g)

½ teaspoon baking powder (2 g)

½ teaspoon baking soda (3 g)

½ teaspoon kosher salt (2 g)

⅔ cup sour cream, at room temperature (160 g)

Grated zest and juice of 1 navel orange

2 cups Orange Curd (page 324)

FOR THE ROSE WATER MERINGUE

1½ cups sugar (300 g)

6 large egg whites

1½ tablespoons light corn syrup (26 g)

½ cup water (120 g)

1 teaspoon rose water, or to taste (5 g)

To make the cupcakes, preheat the oven to 350°F. Line a 12-portion standard muffin tin with paper liners.

In a standing mixer bowl, toss the butter with the sugar until coated. Attach the bowl and paddle to the mixer and beat the butter and sugar on medium speed for about 5 minutes, until a thick paste forms and there are no visible butter lumps. Add the almond flour and mix until well combined. With the motor running, add the eggs, one at a time, stopping the mixer and scraping down the bowl with a rubber spatula between additions. Add the almond extract and mix well.

Meanwhile, in a separate bowl, sift together the all-purpose flour, baking powder, and baking soda; sprinkle the salt evenly over the top. With the mixer on low speed, slowly add the dry ingredients and mix just until incorporated; scrape down the bowl as necessary. Remove the bowl from the mixer and with a rubber spatula fold the sour cream and orange zest and juice into the batter until just combined; do not overmix.

Divide the batter evenly among the liners, filling them about three-quarters full. Bake the cupcakes in the center of the oven for about 20 minutes, until set, firm to the touch, and a cake tester inserted in the center comes out clean. Cool the cupcakes in the pan for 10 minutes before transferring them to a rack to cool completely.

Using an apple corer or ¾-inch plain cutter, hollow out the center of each cupcake, cutting about three quarters of the way down, keeping the structure intact. Transfer the orange curd to a pastry bag fitted with a small plain tip and fill each cupcake just until the curd is level with the top of the cupcake.

To make the rose water meringue, put 2 tablespoons of the sugar and the egg whites into a standing mixer with the whisk attachment and turn the mixer on to low speed. Put the remaining sugar, corn syrup, and water into a medium saucepan and stir with your finger until sandy. Wet your finger and wipe down the sides of the pan. Put the pan over medium-high heat; when the sugar is dissolved, dip a clean pastry brush in cold water and wipe down the sides of the pan.

When the sugar reaches a rolling boil, increase the mixer speed to medium. Continue cooking the sugar, brushing the pan sides if any crystals form, until it reaches 250°F (firm-ball stage). Increase the mixer speed to medium-high. The whites should be fluffy and shiny but still soft. With the motor running, carefully pour the hot sugar syrup in a slow, steady stream into the mixer—pour it directly onto the whites between the mixer bowl edge and outer reach of the whisk. Add the rose water, increase the mixer speed to high, and whip the meringue for about 6 minutes, until cool to the touch. If the meringue level begins to recede in the mixing bowl, stop whipping immediately.

Transfer the meringue to a pastry bag fitted with a large plain or star tip and pipe it in patterns on top of each cupcake. Serve immediately or refrigerate and serve within 1 day.

Note: *To add another level of sophistication, brown the tops of the iced cupcakes with a kitchen blowtorch or remove the paper liners and place the cupcakes about 3 inches away from the broiler in your oven very briefly until the tops brown.*

CHOCOLATE CUPCAKES

Here's an easy recipe for a moist chocolate cupcake made with buttermilk and mayonnaise, which gives them a deep flavor and dense, rich texture like devil's food cake. They can be frosted with any of the buttercreams on pages 319 to 321. You could also easily fold some fresh raspberries into the batter or, once baked, squeeze a little Raspberry-Mint Jam (page 326) into the center and decorate with basic Vanilla Buttercream (page 319). **MAKES 24 CUPCAKES**

¾ pound (3 sticks) cold unsalted butter, diced (339 g)

2 cups sugar (400 g)

5 large eggs, at room temperature

⅓ cup mayonnaise, at room temperature (75 g)

2 teaspoons vanilla extract (10 g)

2 cups cake flour (220 g)

1 cup plus 2 tablespoons cocoa powder (107 g)

1 teaspoon baking powder (4 g)

½ teaspoon kosher salt (2 g)

1 cup low-fat buttermilk (247 g), at room temperature

Preheat the oven to 350°F. Line two 12-portion standard muffin pans with paper liners.

Toss the butter with the sugar in a standing mixer bowl until coated. Attach the bowl and paddle to the mixer and beat the butter and sugar on medium speed for about 5 minutes, until a thick paste forms and no butter lumps remain. Add the eggs, one at a time, mixing well between additions and stopping to scrape the bowl down with a rubber spatula. Add the mayonnaise and vanilla and mix well.

Meanwhile, in a separate bowl, sift together the flour, cocoa, and baking powder; sprinkle the salt over the top. With the mixer on low speed, alternately add the dry ingredients and buttermilk in 3 additions, starting and ending with the dry ingredients. Stop the mixer and scrape down the bowl several times.

Divide the batter evenly among the lined pans, filling each liner three-quarters full. Bake for 25 to 30 minutes, rotating the pans halfway through, until firm to the touch and a cake tester inserted in the center of a cupcake comes out clean.

Cool the cupcakes in the pans for 10 minutes before transferring them to a rack to cool completely. Once cooled, fill or frost as desired. Undecorated cupcakes can be wrapped tightly and frozen for up to 2 weeks.

Caramel-Chocolate Cupcakes with Sea Salt

Bake and cool the chocolate cupcakes as directed and hollow out the centers as for the Almond-Orange Cupcakes (page 192). Fill a pastry bag fitted with a plain ½-inch tip with 3 cups Whipped Caramel Cream (page 322), dip them in Shiny Chocolate Glaze (page 328), and garnish them with a sprinkling of cacao nibs and crunchy Maldon sea salt.

THIN ALMOND SPONGE CAKE

This is a nut-flour-based meringue cake, called a *dacquoise* (*dah-KWAZ*) in French. It can be baked in a regular cake pan to eat as is or baked in sheet pans in a thin layer to be rolled up or used to make a layer cake or other layered desserts. Due to the meringue in the batter, this sponge cake is malleable and can be cut, formed, and rolled into many other shapes. **MAKES ONE 11 × 17-INCH THIN CAKE, ABOUT 20 SERVINGS**

1½ cups finely ground almond flour (150 g)

1½ cups confectioners' sugar (180 g)

7 large egg whites

Pinch of cream of tartar

⅛ teaspoon kosher salt

⅓ cup granulated sugar (65 g)

⅓ cup sliced almonds (35 g)

Preheat the oven to 375°F. Line a 11 × 17-inch rimmed baking sheet with a silicone baking mat or parchment paper.

Sift together the almond flour and confectioners' sugar twice (1) and then return it to the sifter.

Put the egg whites, cream of tartar, salt, and about a third of the granulated sugar into the bowl of a standing mixer and whisk the ingredients by hand with the whisk attachment to combine. Attach the bowl and whisk to the mixer and turn the mixer on to medium speed. Whip until there is no liquid egg white left in the bowl and the whites are beginning to

gain volume. Gradually sprinkle another third of the granulated sugar over the whipping whites. Continue whipping until the whites have more volume and the meringue is beginning to hold the trail of the whisk. Gradually sprinkle the remaining granulated sugar over the whipping eggs. When the whites begin to turn glossy but still hold soft peaks (2), increase the speed to high and whip for 30 seconds to ensure the whites are evenly whipped in all areas of the bowl.

With a large, flat rubber spatula, transfer the meringue to a very large mixing bowl. Evenly sift about a quarter of the dry ingredients over the whites (3) and fold about 6 times, turning the bowl as you fold. Repeat twice. Sift the remaining dry ingredients over the whites and gently fold together until completely incorporated and no bits of flour remain. Transfer the batter to the lined sheet pan and gently spread it over the surface of the pan (4, 5). Use your finger to wipe away some batter and create a "moat" around the cake batter at the edge of the pan. This will help prevent the cake from sticking to the pan edges.

Sprinkle the sliced almonds evenly over the surface of the batter. Bake for 18 to 20 minutes, rotating the pan halfway through, until light golden brown and springy to the touch but not dry.

Immediately use a small sharp knife to release any of the cake that is sticking to the sides of the pan. Use an offset spatula to lift one corner of the cake and carefully pull the cake (along with the baking mat or parchment) onto a cooling rack to cool completely. Once cool, cover the cake with a sheet of parchment and invert an empty sheet pan onto the top of the cake. Invert the cake, peel off the parchment or baking mat, and invert the cake back onto the cooling rack. Cut or use the cake as desired.

Note: *You can substitute finely ground hazelnut flour, which can be found at health food stores or ground at home in a food processor, and finely chopped toasted hazelnuts (see page 142) for the almond flour and sliced almonds.*

Almond-Apricot Jelly Roll

SERVES 12

Bake and cool Thin Almond Sponge Cake (page 199) as directed. Whisk together 1 cup (240 g) heavy cream with 2 teaspoons (10 g) (or to taste) amaretto and 1 tablespoon (8 g) confectioners' sugar until firm peaks form. Invert the cake onto a piece of parchment paper, and spread about ⅔ cup (200 g) apricot jam in a very thin layer over it. Using an offset spatula, spread the whipped cream evenly over the surface. With the long side facing you and using the parchment as a guide, roll the cake up as snugly as possible without squeezing out the cream. Refrigerate, seam side down, for at least 1 hour before slicing, dusting with confectioners' sugar, and serving.

OLIVE OIL SPONGE CAKE

I adapted this cake from a Spanish recipe, and so I like to use a nice grassy green Spanish olive oil here. The crumb is firm but melts in your mouth when you eat it, and the cake rides the line between sweet and savory. I love pairing this cake with roasted or poached fall fruits, like pears or quince. **MAKES ONE 9-INCH CAKE; SERVES 12**

¼ cup extra-virgin olive oil, plus more for the pan (48 g)

1½ cups cake flour, plus more for the pan (165 g)

4 large eggs, at room temperature

¾ cup plus 1 tablespoon sugar (162 g)

½ cup whole milk, at room temperature (120 g)

¾ cup finely ground almond flour (75 g)

5 teaspoons baking powder (20 g)

½ teaspoon kosher salt (2 g)

Grated zest of 1 orange

¼ cup grapeseed oil (48 g)

Preheat the oven to 400°F. Brush a 9-inch cake pan with olive oil and dust with cake flour.

In a standing mixer with the whisk, whip the eggs and sugar together on medium speed for about 5 minutes, until light and pale in color. Reduce the mixer speed to low and slowly drizzle in the milk until combined.

Meanwhile, in a separate bowl, sift the 1½ cups cake flour, almond flour, and baking powder together; sprinkle the salt evenly over the top. With the motor on low speed, slowly add the dry ingredients to the wet and mix until just combined. Turn off the mixer

and scrape down the bowl with a rubber spatula. Turn the mixer back on to low speed, add the orange zest, and slowly drizzle in the ¼ cup olive oil and the grapeseed oil until just combined.

Pour the mixture into the prepared pan and bake in the center of the oven for 35 to 40 minutes, rotating the pan halfway through, until the crust is deep golden brown, a cake tester comes out clean, and the cake springs back when pressed.

Cool the cake in the pan for 10 minutes before inverting on a rack to cool completely.

VANILLA SPONGE CAKE

Based on the great French cake génoise, this is a whole-egg foam cake that is a great foundation for layer cakes. This sponge cake is like a blank canvas, ready to showcase any flavor combination you can dream up. Typically génoises are brushed with flavored syrups and iced with buttercream. **MAKES TWO 9-INCH CAKES; SERVES 12 TO 16**

4 tablespoons (½ stick) unsalted butter, melted and slightly warm, plus more for the pan (57 g)

2 cups all-purpose flour, plus more for the pan (250 g)

8 large eggs, at room temperature

1 cup sugar (200 g)

Seeds from 1 vanilla bean

½ teaspoon kosher salt (2 g)

Preheat the oven to 375°F. Grease two 9-inch round cake pans, line with parchment paper, grease the paper, and dust the pans with flour.

Fill a medium saucepan one-third full of hot water and bring to a boil; reduce the heat to a gentle simmer. In a standing mixer bowl, whisk the eggs, sugar, and vanilla seeds together (1) and set the

bowl over the simmering water, making sure the bottom does not touch the water. Whisk the mixture constantly until the sugar is completely dissolved, the mixture begins to thicken, and the eggs are hot to the touch (2).

Transfer the bowl to the mixer, attach the whisk, and whip on medium speed until the mixture begins to

gain volume. Increase the speed to high and whip for 4 to 5 minutes, until the mixture triples in volume, is cool to the touch, and holds the trail of the whisk (3). Watch the bowl carefully; if the volume of the eggs begins to decrease in the bowl, stop the mixer immediately. Transfer the egg foam to a very large mixing bowl.

Put the 2 cups flour into a sifter and sift enough flour over the egg mixture just to cover the surface; sprinkle the salt over the flour. Fold the flour into the eggs in long, slow strokes, rotating the bowl as you fold (4). Continue adding the flour in 3 more additions, folding and rotating the bowl one turn for each addition of flour (do not overmix) (5). While turning the bowl, drizzle the 4 tablespoons melted butter over the batter (6). Fold the batter from the outside in to incorporate the butter (7), folding just until no lumps of flour remain. Be sure to pull the spatula all the way through the batter to the bottom of the bowl, as the butter can settle below the batter.

Divide the batter between the prepared pans and smooth the top with a small offset spatula. Bake the cakes in the center of the oven for 16 to 18 minutes, rotating the pans halfway through, until golden, the top is springy to the touch, and the sides are beginning to pull away from the pan. Cool the cakes for 10 minutes in the pans on a rack. Run a sharp knife around the edges to release them before inverting and cooling them completely on the rack.

FLOURLESS CHOCOLATE MERINGUE CAKE

French meringue makes this cake as light as air, but still rich and chocolaty. The whipped egg whites give the cake its structure, and it will puff up like a soufflé in the oven before settling back into the pan once cool. It's not as dense as a devil's food or other butter/oil chocolate cake, but it still delivers big chocolate flavor.

MAKES ONE 9-INCH CAKE; SERVES 8 TO 10

6 tablespoons (¾ stick) unsalted butter, plus more for the pan (84 g)

Cocoa powder, for dusting

7 ounces bittersweet chocolate (72% cacao), chopped (200 g)

7 large egg whites

Pinch of cream of tartar

⅓ cup plus 1 tablespoon sugar (65 g + 12 g)

4 large egg yolks

½ teaspoon kosher salt (2 g)

Preheat the oven to 350°F. Grease a 9-inch springform pan and dust it with cocoa powder.

Fill a medium saucepan one-third full of water and bring to a boil. Put the chocolate and 6 tablespoons butter in a large heatproof bowl and set it over the water, making sure the bowl doesn't touch the water. Turn off the heat and let stand, stirring occasionally, until the butter and chocolate are melted and smooth. Remove from the heat and cool to room temperature.

Put the egg whites and cream of tartar into the bowl of a standing mixer fitted with the whisk attachment and turn the mixer on to medium-low speed. Slowly sprinkle about a third of the ⅓ cup sugar into the whites and whip until the mixture is foamy. With the motor running, gradually drizzle in another third of the sugar in the measuring cup. Increase the speed to medium, and when the whites have soft peaks, sprinkle in the remaining sugar in the cup and whip until soft, glossy peaks form.

Meanwhile, in a medium bowl, whisk the egg yolks, the remaining 1 tablespoon sugar, and the salt together until pale and thick. Fold the cooled chocolate into the yolk mixture until combined. Add about 1 cup of the whites and fold gently until just combined; add the remaining whites and fold gently until no streaks of whites remain. Transfer to the prepared pan and spread the batter evenly with a spatula, smoothing out the top.

Bake in the center of the oven for about 25 minutes, rotating the pan halfway through baking, until set and a tester inserted into the thickest part of the cake comes out clean. Let the cake cool for 15 minutes before removing the springform ring. The cake can be served slightly warm or at room temperature, dusted with cocoa powder if desired.

Note: To add a crunchy texture, you can coat the pan with some turbinado sugar after greasing it.

Gluten-Free VANILLA BIRTHDAY CAKE

I first met Jacqueline Raposo at a baking competition. I was impressed by her entry, a pie, because it was gluten-free, using nontraditional gluten-free ingredients, and she won the whole competition. She now has a great blog called "The Dusty Baker," where she shares her creative gluten-free and often dairy-free recipes. Based on one of her recipes, this angel-food-like light cake works in a layered birthday cake. All of these ingredients can be found at natural grocery stores. **MAKES ONE 2-LAYER 8-INCH CAKE; SERVES 10 TO 12**

2 tablespoons (¼ stick) unsalted butter, plus more for the pans (28 g)

1 cup gluten-free cake flour (160 g)

½ teaspoon fine sea salt (2 g)

½ teaspoon xanthan gum (2 g)

⅛ teaspoon freshly grated nutmeg

3 tablespoons unsweetened almond milk (50 g)

1 teaspoon vanilla extract (2 g)

5 large eggs

¾ cup sugar, preferably beet sugar (150 g)

Pinch of cream of tartar

3 cups Vanilla Buttercream (page 319), preferably made with beet sugar

3 cups Red Berry Pudding (page 62), made with gluten-free cornstarch and beet sugar

2 pints fresh blackberries (560 g)

Grated lime zest, for garnish

Preheat the oven to 350°F. Grease two 8-inch cake pans with butter. Cut two 8-inch parchment paper circles and line the bottoms of the pans; grease the paper with butter.

In a small bowl, whisk together the flour, salt, xanthan gum, and nutmeg.

Put the almond milk and the butter into a small saucepan and heat over medium-low heat until very warm and the butter is melted; stir in the vanilla. Let cool slightly.

Separate 3 of the eggs. In a standing mixer bowl, whisk together the whole eggs, egg yolks, and about 6 tablespoons of the sugar until combined. Attach the bowl and whisk to the mixer and whip on medium speed until pale yellow and creamy, about 5 minutes.

Transfer the egg foam to a very large mixing bowl. Wash and dry the mixer bowl and whisk.

Put the egg whites and cream of tartar in the mixer bowl and beat the whites on medium speed until foamy, about 2 minutes. With the mixer running, slowly sprinkle in the remaining 6 tablespoons sugar, a tablespoon at a time, and continue beating for 3 to 5 minutes, until soft, moist peaks form. Do not overbeat. Pour the meringue onto the egg foam in the mixing bowl.

Sift the dry ingredients evenly over the meringue and beaten eggs and, using a large rubber spatula, fold together very gently, about 10 turns of the bowl. Make a well in the center of the batter and pour in the slightly warm almond milk mixture.

Fold the ingredients together lightly until just combined; do not overmix.

Evenly divide the batter between the prepared pans and bake in the center of the oven for 22 to 25 minutes, until slightly firm, springy to the touch, and the sides are pulling away from the pan.

Remove the pans from the oven and immediately run a small icing spatula or thin knife around the edges of each cake to loosen it from the pan. Let stand for about 2 minutes before inverting the cakes onto a plate. Invert them back, right side up, onto a cooling rack to cool completely.

Put the buttercream and pudding into separate piping bags fitted with plain ½-inch tips. Starting with buttercream on the outer edge of each cake, pipe alternating rings of buttercream and pudding on the top of each. Press blackberries, upright, just touching each other, into the buttercream rings. The cakes can be stacked like a layer cake and sliced or kept separate. Garnish the cake with fresh lime zest before serving.

Spicy Malted Chocolate Chipotle BROWNIES

This decadent brownie is not for the faint of heart—this is a bar with an attitude. It is dense, intense, and has a one-two punch of heat from chipotle and paprika powders. The earthy richness of the malt gives the brownies almost a fermented flavor; the heat and the maltiness linger long after you finish one. A little bite goes a long way. **MAKES ABOUT 2 DOZEN 2-INCH-SQUARE BROWNIES**

½ pound (2 sticks) unsalted butter, plus more for the pan (226 g)

2 to 3 tablespoons Demerara sugar, for the pan

10 ounces bittersweet chocolate (66 to 72% cacao), chopped (284 g)

2 ounces unsweetened chocolate, chopped (57 g)

3 tablespoons barley malt syrup (75 g)

4 large eggs

2 cups granulated sugar (400 g)

2 teaspoons vanilla extract (10 g)

1½ cups all-purpose flour (190 g)

1 teaspoon baking powder (4 g)

1½ teaspoons chipotle chile powder (3 g)

1½ teaspoons smoked paprika (3 g)

¾ teaspoon cayenne pepper (1 g)

1 teaspoon kosher salt (4 g)

Preheat the oven to 350°F. Butter an 8 × 11-inch baking dish or cake pan and coat it generously with Demerara sugar, tapping out the excess.

Put the bittersweet and unsweetened chocolate and the ½ pound butter into a large heatproof bowl. Fill a saucepan one-third full of water and bring it to a simmer. Set the bowl over the simmering water, making sure the bottom of the bowl does not touch the water. Stir the chocolate occasionally until completely melted. Remove from the heat, stir in the malt syrup, and cool to room temperature.

Put the eggs, granulated sugar, and vanilla into a standing mixer bowl and set it over the simmering water, making sure the bowl does not touch the water. Whisk constantly until the sugar has dissolved and the mixture is hot to the touch (180°F). Transfer the bowl to the mixer, attach the whisk, and whip on high speed until pale, fluffy, and cooled to room temperature, about 10 minutes.

Meanwhile, sift together the flour, baking powder, chile powder, paprika, and cayenne into a bowl; sprinkle the salt on top. With a large, flat rubber spatula, fold the whipped egg mixture into the cooled chocolate until just combined but still streaky. Sprinkle the dry ingredients in 4 additions over the chocolate, folding until just combined between additions.

Transfer the batter to the prepared pan and smooth the top with the spatula. Bake in the center of the oven for about 50 minutes, until a toothpick or cake tester comes out clean.

Cool the brownies completely in the pan before cutting into 2-inch squares.

Butternut-Maple BLONDIES

There are really no rules on what you can and can't use in a great dessert, and I find that vegetables offer flavors, textures, and colors that work well in the sweet environment. They also can add tons of moisture to a dessert, as the squash does for these blondies. Here the rich, moist squash eliminates the need for the heavy, flavorless corn syrup usually found in blondie recipes. **MAKES ABOUT 12 BLONDIES**

One 2-pound butternut squash, halved and
  seeded (907 g)

¾ cup (1½ sticks) cold unsalted butter, diced,
  plus more for the pan (170 g)

2 to 3 tablespoons Demerara sugar, for the pan

1 cup (packed) dark brown sugar (232 g)

2 large eggs, at room temperature

2 tablespoons pure maple syrup (34 g)

1 teaspoon vanilla extract (5 g)

2 cups all-purpose flour (250 g)

1½ teaspoons baking powder (6 g)

¾ teaspoon ground cumin (1.5 g)

¾ teaspoon ground ginger (1.5 g)

¼ teaspoon ground mace

½ teaspoon kosher salt (2 g)

6 ounces white chocolate, coarsely chopped
  (170 g)

Preheat the oven to 400°F.

Line a baking sheet with parchment paper and put the squash halves on it, cut side down. Roast until the flesh is fork-tender, 25 to 30 minutes. Remove from the oven and, when cool enough to handle, scoop the flesh from the skins into a food processor and purée until smooth.

Transfer the squash to a saucepan and simmer over low heat, stirring frequently, for 10 minutes to remove excess moisture. Remove from the heat, measure 1 cup for the blondies, and reserve the remaining purée for another use.

Reduce the oven temperature to 350°F. Grease an 8 × 11-inch baking dish or cake pan with butter and coat it generously with the Demerara sugar, tapping out the excess.

In the bowl of a standing mixer with the paddle attachment, toss the ¾ cup butter and the brown sugar together with your hands until the butter is coated. Beat the butter and sugar on medium speed for about 5 minutes, until lightened and no clumps of butter remain. Add the eggs, one at a time, mixing well and scraping down the bowl with a rubber spatula between additions. Add the syrup and vanilla and mix well.

Sift the flour, baking powder, cumin, ginger, and mace together; sprinkle the salt over the top. With the mixer on low speed, gradually add the dry ingredients, a little at a time, mixing until just combined. Add the cooled squash and mix until just combined. Remove the bowl from the mixer and fold in two thirds of the white chocolate pieces.

Evenly spread the batter into the prepared pan and sprinkle the remaining chocolate pieces evenly over the top. Bake on the center rack until a cake tester inserted in the center comes out clean, about 45 minutes.

Cool completely in the pan on a rack before cutting into 12 equal-sized pieces.

Spiced Apple and Pistachio Streusel MUFFINS

My dad is a pistachio fanatic. When we had movie night at home, he made my brother and me sit and shell huge bags of them so he wouldn't have to crack a single one during the movie. Once when my mom was making apple crisp, she ran out of walnuts, so she replaced them with some of Dad's preshelled pistachios, and we had to start all over again shelling a new bag. But the combination of the two stuck—they taste great together, especially in these moist streusel-topped muffins. **MAKES 1½ DOZEN MUFFINS**

FOR THE STREUSEL

½ cup plus ⅓ cup all-purpose flour (109 g)

½ cup shelled unsalted pistachios, coarsely chopped (70 g)

¼ cup granulated sugar (50 g)

2 tablespoons (packed) light brown sugar (28 g)

½ teaspoon kosher salt (2 g)

¼ teaspoon baking powder (1 g)

4 tablespoons (½ stick) unsalted butter, melted (57 g)

FOR THE MUFFINS

8 tablespoons (1 stick) cold unsalted butter, diced (113 g)

1 cup granulated sugar (200 g)

¼ cup sour cream, at room temperature (60 g)

2 large eggs, at room temperature

1 teaspoon vanilla extract (5 g)

1 teaspoon fresh lemon juice (5 g)

2 cups all-purpose flour (250 g)

1½ teaspoons baking powder (6 g)

½ teaspoon baking soda (3 g)

½ teaspoon ground cinnamon (1 g)

¼ teaspoon freshly grated nutmeg (1 g)

½ teaspoon kosher salt (2 g)

2 medium Granny Smith apples

To make the streusel, put the flour, pistachios, granulated sugar, brown sugar, salt, and baking powder in a small bowl and stir well to combine. Drizzle the butter over the mixture and use your fingers to squeeze it into pea-sized clumps. Spread the mixture out on a small plate or pan and freeze it while you make the muffin batter.

To make the muffins, preheat the oven to 350°F. Line three 6-portion standard muffin tins with paper liners.

In a standing mixer bowl, toss the butter and granulated sugar together until the butter is coated. Attach the bowl and paddle to the mixer and beat the butter and sugar on medium speed for about 5 minutes, until a sugary paste forms and there are no visible clumps of butter.

Whisk the sour cream, eggs, vanilla, and lemon juice together in a small bowl. Reduce the mixer speed to low and slowly drizzle in the egg mixture. With a rubber spatula, scrape down the sides of the bowl.

In a separate bowl, sift the flour, baking powder, baking soda, cinnamon, and nutmeg together; sprinkle the salt over the top. With the mixer on low speed, gradually add the dry ingredients to the butter; mix until just incorporated.

Cut the apples away from the core into 4 quarters. Set a box grater over a plate and grate the apples, skin side out, until all of the flesh is grated, leaving just some of the peel; discard the peels. Immediately fold the grated apples into the batter.

Divide the batter evenly among the lined muffin tin cups. Remove the streusel from the freezer and loosen it with your fingers. Evenly sprinkle the streusel mixture over the muffin batter in the pans. Bake in the center of the oven until golden brown and a knife inserted in the center of a muffin comes out clean, about 25 minutes.

Cool the muffins in the pan. Serve slightly warm or at room temperature.

Zucchini and Roasted Corn MUFFINS

Two of my favorite baked goods are corn bread and zucchini bread. But I hate when I order one of them and all I taste is sugar, so I thought it would be cool to create a muffin in which these two vegetables are the star. By using fresh roasted corn in addition to cornmeal, I coax even more flavor out of these sweet-meets-savory muffins. **MAKES 1½ DOZEN MUFFINS**

FOR THE VEGETABLES

1 small zucchini (about 8 ounces) (225 g)

1¼ teaspoons kosher salt (5 g)

2 cups fresh corn kernels (cut from about 3 large ears) (285 g)

2 tablespoons (¼ stick) unsalted butter (28 g)

2 tablespoons sugar (25 g)

FOR THE MUFFINS

8 tablespoons (1 stick) cold unsalted butter, diced (113 g)

½ cup sugar (100 g)

¼ cup Greek yogurt, at room temperature (63 g)

2 large eggs, at room temperature (100 g)

1 teaspoon vanilla extract (5 g)

Grated zest of 1 lime

2 cups all-purpose flour (250 g)

½ cup fine cornmeal (90 g)

1½ teaspoons baking powder (6 g)

½ teaspoon baking soda (3 g)

1½ teaspoons kosher salt (6 g)

¾ teaspoon chili powder (1 g)

¾ teaspoon coarsely ground black pepper (2 g)

½ cup crumbled cotija cheese or queso fresco (optional) (60 g)

To prepare the vegetables, grate the zucchini on the large holes of a box grater into a colander set over a bowl. Sprinkle 1 teaspoon of the salt over the zucchini, toss, and spread the zucchini over the surface of the colander to drain. Let stand for at least 10 minutes.

Meanwhile, put the corn kernels in a large skillet and add the remaining ¼ teaspoon salt, the butter, and the sugar. Cook over medium heat, stirring frequently, for about 10 minutes, until the corn starts to caramelize. Transfer to a medium bowl to cool.

Using your hands, firmly squeeze the excess moisture from the salted zucchini to extract as much liquid as possible; toss the zucchini with the corn.

To make the muffins, preheat the oven to 350°F. Line three 6-portion standard muffin tins with paper liners.

In a standing mixer bowl, toss the butter and sugar together until the butter is coated. Attach the bowl and paddle to the mixer and beat the butter and sugar on medium speed for about 5 minutes, until a sugary paste forms and no visible clumps of butter remain.

Whisk together the yogurt, eggs, vanilla, and lime zest in a small bowl. Reduce the mixer speed to low and slowly drizzle in the egg mixture. With a rubber spatula, scrape down the sides of the bowl.

In a small bowl, whisk together the flour, cornmeal, baking powder, baking soda, salt, chili powder, and black pepper. With the mixer on low speed, gradually add the dry ingredients to the butter mixture; mix until just incorporated. Remove the bowl from the mixer and, using a rubber spatula, fold the corn and zucchini into the batter until well combined.

Divide the batter evenly among the lined muffin tin cups and evenly scatter the cotija, if using, over the surface of the muffins. Bake in the center of the oven for 20 to 25 minutes, until golden brown and a knife inserted in the center of a muffin comes out clean.

Cool the muffins in the pan. Serve warm or at room temperature.

CHAPTER 5

COOKIES, TEA CAKE

S, *and* BISCUITS

Less is more when it comes to dessert. I'd much rather have a small, balanced bite or two than a giant piece of cake smothered in supersweet frosting and ice cream. Desserts, even small ones, should have deep flavor. In every pastry kitchen I've worked in, I have prepared petits fours and miniature desserts like cookies for the end of the meal. As they are the final bite diners take at the end of the evening, they have to leave a good, lasting impression. So these little gems deserve as much attention as a plated, composed dessert.

People assume that cookies are simple to make, which some are, but that doesn't mean their flavor should be simple. Trust me, I've had plenty of bad cookies, and there's nothing worse. Over- or underbaked cookies are terrible. Cookie texture is every bit as important as good, fresh ingredients, and just baking them incorrectly can really affect how they taste.

I've made thousands of cookies using several techniques: rolled, where the dough is rolled out with a rolling pin from which cookies are cut and baked; dropped, where the dough is scooped with a spoon directly onto a baking sheet and baked from a ball shape; bars, where dough is pressed into a baking sheet or dish, baked, and sliced later; refrigerator (sometimes called *icebox*) cookies, where dough is rolled into cylinders, chilled, sliced, and baked; and sandwich cookies, where the mighty macaron is the king. Every cookie type has specific techniques to pay attention to that can mean the difference between a crumbly mess and a sophisticated experience in one bite.

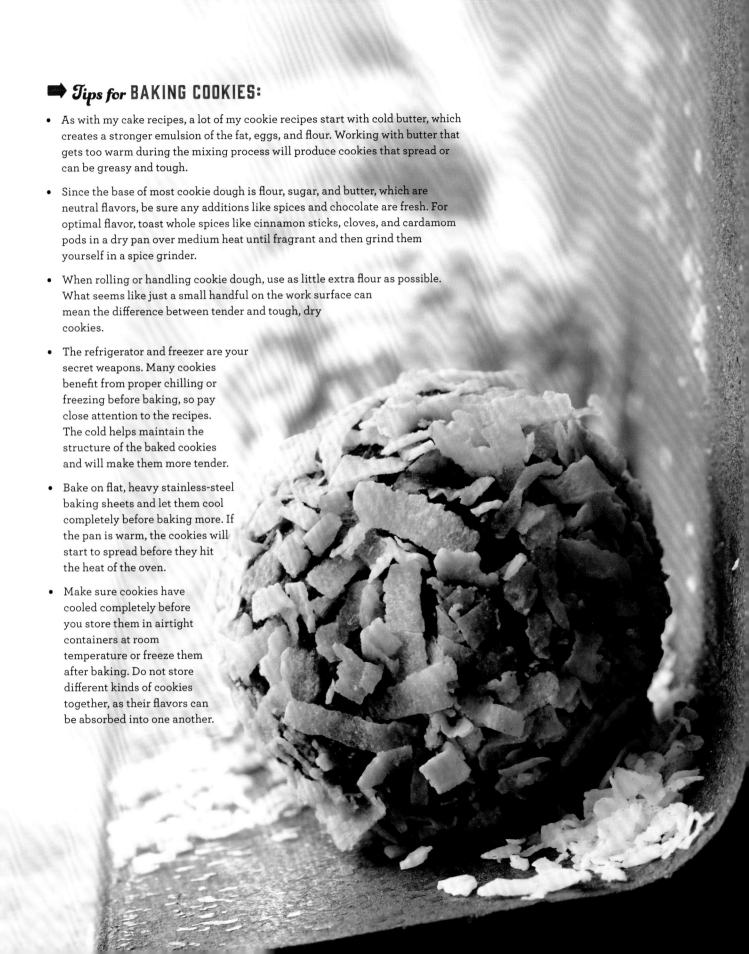

➡ *Tips for* BAKING COOKIES:

- As with my cake recipes, a lot of my cookie recipes start with cold butter, which creates a stronger emulsion of the fat, eggs, and flour. Working with butter that gets too warm during the mixing process will produce cookies that spread or can be greasy and tough.

- Since the base of most cookie dough is flour, sugar, and butter, which are neutral flavors, be sure any additions like spices and chocolate are fresh. For optimal flavor, toast whole spices like cinnamon sticks, cloves, and cardamom pods in a dry pan over medium heat until fragrant and then grind them yourself in a spice grinder.

- When rolling or handling cookie dough, use as little extra flour as possible. What seems like just a small handful on the work surface can mean the difference between tender and tough, dry cookies.

- The refrigerator and freezer are your secret weapons. Many cookies benefit from proper chilling or freezing before baking, so pay close attention to the recipes. The cold helps maintain the structure of the baked cookies and will make them more tender.

- Bake on flat, heavy stainless-steel baking sheets and let them cool completely before baking more. If the pan is warm, the cookies will start to spread before they hit the heat of the oven.

- Make sure cookies have cooled completely before you store them in airtight containers at room temperature or freeze them after baking. Do not store different kinds of cookies together, as their flavors can be absorbed into one another.

Killer CHOCOLATE CHIP COOKIES

People constantly ask me how I stay thin working as a pastry chef. While I do love sugar, I am able to restrain myself around most desserts. Cookie dough, though, is the devil, and baking it into these crunchy cookies, which are great for dunking in milk, doesn't help much either. They have a fine crumb and crisp texture, due to the addition of cake flour, and have a more intriguing flavor from a good hit of kosher salt and a pinch of cinnamon. This recipe makes a big batch of dough, enough to share, even if you have willpower like mine.

MAKES ABOUT 4 DOZEN 2-INCH COOKIES

½ pound (2 sticks) cold unsalted butter, diced (226 g)

1 cup granulated sugar (200 g)

1 cup (packed) light brown sugar (232 g)

¾ teaspoon vanilla extract (4 g)

¼ teaspoon almond extract

1 large egg

2 large egg yolks

2 cups all-purpose flour (250 g)

1 cup cake flour (110 g)

1 teaspoon baking powder (4 g)

1 teaspoon baking soda (6 g)

½ teaspoon ground cinnamon (1 g)

1½ teaspoons kosher salt (6 g)

14 ounces bittersweet chocolate (70% cacao), coarsely chopped (397 g)

Maldon sea salt (smoked, if you can find it), for garnish

Preheat the oven to 350°F. Line 2 baking sheets with silicone baking mats or parchment paper.

Put the butter, granulated sugar, and brown sugar into a standing mixer bowl and toss with your fingers until the butter is coated. Attach the bowl and paddle to the mixer and beat the butter and sugar on medium-low speed until a thick paste forms with no visible butter lumps. Add the vanilla and almond extracts and mix well. With the motor on low speed, add the egg and egg yolks, one at a time, mixing well between additions. Stop the mixer and scrape down the bowl with a rubber spatula.

Meanwhile, in a separate bowl, sift together the flours, baking powder, baking soda, and cinnamon; sprinkle the kosher salt over the top. With the mixer on low speed, slowly add the dry ingredients to the butter mixture, stopping frequently to scrape down the bowl. Mix until just combined; remove the bowl from the mixer and fold the chocolate into the dough by hand.

Using a small (½-ounce) ice cream scoop, scoop level balls of dough and arrange them about 2 inches apart on the lined cookie sheets. Use the bottom of a glass to flatten the dough balls slightly and then sprinkle a little Maldon salt over each cookie. Bake for 12 to 13 minutes, rotating the pans once, until just set and the bottoms are beginning to brown. Cool for 10 minutes on the pans before transferring to a rack to cool completely.

Store the cookies in an airtight container for up to 3 days. If they last that long.

Note: *This dough freezes well, either in bulk, which can be defrosted, scooped, and baked, or prescooped and shaped into balls that you can just put on a lined baking sheet and bake whenever you are craving them, adding another minute or two to the baking time.*

RICH BUTTER COOKIES
with Pink Peppercorns and Sea Salt

The base of this cookie is a sablé dough that I learned from Thomas Haas, a fourth-generation pastry chef hailing from the Black Forest region of Germany and one of my mentors as a young pastry cook. Because the egg is precooked before it is added to the dough, it lends richness but does not bind the dough, which is very tender. Unlike their cousins, pink peppercorns are not "peppery" but more fragrant and almost floral in comparison. Add a pinch of sea salt to the tops of the cookies and they contain everything a good dessert should have—tender crumb, crunch, a bit of flowery spice, sweetness, and saltiness all in one bite.

MAKES ABOUT 3 DOZEN COOKIES

1¼ cups (2½ sticks) cold unsalted butter, diced (283 g)

1¼ cups sugar (250 g)

½ teaspoon kosher salt (2 g)

Yolks of 4 hard-boiled large eggs

Seeds from 1 vanilla bean

3 cups all-purpose flour, plus more for rolling (375 g)

1 large egg, beaten

2 tablespoons crushed pink peppercorns, for garnish

Coarse sea salt, for garnish

Put the butter, sugar, and kosher salt in a standing mixer bowl and toss with your fingers to coat. Attach the bowl to the mixer with the paddle and beat on medium-low speed until a sugary paste forms with no visible lumps of butter.

Meanwhile, using a rubber spatula, press the egg yolks through a fine-mesh strainer into a bowl and scrape any egg yolk stuck to the strainer into the bowl. Add the yolks and vanilla seeds to the butter and mix until well incorporated.

Turn the mixer to low and gradually add the flour; stop to scrape down the bowl with a rubber spatula several times. Mix until just incorporated. Put a sheet of parchment paper on a work surface, dump the dough onto it, and cover with another sheet of parchment. Use a rolling pin to roll the dough ¾ inch thick. Transfer the dough to a sheet pan and freeze until firm, at least 1 hour.

Remove the dough from the freezer and let stand for 10 minutes. When partially thawed, roll the dough between the parchment sheets until it is ½ inch thick. (Peel back the parchment and dust the dough with flour if it sticks to the paper.)

Line 2 baking sheets with silicone mats or parchment. Use a 2½-inch plain cutter to cut out rounds of dough and transfer them to the lined sheets, about 1 inch apart. Reroll the scraps and cut cookies until the dough is used up. Cover the pans and freeze for 30 minutes, until ready to bake.

To bake the cookies, preheat the oven to 375°F.

Remove the cookies from the freezer and brush them with the beaten egg. Sprinkle a pinch of pink peppercorns over the top along with a few flakes of coarse salt. Bake for 18 to 20 minutes, rotating the pans halfway through, until the edges of the cookies are light golden brown. Cool for 10 minutes on the pan before transferring to a rack to cool completely.

Note: *If you have 2- or 2½-inch pastry rings, butter them and cut the cookies to that exact dimension using the appropriately sized cutter. Since this dough has so much butter, it spreads easily, so baking them in rings helps keep them perfectly straight so you can see the rich, cakey layers from the side when you unmold them.*

Ginger-Curry SUGAR COOKIES

Plain sugar cookies, no matter how well they are made, are a bit boring to me. You may think I have gone off the rails by adding curry powder to cookies, but along with the ground and candied ginger, the combo really wakes up a classic American cookie. Give these a shot! **MAKES ABOUT 4 DOZEN COOKIES**

10 tablespoons (1¼ sticks) cold unsalted butter, diced (140 g)

1 large egg

Seeds from 1 vanilla bean

1½ cups plus 1 tablespoon all-purpose flour (208 g)

¾ cup confectioners' sugar (90 g)

1½ teaspoons ground ginger (3 g)

1 teaspoon mild curry powder (2 g)

½ teaspoon kosher salt (2 g)

Demerara sugar, for rolling

2 large egg yolks, beaten

Maldon sea salt, as needed

24 one-inch pieces crystallized ginger, halved crosswise

In the bowl of a standing mixer fitted with the paddle attachment, beat the butter on medium-low speed for about 5 minutes, until a thick paste forms with no lumps of butter. Add the whole egg and vanilla seeds and mix until combined.

Meanwhile, in a separate bowl, sift together the flour, confectioners' sugar, ginger, and curry powder; sprinkle the kosher salt over the top. With the mixer on low speed, slowly add the dry ingredients to the butter and mix until just combined.

Divide the dough between 2 sheets of parchment and form into long thin logs, about 1½ inches in diameter. Fold the paper over the dough roll and use a pastry scraper to tighten the dough log. Use your hands to smooth and form the dough into as perfect a cylinder as you can. Refrigerate until firm.

When ready to bake, preheat the oven to 350°F. Line 2 baking sheets with silicone baking mats or parchment paper.

Using 2 hands, roll the dough logs firmly on a work surface to round out any edges. Sprinkle the Demerara sugar onto another baking sheet. Unwrap the dough and, using a pastry brush, brush the surface with beaten egg yolk. Roll the dough in the sugar and slice it with a sharp knife into ¼-inch-thick slices. Brush the surface of each cookie with beaten yolk, sprinkle a few flakes of Maldon salt on top, and press a piece of crystallized ginger into the center of each cookie.

Space the cookies about 1 inch apart on the lined baking sheets and bake for 15 to 16 minutes, rotating the pans halfway through, until the edges are just beginning to turn golden.

Cool in the pan for 10 minutes before transferring to a rack to cool completely. Store in an airtight container for up to 5 days.

Sesame-Poppy PALMIERS

Palmiers are a classic French cookie, sometimes called *elephant ears,* that are made by folding puff pastry into tight cylinders and slicing them crosswise before baking. I love them because they aren't too sweet, and they get supercrunchy when the sugar caramelizes in the oven. This version is almost savory, and the addition of poppy and sesame seeds makes them even crunchier. You could easily serve these instead of crackers with a bowl of soup or with a cheese plate. **MAKES ABOUT 4 DOZEN PASTRIES**

FOR THE SIMPLE SYRUP

½ cup sugar (100 g)

⅓ cup water (80 g)

FOR THE COOKIES

All-purpose flour, for rolling

1 pound Puff Pastry (page 264) or store-bought all-butter frozen, thawed

2 tablespoons sugar (25 g)

¼ teaspoon kosher salt (1 g)

2 teaspoons poppy seeds (7 g)

2 teaspoons sesame seeds (6 g)

To make the simple syrup, put the sugar and water into a small saucepan and heat over medium heat, stirring, until the sugar is completely dissolved. Cool to room temperature before using.

To make the cookies, lightly flour a work surface and rolling pin. Turn the pastry sheet so long side faces you. Rolling only in one direction, roll the sheet into a 10 × 16-inch rectangle, making sure the edges are very square and straight. With a pastry brush, brush the surface evenly with simple syrup (1). Mix the sugar, salt, poppy seeds, and sesame seeds together in a small bowl and sprinkle the mixture evenly over the surface of the pastry sheet (2).

recipe continues

Working from the outside long edges, measure a 1½-inch-wide strip and fold it in toward the center over the top of the dough. Repeat on the other side. With a clean brush, remove any excess flour stuck to the puff pastry fold (3). Brush the top of the folded dough with simple syrup and fold each side toward the center again (4), creating a horseshoe shape (5). Press the dough together lightly, making sure the folds are uniform and even. Brush any excess flour from the dough. Wrap the dough tightly in parchment paper, transfer to a baking sheet, and freeze until firm, at least 1 hour or covered for up to 1 week.

Preheat the oven to 350°F. Line 2 baking sheets with silicone baking mats or parchment paper.

Remove the dough from the freezer and unwrap it; if it is frozen solid, let stand for about 10 minutes. Using a very sharp knife, cut the dough crosswise into ¼-inch slices, being sure to cut straight down through the dough without sawing (6). Arrange the slices, cut side down, about 2 inches apart on the lined baking sheets. If the dough has thawed, refrigerate the slices until firm, about 15 minutes.

Lay a sheet of parchment on top of each pan of cookies (7) and set another baking sheet on top of them (this will help the cookies bake flat and the sugar to caramelize on the bottom) (8). Bake for 40 to 45 minutes, rotating the pans halfway through, until golden brown. Cool completely on the pan before storing in an airtight container for up to 5 days.

Cottontail COOKIES

These are sometimes also called *Mexican wedding cookies* or *Russian tea cakes*. I was introduced to them as a kid but never made one until my externship while at the Culinary Institute. You would expect the cookies to be supersweet from being rolled in confectioners' sugar, but the rich, roasted nut flavor balances everything and is what seals the deal for me. I like how they break down when you eat them; the texture is just perfect—part crunchy, part chewy. You can taste each element separately, but they have great synergy together. **MAKES ABOUT 2 DOZEN COOKIES**

½ cup whole almonds, toasted (see page 142) (70 g)

½ cup walnut pieces, toasted (see page 142) (60 g)

6 tablespoons (¾ stick) cold unsalted butter, diced (84 g)

6 tablespoons granulated sugar (72 g)

1 tablespoon brandy or whiskey (15 g)

1¼ cups all-purpose flour, sifted (156 g)

½ teaspoon kosher salt (2 g)

About 1 cup confectioners' sugar, for rolling, sifted

Preheat the oven to 350°F. Line a baking sheet with a silicone baking mat or parchment paper.

Put the almonds and walnuts into a food processor and pulse until finely chopped but not powdery.

Put the butter and granulated sugar into a standing mixer bowl and toss with your fingers until the butter is coated. Attach the bowl and paddle to the mixer and beat the butter and sugar on medium-low speed until a thick paste forms with no visible butter lumps. Add the brandy and, with the mixer on low, add the flour and salt, a little at a time, occasionally scraping down the bowl with a rubber spatula; mix just until the dough begins to clump together. Add the nuts and mix on low speed just until combined.

Roll level tablespoon-sized portions of dough into round balls and place them on the lined baking sheet. Bake until light golden brown, 18 to 20 minutes.

Put the confectioners' sugar in a large bowl. Let the cookies cool on the pan for about 5 minutes and then toss them in confectioners' sugar until coated. Shake off the excess and transfer them to a rack to cool completely before rolling them in the sugar again.

Store the cookies at room temperature in an airtight container for up to 5 days.

Pecan SHORTBREAD

This is a good basic shortbread recipe, elevated by toasted pecans. It's a perfect cookie for tea or even with a cheese plate. These also make great wafers for ice cream sandwiches in the dead of summer. This recipe makes a lot of dough; you can keep it in the freezer and bake cookies when you need them. **MAKES ABOUT 4 DOZEN 2-INCH COOKIES**

1¼ cups (2½ sticks) cold unsalted butter, diced (286 g)

¾ cup sugar (150 g)

5 large egg yolks, at room temperature, plus more for glazing

¼ teaspoon lemon extract

¼ teaspoon orange extract

3⅓ cups all-purpose flour, plus more for rolling (417 g)

6 ounces pecans, toasted (see page 142) and finely ground (175 g)

1 teaspoon kosher salt (4 g)

Pecan halves, for garnish (optional)

Put the butter and sugar into a standing mixer bowl and toss with your fingers until the butter is coated. Attach the bowl and paddle to the mixer and beat the butter and sugar on medium-low speed until a thick paste forms with no visible butter lumps.

Whisk the egg yolks, lemon extract, and orange extract together. With the mixer on low speed, slowly drizzle the yolk mixture into the butter and mix until well combined. Scrape down the bowl with a rubber spatula.

In a bowl, whisk together the flour, ground pecans, and salt. With the mixer on low speed, slowly add the dry ingredients to the butter and mix just until combined. Do not overmix. Transfer the dough to a large sheet of parchment paper; press with the spatula to an even layer about 1 inch thick. Lightly dust the surface with flour and lay another sheet of parchment on top of it. Using a rolling pin, roll the dough, flipping it several times in the parchment on the work surface, to an even ¼-inch thickness. Slide

the dough onto a baking sheet and freeze for at least 1 hour or covered for up to 1 week.

Line 2 baking sheets with silicone baking mats or parchment paper.

Using a lightly floured 2-inch round cutter, cut cookies out of the rolled dough and arrange them ½ inch apart on the lined baking sheets. (Alternatively, you can cut them into squares or rectangles with a knife.) If the dough has thawed, briefly freeze the cookies before baking. Continue rerolling and cutting cookies until the dough has been used up. Freeze until ready to bake or covered for up to 1 week.

Preheat the oven to 375°F. Brush the surface of the cookies with beaten egg yolk and position a pecan half on top of each cookie if desired. Bake for 12 to 14 minutes, rotating the pans halfway through, until light golden. Cool on the pan for 5 minutes before transferring to a rack to cool completely. Store in an airtight container for up to 1 week.

Note: *It's important to cut the cookies and bake them while frozen. This helps them retain their shape and sharp, defined edges.*

MACARONS

I had the good fortune of working at one of the most famous macaron palaces in the world—Ladurée, in Paris. At the time, the macarons were still being made by hand and the gentleman who made them spent eight hours every day piping them. He was so fast that it sounded like a machine gun going off as the metal piping tip slapped the baking sheets. My version uses an Italian meringue, which produces stable, consistent macarons and helps create an evenly risen "foot," the ruffled base edge around the bottom of the cookie. One of the crown jewels of French pastry, macarons are not hard to make, as long as you control the variables: your meringue, the humidity level in the room, and the almond flour you use (see Tips for Successful Macarons, page 238). It's also imperative that the measurements are exact, so these ingredients must be weighed. **MAKES ABOUT 150 COOKIES (75 MACARONS)**

FOR THE COOKIE BASE

185 g confectioners' sugar

185 g almond flour

65 g egg whites

FOR THE ITALIAN MERINGUE

185 g plus 1 tablespoon granulated sugar

75 g egg whites

Pinch of cream of tartar

Food coloring, as desired

Line 3 baking sheets with silicone baking mats or Teflon-coated baking paper.

To prepare the cookie base, using a very fine sifter, sift together the confectioners' sugar, almond flour, and cookie flavoring, if using, in a large mixing bowl (1). Add the egg whites and stir gently until the ingredients are evenly moistened.

To make the Italian meringue, put the 185 g sugar in a small saucepan (the smallest pan you have). Add enough water (about 2 tablespoons), stirring with a finger, to make wet sand; wet your finger again and wipe down the sides of the pan. Put the pan over medium heat and bring to a boil. Meanwhile, put the egg whites in a standing mixer bowl with the whisk attachment with the remaining 1 tablespoon sugar

and the cream of tartar and turn the mixer on to medium-low speed.

Once the sugar has dissolved, dip a clean pastry brush in cold water and wash down the sides of the pan. When the sugar is at a rolling boil, raise the mixer speed to medium-high. Cook the sugar to 244°F (firm-ball stage). When the egg whites have volume but are still soft, turn the mixer to low speed and slowly drizzle the sugar directly onto the egg whites between the side of the bowl and the outer reach of the whisk (this prevents splattering). Whip the whites until firm and glossy but not dry, about 5 minutes.

Add a small amount of meringue to the cookie base and stir with a rubber spatula to lighten the

recipe continues

mixture (2). Add food coloring as desired. Add the whites in 3 batches, folding gently between additions to combine. When the egg whites are completely mixed in, pull the spatula through the batter and over the surface as if folding, pulling a ribbon of batter over the surface (3). The ribbon should settle very slowly into the batter. If the ribbon rests on the top without settling, the batter is too stiff; fold the batter 4 or 5 more times to loosen but *not* liquefy it. If the batter is too loose, the cookies will not hold their shape and will spread when baked.

Preheat the oven to 350°F.

Transfer the mixture to a piping bag fitted with a ⅜-inch straight tip (Ateco # 804). Pipe quarter-sized rounds of batter onto the prepared pan, about ½ inch apart. Pipe the batter from an angle, away from you. Stop squeezing the bag and drag the tip counterclockwise through the surface of the batter until the batter stops coming out of the tip (4).

Let stand at room temp until they are dry to the touch and have formed a shell on the surface, 10 to 15 minutes, depending on the humidity level in your kitchen.

Bake 2 pans at once for 8 to 10 minutes, rotating the pans halfway through, until the cookies are risen and set but not brown. Let the cookies cool completely on the pan. Bake the remaining pan.

Store the cookies in the freezer in an airtight container until ready to fill.

Note: *Macarons can also be colored and flavored with powdered ingredients (see variations) that will sift well with the almond flour in the cookie base. You can also sprinkle a little of the flavoring on the top of the cookies directly after piping them.*

Coffee Macarons

Add 2 tablespoons (12 g) fine instant espresso powder to the cookie base. Fill with Chocolate Ganache Filling (page 327) or Coffee Buttercream (page 320).

Chocolate Macarons

Add 2 tablespoons (12 g) cocoa powder to the cookie base and dust the cookies with more powder immediately after piping. Or scatter a few cacao nibs on the wet cookies. Fill with Salted Dulce de Leche Buttercream (page 320) or Chocolate Buttercream (page 320).

Green Tea Macarons

Add 1 tablespoon (8 g) matcha (green tea powder) to the cookie base and dust the piped cookies with a little more powder.

➡ *Tips for* PIPING MACARONS:

- Twist end of pastry bag closed tightly and hold it with both hands.

- Pipe quarter-sized mounds away from you at a 45-degree angle. Stop squeezing bag and flick tip up counterclockwise; "tail" will settle into batter.

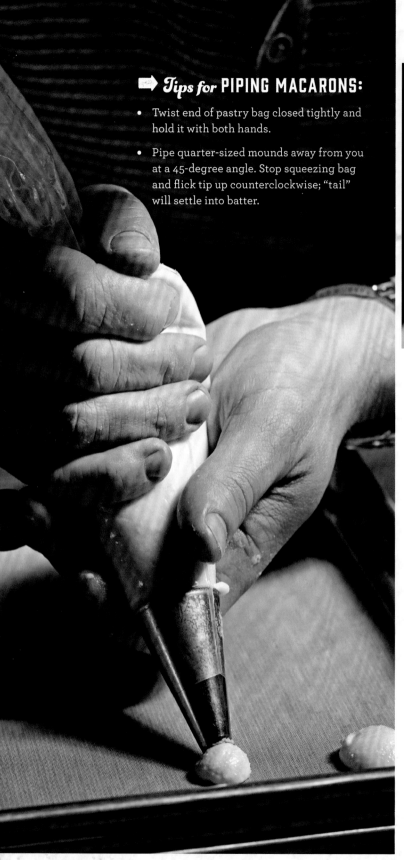

➡ *Tips for* SUCCESSFUL MACARONS:

- For the best results, bake macarons on silicone baking mats or Teflon-coated paper; they help produce a taller, more defined "foot." Macaron batter can stick to parchment paper, inhibiting the rise.

- This is one recipe where you *must* weigh your ingredients—precision is key.

- If your almond flour has an oily feel to it, spread it out on a sheet pan, dry it out in a 225°F oven for 10 or 15 minutes, and then let cool before you use it; otherwise your macarons will be gummy.

- Remember not to overwhip your meringue. It should be firm and glossy but not dry.

- Use only water-based food coloring to tint the cookies—the inexpensive squeeze bottles with pointy caps are fine. Oil-base or paste colors can break the meringue.

- Once the macarons are piped, they need to dry out and form a crust so they will have a crunchy yet soft texture when you bite into them. Don't skip this step.

Macaron Fillings

Macarons can be filled layered with a number of fillings—jam, buttercream, ganache, thick nut pastes (praline), or even just peanut or almond butter. Whatever filling you choose, though, must be thick enough to sandwich between cookies without dripping out. Typically I will color the cookies to match the filling flavor. Plain macarons can be tinted pink and filled with Raspberry-Mint Jam (page 326) or Vanilla Buttercream (page 319). Tint your macarons yellow or orange and fill them with Citrus Vanilla Buttercream (page 320). Pipe the filling with a small pastry bag or resealable plastic food bag onto one cookie before sandwiching another cookie (bottom to bottom) on top. I also like to sprinkle very finely chopped nuts on the cookies the moment they are piped if I am filling them with a nut-flavored filling.

Play Date COOKIES

One of my closest friends, Zohar Zohar, whom I met when I was about twenty in the early years of Daniel, has come full circle in the culinary world. After years of working in the finest restaurants in New York City as a line cook with no formal training, she phased out of that world to begin a family. Finding herself back in the kitchen with her kids doing a lot of baking, she realized she missed the professional environment, so she gave it another go, opening a bakery called Zucker in the East Village, specializing in cookies with the Middle Eastern ingredients of her youth—dates, spices, and figs. This cookie is for those with advanced rolling skills, as the dough should be rolled until it is very thin and see-through, but it is worth the effort. It's my favorite of Zohar's cookies—a tender spiral crust with a spicy date filling. **MAKES ABOUT 2 DOZEN COOKIES**

FOR THE DOUGH

7 tablespoons cold unsalted butter, diced (99 g)

¼ cup granulated sugar (50 g)

3 large egg yolks, at room temperature (60 g)

1½ cups all-purpose flour, plus more for rolling (190 g)

1½ teaspoons baking powder (6 g)

1 to 2 tablespoons cold water (15 to 30 g)

FOR THE FILLING

8 ounces pitted whole dates (about 28) (250 g)

½ cup water (120 g)

½ teaspoon baking soda (3 g)

½ teaspoon ground cloves (1 g)

½ teaspoon ground cinnamon (1 g)

Confectioners' sugar, for dusting

To make the dough, put the butter and granulated sugar into a standing mixer bowl and toss with your fingers until the butter is coated. Attach the bowl and paddle to the mixer and beat the butter and sugar on medium-low speed for about 5 minutes, until a thick paste forms with no visible butter lumps. With the mixer on low speed, add the egg yolks, one at a time, stopping to scrape down the bowl between additions.

Sift the flour and baking powder together, and with the mixer on low speed, add the flour mixture to the butter mixture in 3 batches until just combined. Scrape down the bowl and, with the mixer on low, add enough cold water (1 to 2 tablespoons) just to bring the dough together. Remove the dough from the mixer and divide into 2 equal portions.

Lay 2 sheets of plastic wrap on a work surface and transfer a portion of dough to each; pat each portion into an even rectangle about ½ inch thick. Wrap each dough piece tightly in the plastic wrap, being sure to retain the rectangular shape as neatly as possible. Refrigerate overnight.

Meanwhile, to make the filling, put the dates and water into a small saucepan and bring to a boil over medium heat. Reduce the heat to low and simmer for 3 to 4 minutes, until the dates are very soft and most of the water has been absorbed. Remove from the heat, stir in the baking soda, and let stand for a few minutes to cool. Transfer the dates and liquid to a food processor and purée until very smooth. The mixture should be thick but spreadable, like softened butter; if it is too thick, add a few drops of hot water and purée. Add the cloves and cinnamon and mix until combined. Store in an airtight container at room temperature until you are ready to bake the cookies.

Preheat the oven to 350°F. Line a baking sheet with parchment paper. Remove the dough from the refrigerator and let stand for about 10 minutes, until soft enough to roll. Cut a piece of parchment paper into a 10 × 15-inch rectangle to use as a template.

Put a large sheet of plastic wrap on a work surface and lightly flour it. Unwrap 1 dough piece, put it on the plastic sheet, and sprinkle a light coating of flour over the surface. Dust a rolling pin with flour and roll the dough evenly into a rough 8 × 10-inch rectangle. Flour the top of the dough lightly and put another large sheet of plastic over the top of the dough; roll it several times to adhere the plastic.

Flip the dough over and gently peel back the top sheet of plastic wrap. Very lightly, but evenly, flour the dough; lay the plastic back on top of it. Continue rolling the dough, using the paper template as a guide, until it is a 10 × 15-inch rectangle. Be sure the edges are square and even; if they are uneven, you can peel off the plastic, cut the edges as needed, and use the scraps to patch any parts that are not even, lightly rerolling so the scraps adhere. The thinner you can roll this dough, the better, but if you struggle

to reach the dimensions specified, don't worry. It will still taste delicious. If at any point the dough gets sticky and hard to work with, refrigerate it in the plastic for a few minutes to firm it back up.

Working with half of the date filling, remove the top piece of plastic wrap and, using a small offset spatula, drop small mounds of the filling evenly spaced over the dough and then spread it out with the spatula in a thin, even layer (if the dough is soft and sticky, refrigerate it again so spreading is easier). Using the bottom piece of plastic as a guide, at the long side of the closest edge to you, fold the dough over about $1/16$ inch onto itself. Then lift the plastic and roll the dough up very tightly into a log, stopping periodically to even out and tighten the roll with your hands; the more tightly you roll the dough, the smaller and more delicate the spiral layers will be. Transfer it to a baking sheet, seam side down. Repeat with the second dough rectangle and the remaining filling. Chill the dough rolls for 20 minutes.

Bake until the bottom edge is just beginning to turn very light golden brown, about 20 minutes. Cool for 5 minutes on the pan and then use a serrated knife to cut the logs into slices on the diagonal, about ½ inch thick. Reassemble the dough logs on a plate and let them cool completely. Dust the slices with confectioners' sugar before serving.

See technique photos, pages 242–43

⑦ ⑧

PLAY DATE COOKIES: 1 *Pound wrapped dough with rolling pin several times until soft enough to roll.* **2** *On a floured sheet of plastic, roll dough into a rectangle.* **3** *Continue rolling (between 2 floured plastic sheets) until dough is 10 × 15 inches.* **4** *Remove top plastic sheet and trim edges using template.* **5** *Peel off template.* **6** *Spread half of filling evenly over dough.* **7** *Fold bottom edge over (about ¹⁄₁₆ inch) using plastic as a guide.* **8** *Use your hands to tightly roll dough into a cylinder.*

Chocolate SNOWBALLS

Another one of Zohar's creations (see page 240), these are a crossover—part cookie, part cake. I love them because you can make these very quickly without turning on the oven; they are perfect to make with the kids. Zohar makes them with ground digestif biscuits, which are an English butter cookie that is like a graham cracker but not as sweet. You can find them in most cookie aisles, but if not, a good-quality plain butter cookie will work. They're a simple little cookie to make, but don't be fooled—they pack complex texture and some serious flavor. **MAKES ABOUT 1½ DOZEN COOKIES**

---

7 tablespoons unsalted butter (99 g)

½ cup sugar (100 g)

¼ cup dark cocoa powder (25 g)

¼ cup whole milk (60 g)

1 teaspoon ground espresso powder (2 g)

½ teaspoon vanilla extract (2½ g)

¼ teaspoon kosher salt (1 g)

6 ounces plain butter cookies, finely ground (about 1¼ cups crumbs) (170 g)

½ cup unsweetened desiccated (fine dried flakes) coconut (38 g)

Put the butter, sugar, cocoa powder, and milk into a small saucepan and heat over medium-low heat, stirring occasionally, until the sugar is dissolved and the mixture is smooth. Remove from the heat and stir in the espresso powder, vanilla, and salt.

Put the crumbs into a medium bowl and pour the warm liquid mixture over them; mix well until crumbs are evenly moistened. Line a small sheet pan with parchment paper and spread the mixture out on it in an even, thin layer. Refrigerate for 1 to 2 hours.

Scoop level tablespoon-sized portions and roll them into balls. Toss them in the coconut, rolling firmly with your hands to adhere the coconut. Refrigerate for at least 30 minutes before serving and up to 1 week.

Gluten-Free Chocolate Oatmeal CHUNKERS

I first met Loren Brill at a Martha Stewart event. She approached me and told me about her project called Sweet Loren's, a ready-to-bake frozen dessert line made with healthy, whole-food ingredients without dairy or refined or processed ingredients; many of them are gluten-free. She came to the pastry kitchen armed with samples, and I couldn't believe how good they tasted. I've been a fan of hers ever since. I asked her if she would share a recipe that was representative of her baking philosophy, and she was nice enough to send this cookie recipe, which should make a lot of my buddies out there with dietary issues very happy. No more cardboard-textured, bland-tasting gluten-free cookies. Thanks, Loren! **MAKES ABOUT 3 DOZEN COOKIES**

¾ cup flavorless coconut oil or ¾ cup (1½ sticks) unsalted butter, softened (170 g)

1¾ cups sucanat (natural unrefined cane sugar) (290 g)

2 large eggs

1 cup gluten-free oat flour (110 g)

½ cup plus 2 tablespoons natural cocoa powder (70 g)

½ teaspoon baking soda (2 g)

½ teaspoon Maldon sea salt (3 g)

2 cups gluten-free rolled oats (190 g)

1¼ cups bittersweet chocolate chips or chunks (215 g)

Preheat the oven to 350°F. Line 2 baking sheets with silicone baking mats or parchment paper.

Put the coconut oil into a small bowl and microwave it on low power until liquefied or melt it in a double boiler (if using butter, do not melt it). Transfer it to the bowl of a standing mixer fitted with the paddle and add the sucanat. Mix on medium-low speed until incorporated, about 2 minutes. Stop the mixer and scrape down the sides of the bowl with a rubber spatula. Add the eggs and mix on low speed; scrape down the bowl again. Increase the mixer speed to medium and mix together until creamy and homogenous, 4 to 5 minutes.

In a small bowl, sift together the oat flour, cocoa, and baking soda. With the mixer on low speed, slowly add the dry ingredients, mixing just until combined. Add the salt, mix briefly, and add the oats and chocolate pieces; mix just until combined and incorporated.

Using a small ice cream scoop, measure heaping tablespoon-sized balls of dough and transfer them to the lined baking sheets, 2 inches apart. Cover the sheets with plastic wrap and refrigerate for 30 minutes.

Unwrap the cookies and bake for 14 to 16 minutes, rotating the pans halfway through, until puffed on top and the aroma fills your kitchen. Cool the cookies on the pan for 10 minutes before transferring them to a cooling rack to cool completely.

Spiced Red Plum TEA CAKES

In every restaurant I've worked in, there have been petit four plates—little sweet bites that come to the table at the very end of the meal. I often turned to recipes like this one because the batter can be made ahead and baked at a moment's notice. These little cakes, filled with warm spices and moist from mashed banana, are easy-to-make two-bite sweets that are perfect for tea, coffee, or dessert. **MAKES 12 TEA CAKES**

---

7 ounces almond paste (198 g)

One 2-inch piece of banana, mashed

1 large egg

1 large egg yolk

2 tablespoons all-purpose flour (16 g)

½ teaspoon ground cardamom (1 g)

½ teaspoon Chinese five-spice powder (1 g)

½ teaspoon kosher salt (2 g)

3 tablespoons unsalted butter, melted, plus more for the pan (42 g)

2 red plums

Confectioners' sugar, for dusting

Put the almond paste and banana into the bowl of a standing mixer fitted with the paddle. Mix on low speed until the paste is broken down and the banana is incorporated. With the mixer on low speed, add the whole egg and mix well. Scrape down the bowl with a large rubber spatula. Add the egg yolk and mix well.

In a separate bowl, whisk the flour, cardamom, five-spice powder, and salt together until combined. With the mixer on low speed, add the flour mixture and melted butter and mix until the batter is smooth and uniform. Chill the batter for 1 hour.

Preheat the oven to 325°F. Brush a 12-portion nonstick minimuffin pan with butter. Quarter the plums lengthwise and discard the pits. Cut the wedges in half crosswise.

Transfer the batter to a large piping bag with a large plain tip (or use 2 tablespoons). Pipe the batter into the prepared pan, filling each slot half full. Press a plum wedge, cut edges upright, into the batter in each muffin cup. Bake in the center of the oven until just set and light golden brown, about 35 minutes.

Cool in the pan for 10 minutes. Dust with confectioners' sugar before serving.

Fluffy BUTTERMILK BISCUITS

While I was visiting my buddy and awesome chef Sean Brock for an event, he showed me the way he makes biscuits. Using his grandmother's recipe as a jumping-off point, Sean tinkered and realized that freezing the fat and then shaving it made the biscuits even fluffier and more tender. While this is not Sean's grandmother's recipe, I did borrow that technique to make my biscuits even better. Thanks for the tip, Sean!

MAKES 12 BISCUITS

2¼ cups all-purpose flour, plus more for rolling and cutting (280 g)

4 teaspoons baking powder (16 g)

1 tablespoon granulated sugar (12 g)

1 teaspoon kosher salt (4 g)

6 tablespoons (¾ stick) frozen unsalted butter, plus 2 tablespoons, melted, for brushing (84 g + 28 g)

¾ cup heavy cream (180 g)

½ cup low-fat buttermilk (120 g)

Demerara sugar, for sprinkling (optional)

Maldon or coarse sea salt, for sprinkling (optional)

Sift the 2¼ cups flour, baking powder, and granulated sugar together in a large mixing bowl; sprinkle the kosher salt evenly over the top. Using the large holes of a box grater, grate the frozen butter directly into the dry ingredients. With a fork, toss the flour and butter together until it begins to form clumps somewhere between the size of a pea and the size of a hazelnut. Freeze the mixture in the bowl for 10 minutes.

In a small bowl, stir the cream and buttermilk together and pour about a third of it into the dry ingredients. Using a large rubber spatula, fold very gently just until the liquid is absorbed. Add another third of the liquid and fold; add the remaining liquid and fold gently just until the liquid is absorbed. Do not overmix.

Lightly flour a work surface and turn the dough out onto it. Using a lightly floured rolling pin, gently roll the mixture into a rectangle about ½ inch thick; use your hands to press the edges together to smooth

them. Fold the dough over onto itself and roll it until about ¾ inch thick; gently pat and press the dough together at the edges.

Line a baking sheet with a silicone baking mat or parchment paper. Dip a 2½-inch plain cutter in flour and cut 12 biscuits, pressing the dough scraps back together lightly as needed. Transfer the biscuits to the lined sheet pan, brush the tops with the melted butter, and sprinkle a light layer of Demerara sugar and Maldon salt, if using, on each biscuit. Chill the biscuits in the refrigerator for 20 to 30 minutes.

Preheat the oven to 400°F.

Bake the biscuits in the lower third of the oven until the bottoms are light golden and the tops are just beginning to brown, 18 to 20 minutes. Cool for 5 minutes on the pan before transferring to a cooling rack.

Note: *Don't overblend the butter into the dough—just gently bring it together with specks of butter throughout. In the warmer months of the year, chilling all of the ingredients first also helps produce a more tender biscuit. I don't like making biscuits in a food processor, because it overworks the dough and quickly heats up the ingredients. These biscuits freeze well after baking and can be rewarmed in a low oven.*

Bacon, Cheese, and Scallion Biscuits

Mix the dry ingredients as directed for Fluffy Buttermilk Biscuits, adding ½ teaspoon (2 g) coarsely ground black pepper. When adding the liquid to the dry ingredients, with the last addition of cream, add 4 slices finely chopped cooked bacon, ⅓ cup (40 g) grated sharp white Cheddar, ⅓ cup (40 g) grated Gruyère, and 2 finely sliced scallions to the bowl and fold gently, being careful not to overmix. Brush the biscuits with the melted butter and scatter 1 teaspoon (5 g) of each grated cheese evenly over the tops of the biscuits. Sprinkle some Maldon salt on each biscuit and chill for 20 to 30 minutes. Bake as directed.

CHAPTER 6

TARTS, COBBL

Great desserts, to me, should have varying components.
I often combine six or eight elements on a plate—so I
have a hard time being satisfied with just a slice of plain
cake as dessert, as most normal folks are. Tarts (and
cobblers and crisps, for that matter), however, are
something I can really get behind. There are many
more options for combining textures and complex
flavors; you can play with crunch, smoothness,
tartness, and creaminess all in one little package,
depending on how you manipulate the type of tart
shells you work with and the fillings you choose to put in
them.

A great tart shell has perfectly even thickness on the
sides, bottom, and corners, whether the corners are at 90 degrees,
like tarts formed in rings, or sloped like those made in a fluted tart pan.
The baked crust should be tender and crumbly or flaky, according to the
ingredients and method used to prepare it. There are two basic methods for
mixing tart crust dough, each of which yields a unique result.

CREAMING METHOD

This is the classic technique for making many crusts; you beat the butter and sugar together, add the flour and other dry ingredients, and mix until the dough forms. This technique produces a sturdy, solid, and stable shell for tarts with a crumbly, cookielike texture. Since texture is such an important component of desserts for me, most tarts I create have shells that are partially baked before the filling is added and baked again until both the filling and shell are set. Creamed butter tart dough, usually a little sweeter than the other tart shells, is almost always prebaked, or "blind-baked."

Creamed butter tart shells are typically used for fillings that are precooked, like puddings, pastry cream, or chocolate ganache, which just need to set up in a fully baked crust. They are also best for fillings that need less baking time to set, like almond cream, or fruit that needs a little time in the oven to just soften or caramelize with sugar sprinkled on top.

BRISÉE METHOD

For this technique, butter is cut into dry ingredients either by hand or with a food processor. The goal is to mix just long enough that the dough comes together while still having bits of butter dispersed throughout the dough. This method creates a flakier, more delicate crust, similar to piecrust dough.

As a result, brisée-style crusts, usually not as sweet as creamed butter tart dough, can be used for loose, liquid fillings and are commonly baked with the filling added from start to finish, like nut pies or tarts. This type of dough is also used for double-crust tarts or pies like fruit pies or for fillings containing eggs like lemon or pumpkin custard that require longer baking time to set. Brisée dough is also the usual choice for savory recipes like quiches or vegetable tarts.

Your choice of tart filling or flavor determines the method of dough you should choose. For either method, be sure not to overmix tart dough, as it will make it tough and can cause the tart to shrink. Typically, as with cake batters, I start with cold butter when making either type of dough. If the butter is too warm when you add the dry ingredients, the water and fat emulsion of butter can break. If the butter is not properly layered with the flour and is too soft, the water evaporates too quickly in the oven, rather than mixing with the protein strands in the flour to create a strong, yet tender, bond.

FORMING AND BAKING TART SHELLS: 1 *Roll dough evenly on a floured surface, turning 45 degrees frequently as dough gets thinner.* **2** *Use the pan as a guide; dough should extend at least 2 inches beyond edges of pan.* **3** *Roll dough up onto rolling pin.* **4** *Brush excess flour from bottom of dough.* **5** *Unroll dough over pan and then lift edges to ease dough into pan corners without stretching dough; gently press into corners.* **6** *Holding your hands at 45-degree angles, press around sides of pan to cut away excess dough.* **7** *Using the back of a knife, trim edges neatly at a slight angle with interior edge a little taller than outside edge.* **8** *Prick bottom and sides with a fork.* **9** *Line tart shell with used parchment paper, tucking it into corners.* **10** *Fill with rice at least ½ inch deep.* **11** *Press rice into corners to weight evenly.*

FORMING TART SHELLS

- When making tart dough, pat it out into the shape it will eventually be baked into. A teacher once taught me to "start with a shape, end with the shape." That means that if you are baking a round tart, chill the dough in a round disk shape from the start.

- Chill dough throughout the tart-making process. Meaning: Make the dough and chill; roll the dough and chill; fit the dough into the tart pans and chill again before baking. This helps maintain the shape of the tart shell you are baking and cuts down on shrinkage. Working in phases gives the dough a chance to relax, which results in a tender texture after baking.

- To roll tart dough, remove the dough from the refrigerator and use a rolling pin to tap the dough out slightly while it is still in the plastic wrap. Let it stand for a few minutes to begin warming up.

- Work with dough that is warm enough to roll out with a rolling pin without cracking but not so warm that it gets sticky and you have to add too much flour to get your tart shells formed, which will make the shells tough.

- When the dough is ready to roll (test this by pressing a finger into it—you should be able to make an imprint, but it should not be too soft), dust your work surface very lightly with flour—just enough to prevent sticking. Roll the dough with a lightly floured pin several times forward and backward in front of your body—always roll the rolling pin past the dough so the pressure you are exerting is the same from one side to the other. As the dough begins to grow in size, turn it 45 degrees and roll a few more times. Keep rolling one or two times, turning the dough until it is the thickness you are looking for, generally between ⅛ and ¼ inch thick for tart shells, depending on what size tart you are making. Smaller tarts with less filling benefit from thinner shells; it's all about proportion of filling to crust. Larger tarts can have a thicker crust as the filling will have more weight and density.

- Always chill the rolled dough on a parchment-lined baking sheet for at least 15 minutes before lining tart pans with it.

- Set the chilled dough on a work surface. Set the pan you are lining on top of it and trace around the edges, leaving at least a 2-inch border around all sides. Let the dough stand for a few minutes before carefully transferring it to the pan. Lift the edges of the dough and let it settle it into the corners without forcing or pulling it; use your finger to gently press it into the corners. If you tug on the dough or force it into the pan, the dough will shrink when it bakes. If the dough tears or cracks, simply patch it with another small piece of dough or press the cracks together. Press the dough evenly into the pan corner and sides and trim the edge with a sharp knife. Chill the tart shell for at least 15 minutes before baking.

BAKING TART SHELLS

- Preheat the oven to 375°F. Dock the bottom and sides with a fork; choose a fork with fine tines so you don't poke large holes in the dough. Line the tart dough with a piece of parchment larger than the pan. (I typically use old parchment that has already been used because it is softer or coffee filters that are trimmed down.) Trim the paper to just fit within the shell, then spray the dough with a very thin layer of cooking spray before lining the dough with paper. Don't use aluminum foil—this will deflect heat away from the crust, and the bottom of the tart will not bake at the same rate as the sides. Then sprinkle an even, thin layer of rice or dried beans over the surface of the paper. I don't like using baking weights because they are too heavy and you can't get them into the corners. With rice, you can press it into the edges to weight the crust down evenly so it doesn't bubble up. Set the lined tart pan on a baking sheet.

- Bake the tart shell until the edges are just turning a very light golden color and the bottom of the tart is dry when you carefully lift the parchment to check it, 12 to 15 minutes. Remove the parchment and rice and return the tart shell to the oven. If the recipe has filling that needs additional baking time in the shell, bake just until the edges are light golden brown, about 10 minutes. If the shell is being filled with a filling that requires no additional baking, bake it until it is evenly golden brown on all sides and crisp, 15 to 20 minutes more.

- If the recipe calls for a filling that is very loose or liquid (whether the filling needs additional baking time or not), lightly brush the bottom and sides of the finished tart shell in the pan with beaten egg white to seal the crust, and then bake it 1 to 2 minutes until it does not look wet and the bottom crust is set.

- Unbaked tart shells can be wrapped tightly and frozen for up to 1 month before baking; you can bake them from frozen, but they will require a few more minutes in the oven than usual. Finished, baked tart shells do not freeze well; cooled shells can be covered tightly with plastic wrap and stored at room temperature for up to one day before being filled.

SWEET TART DOUGH

This is my all-purpose sweet dough, called *pâte sucrée* (*paht-sue-CRAY*), or sugar dough, the one I use most often. It is made in the mixer using the creaming method and is very soft; if it gets tough to handle, pop it into the fridge to firm it up. It is a crumbly dough, but once baked it makes a sturdy but tender crust.

MAKES TWO 9-INCH ROUND TART SHELLS OR EIGHT 4-INCH TART SHELLS

¾ cup (1½ sticks) cold unsalted butter, diced (168 g)

⅓ cup sugar (64 g)

2 large egg yolks, at room temperature

2 cups all-purpose flour, plus more for rolling (250 g)

¼ teaspoon kosher salt (1 g)

1 tablespoon cold water (15 g)

Toss the butter with the sugar in a standing mixer bowl until coated. Attach the bowl to the mixer with the paddle and beat the butter and sugar on medium speed for about 5 minutes, until a paste forms with no visible lumps of butter. Add the egg yolks, one at a time, and mix until combined. Stop the mixer and scrape down the bowl with a rubber spatula.

Meanwhile, in a separate bowl, sift the flour and sprinkle the salt over the top. With the mixer on low speed, slowly add the dry ingredients, mixing just until combined. Add the water and mix briefly until the dough comes together. Turn the dough out onto a lightly floured work surface and knead several times until smooth. Divide the dough into 2 equal portions and form each into the shape of the pan you are lining. Wrap the dough tightly in plastic wrap and chill for at least 1 hour and up to 1 day or freeze tightly wrapped for up to 1 month.

Follow the directions for forming tart shells (page 258) and baking tart shells (page 259).

CITRUS TART DOUGH

This dough is flakier than Sweet Tart Dough (opposite), and it puffs a bit as you bake it. In the French kitchen, this would be a type of pâte brisée (*paht-bree-ZAY*), which means "short pastry." It is somewhere between a sweet, sugary dough and piecrust. It is lighter than piecrust dough and a bit more delicate. **MAKES TWO 9-INCH ROUND TART SHELLS OR EIGHT 4-INCH TART SHELLS**

2½ cups all-purpose flour, plus more for rolling (313 g)

⅓ cup sugar (65 g)

½ teaspoon kosher salt (2 g)

¾ cup (1½ sticks) cold unsalted butter, diced (168 g)

2 large egg yolks

¼ cup cold water (60 g)

Grated zest of 1 orange or lemon

Put the flour, sugar, and salt into a food processor and pulse a few times to mix and lighten it. Add the butter and pulse until the mixture has pea-sized clumps. In a separate bowl, whisk the egg yolks, water, and zest together and, while pulsing, drizzle the liquid into the mixture. Pulse until the dough just begins to come together; do not overmix.

Turn the dough out onto a lightly floured work surface and knead once or twice until smooth. Divide the dough into 2 equal portions and form each into

the shape of the pan you are lining. Wrap the dough tightly in plastic wrap and chill for at least 1 hour and up to 1 day or wrap tightly and freeze for up to 1 month.

Follow the directions for forming tart shells (page 258) and baking tart shells (page 259).

Note: This tart dough is very forgiving; if it cracks or tears while rolling or lining pans, patch it and smooth with your fingers.

CHOCOLATE TART DOUGH

When I'm making a rich chocolate tart, I like the flavor to come in waves. Using a crust with cocoa powder adds a different flavor than a chocolate filling does. The dough is also a little drier and more cookielike than most, adding a nice crumbly texture. This tart dough recipe comes from fellow pastry chef Jason Casey, who's like my little brother. What makes it remarkable is that once it is molded into its shell, it doesn't shrink or sag when baked. **MAKES TWO 9-INCH ROUND TART SHELLS OR EIGHT 4-INCH TART SHELLS**

¾ cup (1½ sticks) cold unsalted butter, diced (168 g)

1 cup confectioners' sugar, sifted (120 g)

2 large eggs, at room temperature

2½ cups all-purpose flour, plus more for rolling (313 g)

¼ cup dark cocoa powder (24 g)

½ teaspoon kosher salt (2 g)

Put the butter and sugar into a standing mixer bowl and toss well with your hands until the butter is coated. Attach the bowl and paddle to the mixer and mix on medium-low speed for about 5 minutes, until the butter is smooth with no lumps remaining. Add the eggs, increase the mixer speed to medium, and mix for about 1 minute, until combined and smooth. Stop the mixer and scrape down the bowl with a rubber spatula.

In a separate bowl, sift the flour and cocoa powder together and sprinkle the salt over the top. On low speed, slowly add the dry ingredients to the butter, stopping the mixer several times to scrape it down.

Mix until just combined; do not overmix. The moment the dough begins to clump together, stop the mixer.

Turn the dough out onto a lightly floured work surface and knead several times until smooth. Divide the dough into 2 equal portions and form each into the shape of the pan you are lining. Wrap the dough tightly in plastic wrap and chill for at least 1 hour and up to 1 day or wrap tightly and freeze for up to 1 month.

Follow the directions for forming tart shells (page 258) and baking tart shells (page 259).

PUFF PASTRY

Homemade puff pastry is one of the most tedious types of dough you can make because of the number of times you need to roll, turn, and flip the dough to work the butter into thousands of layers that make it puff in the oven. This method, called *inverted puff pastry,* is the trickiest type, but it also makes the best puff pastry. The butter is rolled from the outside in, rather than a packet of butter that is surrounded by dough and then rolled. Yes, it is a lot of work, but I find store-bought puff just isn't comparable. Once the pastry is made, though, creating tarts with it is much easier than other tart shells and the options for using it are nearly endless. **MAKES ABOUT 3½ POUNDS**

FOR THE BUTTER PACKET

1½ pounds plus 4 tablespoons (6½ sticks) cold unsalted butter, diced (734 g)

1 cup plus 7 tablespoons all-purpose flour, plus more for rolling (180 g)

1 teaspoon kosher salt (4 g)

FOR THE DOUGH

1¼ cups cold water (300 g)

2 teaspoons kosher salt (8 g)

3⅓ cups all-purpose flour, plus more for shaping (437 g)

To make the butter packet, put the butter into the bowl of a standing mixer fitted with the paddle and beat on medium speed for 5 to 6 minutes, until smooth and no lumps remain. Stop the mixer and scrape down the bowl periodically with a rubber spatula. With the mixer on low speed, slowly add the flour and salt and mix, stopping and scraping down the bowl with the spatula several times, until it forms a homogenous mass. Lay a 12 × 16-inch sheet of parchment paper on a work surface and lightly flour it. Put the butter mixture on the paper, and sprinkle a little flour over the surface. Using floured hands, press the butter into a rough, evenly thick rectangle. Sprinkle flour over the surface and lay another 12 × 16-inch sheet of parchment on top of it. Using your hands or a rolling pin, press the dough mixture into an evenly thick 12 × 16-inch rectangle. Make sure the edges are square and the butter is the same thickness throughout. Slide the butter packet onto a sheet pan and refrigerate while you make the dough.

To make the dough, return the bowl to the mixer and pour the water and salt into it. Add the flour, all at once, on top of the water, attach the dough hook, and mix on low speed, stopping and scraping down the bowl with a rubber spatula once or twice, for 6 to 8 minutes, until the mixture forms a relatively smooth dough. Lightly flour a work surface and press the dough into a 7 × 11-inch even rectangle.

Remove the rolled butter packet from the refrigerator and set it on the work surface, long side facing you. Gently peel off the top parchment sheet. Flour the work surface and invert the butter onto it; carefully peel off the parchment. Set the dough, a shorter side facing you, directly in the center of the butter packet. The outer layer of the butter mixture should be flexible enough to fold without cracking. Fold the outside edges up and over the dough until the butter edges meet in the center. Use your fingers to square up the sides and roll the rolling pin over the top a few times to seal the edges. Transfer the dough to a baking sheet and chill for 20 minutes.

Remove the dough from the refrigerator and lightly dust the work surface with flour. The butter packet should be firm to the touch but not so firm that it will crack if you roll it and not so soft that it sticks to the work surface. Turn the dough so a longer side is facing you and roll the dough, squaring up the sides evenly as you roll, until it is a rectangle, 14 inches high by 24 inches wide, ¼ inch thick. If at anytime the dough sticks to the work surface, use a large offset metal cake icing spatula to release it. Flour under the dough and continue rolling. Make sure the edges and sides are square and even. As if you are folding a letter, fold the left side of the dough inward toward the center one third of the way. Fold the right side over the top of the dough so that the right edge of the dough meets the fold on the left side. Make sure the edges are square using your hands or the rolling pin. This is called a *single turn*.

Turn the dough 90 degrees so that a long side is again facing you. Lightly dust the work surface and dough with flour and roll the dough out again into an even rectangle 14 inches high by 24 inches wide, ¼ inch thick. Square the edges and sides neatly with the rolling pin. On the left vertical side of the dough, fold a 3-inch lip of dough over itself, pressing on the fold lightly with your hands. Now take the opposite vertical edge (right side) of dough and fold it over itself until the right edge meets the left edge you just folded; the two outer edges you started with should now be touching each other. Press on the seams and folds lightly to adhere them, squaring up all sides. Working from the right side, fold the dough in half again over itself vertically, making sure the outer folded edges of the dough meet on the left side. Press the seams lightly with your hands to adhere them and square up the sides. This is called a *double turn*. Transfer the dough to a parchment-lined baking sheet, cover with plastic wrap, and refrigerate for at least 20 minutes.

Remove the dough from the refrigerator, dust the work surface again lightly with flour, and place the dough on the surface with a long side facing you. Roll the dough out again as described above and follow the instructions for a *double turn*.

Rotate the dough 90 degrees, so that a long side is facing you, and repeat the process for a *single turn* as described above. The dough is now ready to be chilled for up to 1 day and used or wrapped tightly in plastic wrap and frozen for up to 1 month. Thawed puff pastry should be used within 1 day.

See technique photos, pages 266–67

PART I: DOUGH & BUTTER PACKET

1 Center dough on butter packet and fold right side of butter packet over dough. **2** Lift left side of butter packet over dough, meeting in center. **3** Press seams and edges together to enclose dough. **4** Roll rolling pin over dough several times to seal.

PART II: SINGLE TURN

5 Roll dough out to 14 x 24-inch rectangle, longest side facing you. **6** Fold one side one-third over center of dough. **7** Fold opposite side over dough like a letter. **8** Use your hands to even edges and folds.

PART III: DOUBLE TURN

9 Fold a 3-inch flap of dough over right side of dough. **10** Fold opposite edge over dough until edges meet. **11** Fold in half, taking one edge over to meet opposite edge. **12** Use your hands to align and even dough.

Double-Lemon TARTS

Hands down, my favorite type of tart to eat is a bright, acidic, well-made fresh lemon tart. I love the aggressive flavor of lemon, and judging by the number of lemon desserts ordered in the restaurants I've worked in over the years, so does everyone else. The double punch of lemon comes from a rich, tart lemon custard baked in a citrus shell topped with thick lemon curd. It's a pucker maker. These are best made the day you want to serve them. You'll use only half of the curd for the tarts, but that leaves you some for your English muffin in the morning. **MAKES SIX 4-INCH TARTS**

FOR THE LEMON CURD

½ cup fresh lemon juice (from 3 to 4 large lemons) (120 g)

1 cup plus 2 tablespoons sugar (225 g)

4 large eggs

3 large egg yolks

8 tablespoons (1 stick) unsalted butter, diced, softened (113 g)

Grated zest of 2 lemons

FOR THE FILLING

1 lemon

1 large egg

1 large egg yolk

⅓ cup sugar (65 g)

Seeds from 1 vanilla bean

½ cup heavy cream (120 g)

Citrus Tart Dough (page 261), formed into 6 4-inch tart shells and blind-baked (see page 259)

Softly whipped cream or crème fraîche, for serving (optional)

To make the lemon curd, put the lemon juice and sugar into a heatproof bowl and set it over a pan of barely simmering water, making sure the bowl does not touch the water. Whisk until the sugar is melted. In another bowl, whisk the whole eggs and egg yolks together until smooth. While whisking, add the eggs to the juice mixture and continue whisking for about 10 minutes, until the mixture is the consistency of pudding and reaches 180°F on a candy thermometer.

Meanwhile, put the butter into a medium bowl and mash it vigorously with a rubber spatula until it is smooth and malleable. Pour the lemon mixture

through a fine-mesh strainer set over a clean bowl, pressing on the strainer with a rubber spatula, and let the curd cool until it is just warm to the touch. Prepare an ice bath in a large bowl. Add the lemon zest and a little of the butter to the curd and stir slowly until the butter is completely incorporated. Keep adding butter, a little at a time, stirring until no lumps remain. Cover the surface with plastic wrap and set the bowl in the ice bath. Cool completely, remove from the ice bath, and refrigerate the curd for up to 3 days.

To make the filling, grate the zest from the lemon, peel the pith from the lemon, and discard the pith. Separate the fruit into sections, remove the seeds, and put the lemon zest and flesh, egg, egg yolk, sugar, vanilla seeds, and cream into a blender and purée until smooth. Pass the mixture through a fine-mesh strainer and use immediately or refrigerate until ready to bake.

To make the tarts, preheat the oven to 300°F.

Put the tart shells on a baking sheet and fill each one halfway with the lemon filling. Bake for about 30 minutes, until the custard is just set and the crust is golden. Remove the tarts from the oven and cool completely.

When ready to serve, whisk the cold lemon curd to loosen it. Put a heaping 2 tablespoons on top of each cooled tart and spread it gently with a small offset spatula or pipe it on, using a piping bag with a small straight tip, in concentric circles.

Serve topped with whipped cream if desired.

Note: *You can go even another step here and use a blowtorch to caramelize the surface of the curd or top the tarts with Swiss meringue (see pages 72–73) and blowtorch them. Mini lemon meringue pies all around!*

ORANGE-HAZELNUT TARTS *with Blueberries*

Virtually every European bakery has a dessert or two with the classic flavor pairing of orange and hazelnuts. Rich, earthy roasted hazelnuts coupled with the flowery, perfumelike flavor of orange are a match made in heaven. These tarts have a tart, moist, marzipan-like orange filling topped with plump blueberries that are baked just long enough to soften and intensify their sweetness. **MAKES EIGHT 4-INCH TARTS**

½ cup blanched (peeled) whole hazelnuts (60 g)

3 tablespoons orange marmalade (90 g)

8 tablespoons (1 stick) cold unsalted butter, diced (113 g)

5 tablespoons granulated sugar (60 g)

2 tablespoons all-purpose flour (16 g)

½ teaspoon kosher salt (2 g)

2 large eggs

Citrus Tart Dough (page 261), formed into 8 4-inch tart shells and blind-baked (see page 259), with an egg wash

4 cups blueberries (560 g)

Confectioners' sugar, for dusting

In a food processor, pulse the hazelnuts until coarsely ground. Add the orange marmalade and purée until smooth. Add the butter, granulated sugar, flour, salt, and eggs and pulse until well combined. Transfer the filling to a bowl and use immediately or refrigerate for up to 1 day.

Preheat the oven to 375°F.

Put the tart shells on a baking sheet. Divide the filling evenly among the tart shells and bake for about 20 minutes, rotating the pan halfway through, until set and golden brown. Remove the tarts from the oven and mound about ½ cup blueberries evenly over the top of each tart. Return the pan to the oven and bake just until the blueberries are hot and turn deep purple but do not break open, about 5 minutes.

Let the tarts cool completely before unmolding. Dust confectioners' sugar over the top before serving.

CARAMEL–WALNUT TART *(Engadiner)*

This awesome dessert is based on a Swiss nut tart called an Engadiner, which has a rich, nutty caramel filling and a double crust. My first exposure to this came courtesy of Chef Markus Farbinger, an Austrian chef instructor at the Culinary Institute of America. For the holidays, the students and faculty made these tarts as gifts to give away to friends and patrons of the school. We had to make thousands of them, and you would think after making so many I would be sick of them. But to this day it is still a favorite. **MAKES ONE 8-INCH TART; SERVES 8**

FOR THE TART DOUGH

14 tablespoons (1¾ sticks) cold unsalted butter, diced (196 g)

7 ounces almond paste (198 g)

Seeds from 1 vanilla bean

1¾ cups all-purpose flour, plus more for rolling (219 g)

1 teaspoon kosher salt (4 g)

FOR THE FILLING

1 cup sugar (200 g)

3 tablespoons water (45 g)

1½ tablespoons light corn syrup (27 g)

1 teaspoon kosher salt (4 g)

¾ cup plus 3 tablespoons heavy cream (225 g)

3 cups coarsely chopped walnuts, toasted (see page 142) (366 g)

FOR THE GLAZE

1 large egg

1 teaspoon whole milk (5 g)

To make the tart dough, put the butter, almond paste, and vanilla seeds into a standing mixer bowl fitted with the paddle and beat on medium-low speed for about 5 minutes, until the butter and almond paste are combined with no butter clumps visible. With the mixer on low speed, slowly add the flour and salt and mix, stopping to scrape down the bowl with a rubber spatula occasionally, until the dough is smooth. Divide the dough into 2 equal portions, form each into a disk, and wrap each tightly in plastic wrap. Refrigerate for at least 1 hour.

On a lightly floured work surface, roll one of the dough disks into an 11-inch circle and carefully press it into an 8-inch removable-bottom fluted tart pan, allowing the excess dough to hang over the edges of the pan. Roll the other portion of dough into a 10-inch circle and transfer it to a lightly floured baking sheet. Chill the bottom and top crusts in the refrigerator while you make the filling.

To make the filling, put the sugar, water, corn syrup, and salt into a medium heavy saucepan and stir with your finger until the mixture is sandy. Wipe the edges of the pan with a wet finger and put the pan over medium-high heat and bring to a boil. Once the sugar is dissolved, brush the edges of the pan with a clean pastry brush dipped in cold water. Cook, without stirring, for about 5 minutes, until the sugar turns a deep mahogany brown and is beginning to smoke.

Meanwhile, warm the cream in another saucepan over medium heat until warm. When the caramel is ready, slowly and carefully whisk in the warm cream. Bring the mixture back to a boil and stir in the walnuts. Remove from the heat and pour the filling into a large bowl to cool completely.

Preheat the oven to 375°F.

To assemble the tart, pour the cooled filling into the bottom tart shell and spread it evenly over the crust. Carefully lay the pastry circle on top of the filling and press on it lightly to compact the filling and seal it at the edges. Lightly press the bottom and top crust together at the edges, trimming away any excess dough. Be sure the top and bottom crusts are adhered to each other. The tart can be decorated by scoring it gently with the back edge of a paring knife if desired; be sure not to cut all the way through the dough.

To make the glaze, in a small bowl, whisk the egg and milk together. Brush the entire surface of the tart with the egg glaze and set the tart on a baking sheet.

Bake the tart on the center rack for 35 to 40 minutes, until the crust is deep golden brown. Cool the tart completely in the pan before slicing. Keep tightly covered at room temperature for up to 3 days.

Strawberry-Tarragon TART

This recipe was inspired by the amazing fraise des bois (small wild strawberry) tarts I constructed working at Ladurée in Paris under Chef Pierre Hermé. Make this tart in the spring, when small, juicy strawberries are ripe and can be found at farmer's markets; don't use the huge berries with the thick white cores found year-round. You could also use fresh ripe local cherries in midsummer. The soft, aniselike flavor of tarragon goes great with either of these juicy red fruits. **MAKES ONE 9-INCH TART; SERVES 10 TO 12**

1½ to 2 pounds small, uniformly sized ripe strawberries, hulled (680 g to 907 g)

½ cup granulated sugar (100 g)

½ cup water (120 g)

1 cup plus 1 tablespoon fresh tarragon leaves (30 g + 2 g)

1 recipe Tarragon-Vanilla Pastry Cream (page 48)

Citrus Tart Dough (page 261), formed into a 9-inch tart shell and fully baked (see page 259)

Chopped pistachios, for garnish (optional)

Confectioners' sugar, for dusting

Halve the strawberries lengthwise, if they are any larger than a big raspberry, and put them in a large bowl. In a small saucepan, heat the granulated sugar and water over medium heat until the sugar is completely dissolved; let cool. Pour the syrup into a blender and add 1 cup (30 g) of the tarragon leaves; blend until very smooth. Pour the syrup over the strawberries and let stand at room temperature, stirring occasionally, for 30 minutes.

To make the tart, put the pastry cream into a small bowl and whisk it lightly to loosen it. Spread the cream in an even layer in the bottom of the baked tart shell. Drain the berries and arrange them in concentric circles, tips upright, on the pastry cream, as close together as possible but in a single layer. Chill the tart for up to 1 day.

Sprinkle the remaining 1 tablespoon (2 g) tarragon leaves and the pistachios, if using, over the tart and dust it lightly with confectioners' sugar before slicing and serving.

Note: *To get that perfectly shiny glazed look of a tart from a bakery, warm some seedless wild strawberry jelly or jam in a small pan and add a little water to thin it. Use a small brush to apply a very thin coat of jam on the berries; the thinner the better. The fruit should glisten but not have clumps of jelly stuck to it or the tart.*

Mango-Coconut Mousse TART

This tart is like a bar cookie in that it is baked in a baking dish rather than a tart pan. The crust dough is very lightly mixed together into crumbs with your hands (like a streusel topping for a fruit crisp), gathered together, chilled, and then grated into the dish in an even layer with a box grater before baking. This dough technique produces a very soft, delicate crust laced with coconut. Tart mango mousse, sweetened with cream of coconut, creates a refreshing tropical filling. **SERVES 12 TO 15**

FOR THE CRUST

7 tablespoons unsalted butter, softened (99 g)

¼ cup sugar (50 g)

1¼ cups all-purpose flour (156 g)

1 cup sweetened shredded coconut (70 g)

1 teaspoon kosher salt (4 g)

FOR THE MOUSSE

2 large mangos, peeled, pitted, and chopped, plus sliced mango for garnish (optional)

4 ounces (½ cup) canned cream of coconut (113 g)

¼ teaspoon kosher salt (1 g)

1¼-ounce packet powdered gelatin (7 g)

1¼ cups heavy cream (300 g)

3 large egg whites

¼ cup sugar (50 g)

Freshly shaved or toasted dried coconut strips, for serving (optional)

To make the crust, put the butter and sugar in a mixing bowl and beat it together by hand with a wooden spoon until lightened and no butter lumps remain. Add the flour and mix until it begins to hold together. Add the coconut and salt and mix gently with your fingers until combined and crumbly. Pour the mixture onto a sheet of plastic wrap. Gather the corners of the plastic and twist them together until it pulls the dough together; lightly compact it until it forms a tight ball. Chill until completely firm, at least 2 hours and up to 1 day; the dough can also be frozen for up to 1 week.

Preheat the oven to 375°F.

Remove the dough from the refrigerator, unwrap, and using the large holes of a box grater, grate the dough evenly into a 9 × 13-inch baking dish. The dough will be crumbly; evenly spread it into the bottom of the dish, making sure the surface is covered, but do not press on it. Bake in the center of the oven, rotating the pan once, until golden brown, about 20 minutes. Cool the crust to room temperature.

To make the mousse, put the chopped mangos into a blender and purée until smooth. Pour the mixture through a fine-mesh strainer, pressing on the solids with a rubber spatula. Discard the solids and measure 1½ cups of the purée; reserve the remaining purée for another use.

Put the purée into a small saucepan and stir in the cream of coconut and salt. Evenly sprinkle the gelatin over the surface, stir, and let stand for 10 minutes.

Heat the mixture over medium heat, stirring, until very hot and the gelatin is completely dissolved. Set aside to cool to room temperature.

In a standing mixer with the whisk, or by hand, whisk the cream to soft peaks; refrigerate until ready to use.

Put the egg whites and sugar into a standing mixer bowl. Fill a saucepan one-third full with water and bring to a simmer over medium heat. Set the mixing bowl with the whites over the simmering water, making sure the bottom of the bowl does not touch the water. Whisk constantly until the mixture is very hot to the touch and the sugar is completely dissolved, about 5 minutes. Transfer to the mixer, attach the whisk, and whip on medium-high for about 5 minutes, until the mixture holds medium-firm peaks but is still slightly warm.

With the mixer on low speed, add the cooled mango purée in a slow, steady stream and mix until just combined. Do not overmix or the meringue will be deflated and the dessert will be too dense. Transfer the mango meringue to a large mixing bowl.

Remove the cream from the refrigerator and fold about half of it into the meringue to lighten. Gently fold the remaining cream into the mango mixture, turning the bowl, until the mixture is even and no streaks of meringue remain. Pour the mixture over the cooled crust and spread it gently and evenly with a small offset spatula. Chill until set, about 4 hours and preferably overnight.

To serve, slice the tart into small squares and garnish with thinly sliced mango and toasted coconut strips if desired.

Rustic Fig and Spiced Almond Cream TART

My pop is a Fig Newton maniac. It was one of the few cookies allowed in the house, because my mom thought they were the least unhealthy of anything in the cookie aisle. It wasn't until later in my life that I tasted a real fig and started making jams, compotes, tarts, ice cream, sorbet, and fig-infused Armagnac with them. They pair so well with almonds and fall spices in this crunchy, impressive free-form tart.

SERVES 8 TO 10

FOR THE SPICED ALMOND CREAM

1 cup Almond Cream (page 325) (220 g)

¾ teaspoon ground cinnamon (2 g)

½ teaspoon kosher salt (2 g)

½ teaspoon freshly ground white pepper (1 g)

¼ teaspoon freshly grated nutmeg

¼ teaspoon ground star anise

⅛ teaspoon ground allspice

⅛ teaspoon ground cloves

FOR THE TART

All-purpose flour, for rolling

1 pound Puff Pastry (page 264) or all-butter store-bought, thawed

1 large egg, beaten

4 tablespoons (½ stick) unsalted butter (56 g)

2 tablespoons honey (40 g)

2 tablespoons balsamic vinegar (30 g)

2 dozen fresh figs, halved through the stem

4 large sprigs fresh rosemary

2 tablespoons sliced almonds, coarsely chopped (15 g)

Demerara sugar, for sprinkling

To make the spiced almond cream, in a small bowl, whisk the almond cream, cinnamon, salt, white pepper, nutmeg, star anise, allspice, and cloves together until combined.

To make the tart, preheat the oven to 400°F. Line a baking sheet with a silicone baking mat or parchment paper.

Lightly flour a work surface and roll the puff pastry with a rolling pin into roughly a 10 × 15-inch rectangle. Transfer the dough to the baking sheet and prick the surface all over with a fork. Lightly brush the outer edges (about ½ inch) with beaten

egg. Using your fingers, fold over about ½ inch of the dough around the edges, creasing it over on itself every ½ inch or so to make a scalloped edge. Press it very firmly to adhere the creases. Refrigerate for 10 minutes.

Meanwhile, in a small saucepan, melt the butter, honey, and balsamic together over medium heat until very warm and smooth. Put the figs and rosemary sprigs in a large bowl and pour the butter mixture over them. Gently toss the figs with a rubber spatula to coat.

Remove the puff pastry from the refrigerator and, using a small offset spatula or a piping bag fitted with a wide, flat basket-weave tip, spread the almond cream evenly over the pastry inside the framed edges. On top of the almond cream, arrange the fig halves all facing the same direction, standing upright and slightly leaning against one another. Brush the figs with any remaining glaze in the bowl and sprinkle the almonds evenly over the tart. Lay the rosemary sprigs across the figs.

With a clean pastry brush, brush the edges of the tart with the beaten egg wash and sprinkle Demerara sugar generously over the edges. Bake the tart in the center of the oven for 35 to 40 minutes, until the puff pastry is deep golden brown.

Let the tart cool for 10 minutes before slicing. Serve warm or at room temperature.

Smoky Chocolate-Ginger Ganache TART

Chocolate ganache, which is basically chocolate and cream, takes on other flavors beautifully. For this tart I steep the cream with loose Lapsang Souchong tea, which is a roasted black tea with a distinct smokiness. Bittersweet chocolate, smoky tea, and ginger combine to make an incredibly sophisticated dessert. **MAKES ONE 9-INCH TART; SERVES 10 TO 12**

1⅓ cups heavy cream, plus more as needed (320 g)

1 (6-inch) piece of fresh ginger, peeled and sliced (112 g)

3 tablespoons Lapsang Souchong tea leaves (15 g)

1 teaspoon ground ginger (2 g)

10½ ounces bittersweet chocolate (66% cacao), chopped (300 g)

3 ounces milk chocolate, chopped (85 g)

5 tablespoons unsalted butter, softened (70 g)

Chocolate Tart Dough (page 263), fitted into a 9-inch tart pan and baked (see page 259)

Crushed cacao nibs, for garnish (optional)

To make the ganache, in a saucepan, heat the cream over medium heat until nearly boiling. Remove it from the heat and stir in the fresh ginger, tea leaves, and ground ginger. Cover and let stand for 20 minutes.

Bring a saucepan one-third full of water to a boil. Put the dark and milk chocolates into a large heatproof bowl and set it over the simmering water, making sure the bowl does not touch the water; turn off the heat. Let stand for 3 to 4 minutes, until the outer edges of the chocolate have melted. Remove the bowl from the pan.

Strain the cream through a fine-mesh strainer set over a measuring cup; press on the ginger with a spatula to remove as much liquid as possible. Add more cream to equal 1⅓ cups and then return it to the saucepan. Heat the cream over medium heat until steaming but just under a boil. Pour about a third of the hot cream into the center of the chocolate. Using a rubber spatula, stir in very small circles in the center, until the liquid is smooth in the center.

Add another third of the hot cream and stir, this time expanding the circle to halfway to the sides of the bowl. Pour the remaining cream into the center of the bowl and stir from the center out, pulling any remaining chocolate pieces into the liquid. Continue stirring, scraping the sides of the bowl, until the ganache is completely smooth and shiny. Let the ganache stand until it is just slightly above body temperature, about 100°F.

Meanwhile, in a small bowl, mash the butter with a rubber spatula until smooth and malleable. Add half of the butter to the ganache and stir to combine; add the remaining butter and stir gently until smooth.

Pour the ganache into the tart shell and let stand at room temperature until set, at least 2 hours.

Slice the tart while at room temperature with a warm, dry knife. Garnish with cacao nibs, if using, and serve. Store any leftover tart covered in the refrigerator; bring to room temperature before serving.

Gooey Chocolate-Caramel TART

It doesn't get any more decadent or rich than this tart. The crust is a hazelnut streusel, topped with a deep chocolate-caramel ganache and swirls of soft caramel. This is a version of one of the desserts I created for a chocolate-caramel tasting menu at Jean-Georges. This is a technically advanced dessert to prepare but an absolute home run. **MAKES ONE 9-INCH TART; SERVES 12**

FOR THE HAZELNUT STREUSEL CRUST

1 cup blanched (peeled) hazelnuts, toasted (see page 142) (135 g)

4 tablespoons (½ stick) cold unsalted butter, diced (57 g)

¼ cup (packed) dark brown sugar (58 g)

½ cup all-purpose flour (63 g)

½ teaspoon kosher salt (2 g)

FOR THE CHOCOLATE-CARAMEL GANACHE

5 ounces unsweetened chocolate, chopped (142 g)

5 ounces bittersweet chocolate (72% cacao), chopped (142 g)

½ cup heavy cream, at room temperature (120 g)

6 tablespoons (¾ stick) unsalted butter (84 g)

1 cup sugar (200 g)

1 tablespoon light corn syrup (17 g)

½ teaspoon kosher salt (2 g)

2 tablespoons water (30 g)

3 large eggs

Seeds from 1 vanilla bean

¾ cup Spreadable Caramel (page 151), at room temperature (210 g)

Crème fraîche or whipped cream, for garnish

Maldon sea salt, for garnish

Grated bittersweet chocolate, for garnish

To make the crust, put the hazelnuts in a food processor and pulse them until coarsely ground. Remove about a quarter of the nuts from the processor and reserve. Pulse the remaining nuts until finely ground (do not overgrind—they will begin to break down and turn into hazelnut butter).

Toss the butter and brown sugar together in a standing mixer bowl to coat. Attach the bowl to the mixer with the paddle attachment and beat the butter on medium speed for about 5 minutes, until a thick paste forms with no visible butter lumps. Add the finely ground hazelnuts, flour, and salt and mix on low speed briefly, until just combined; add the coarsely chopped hazelnuts and mix on low speed to combine. Scrape the dough onto a sheet of plastic wrap and press it into a 1-inch-thick block. Wrap it tightly and refrigerate until firm, at least 2 hours and up to 1 day; the dough can also be frozen for up to 1 week.

Preheat the oven to 375°F.

Grate the chilled hazelnut dough into a 9-inch springform pan (it will be crumbly). Very gently and evenly press the dough into the pan bottom and corners in a single layer to form a crust. Do not overpack the dough or it will be tough. Chill the pan for 10 minutes.

recipe continues

Set the pan on a baking sheet and bake in the center of the oven for about 20 minutes, until set and light golden brown. Cool the crust completely in the pan.

Meanwhile, to make the chocolate-caramel ganache, put the unsweetened and bittersweet chocolates into a heatproof bowl and set it over a pan of simmering water, making sure the bowl does not touch the water. Stir until melted and hot; remove from the heat and let stand until just warm.

In a small saucepan, heat the cream and butter over low heat until hot and the butter is melted; do not boil.

In another medium saucepan, stir the sugar, corn syrup, salt, and water together with your finger until the mixture is sandy and evenly moistened. Wet 2 fingers and wipe down the sides of the pan to remove any sugar crystals. Heat over medium heat; when the mixture boils and the sugar is completely dissolved, brush down the sides of the pan with a clean pastry brush dipped in cold water. Continue cooking, without stirring, swirling the pan occasionally, for 6 to 8 minutes, until the sugar is a deep, dark mahogany color. Remove from the heat and carefully pour in the warm cream mixture; the caramel will sputter. Return the pan to low heat and cook, stirring, for a minute or so, until very smooth. Remove from the heat.

Meanwhile, put the eggs and vanilla seeds into the bowl of a standing mixer fitted with the whisk attachment and whip on medium speed until lightened and foamy and the eggs just begin to hold the trail of the whisk. With the mixer on low speed, slowly drizzle the warm caramel into the egg foam, pouring it directly on the eggs between the outer reach of the whisk and the side of the bowl. Increase the mixer speed to medium-high and whip for about 5 minutes, until the mixture is room temperature.

With the mixer on low speed, slowly add the warm chocolate and mix until just combined. Transfer the mixture to a large piping bag fitted with a ½-inch plain piping tip. Pipe the chocolate mixture evenly into the cooled crust; top the pan to settle it and let stand for about 10 minutes.

Meanwhile, put the spreadable caramel into another piping bag fitted with a ½-inch plain tip. Starting in the center of the tart, pipe the caramel in an even spiral, leaving room so that the chocolate mixture shows between the caramel lines. The caramel will settle slightly into the chocolate; you want to see both mixtures show through in the final tart. Let the tart stand at room temperature for about 1 hour, until completely cooled; refrigerate until ready to serve, at least 1 hour and up to 3 days.

Remove the tart from the refrigerator at least 1 hour before serving to come to room temperature. Slice the tart with a warm, dry, thin knife and serve garnished with small dollops of crème fraîche, Maldon salt, and grated chocolate sprinkled over the top.

Note: *To make the chocolate "wing" garnish as pictured on page 282, melt 4 ounces bittersweet chocolate. Drop heaping tablespoons of the melted chocolate onto a sheet of parchment and, using the back of a spoon, pull a swish of chocolate out of the pool to create a teardrop shape, about 2 to 3 inches long, making sure not to press too hard on the spoon so that the chocolate is connected from the pool outward into the wings. Let stand until set or refrigerate until firm. Gently remove the wings from the paper with a small spatula. To apply them to the tart, while the tart is still cold, heat the blade of a knife and touch the ganache on the sides of the tart with it to melt about a ½-inch spot; carefully stick a chocolate wing to the melted spot and hold it in place a few seconds to adhere it. Cover the sides of the tart with the wings.*

Pear and Blackberry COBBLER

I don't make a lot of classic American desserts like cobblers or crisps, but they're perfect after a meal at home. Crunchy streusel is a great textural contrast to soft, floral pears and tart berries. **SERVES 6 TO 8**

FOR THE STREUSEL TOPPING

8 tablespoons (1 stick) unsalted butter, softened (113 g)

½ cup granulated sugar (100 g)

Grated zest of ½ lemon

1 tablespoon fresh lemon juice (15 g)

1¼ cups all-purpose flour (156 g)

½ teaspoon baking powder (2 g)

½ teaspoon kosher salt (2 g)

FOR THE FILLING

18 ounces blackberries (about 3½ cups) (510 g)

3 firm red pears, peeled, cored, and cut into ½-inch chunks

1 tablespoon granulated sugar (12 g)

FOR THE COBBLER BATTER

Unsalted butter, for the baking dish

1 cup plus 2 tablespoons all-purpose flour (142 g)

¾ cup granulated sugar (150 g)

1 teaspoon baking powder (4 g)

1 teaspoon kosher salt (4 g)

2 large eggs

½ cup whole milk (120 g)

1 teaspoon vanilla extract (5 g)

Grated zest of ½ lemon

Confectioners' sugar, for dusting

To make the streusel topping, in a bowl with a rubber spatula, beat the butter, granulated sugar, and lemon zest and juice together until sandy. Stir the flour, baking powder, and salt together and add to the butter. Using your fingers, work the ingredients together until pea-sized clumps form. Spread into a single layer in the bowl and freeze for up to 1 day.

To make the filling, toss the fruit gently with the granulated sugar. Set aside for 10 minutes.

Preheat the oven to 375°F. Butter a 1½-quart baking dish.

To make the cobbler batter, in a standing mixer fitted with the paddle attachment, combine the flour, granulated sugar, baking powder, and salt. In a small bowl, whisk the eggs, milk, vanilla, and lemon zest until combined. With the mixer on low speed, slowly drizzle in the egg mixture and mix just until combined. Do not overmix.

Transfer the fruit and any accumulated juices to the baking dish and spread evenly. Pour the cobbler batter over the fruit, smoothing the top. Sprinkle the streusel over the batter. Bake for 45 to 50 minutes, rotating the dish halfway through, until the streusel is golden brown and a tester comes out with no crumbs. Let stand for 15 minutes before dusting lightly with confectioners' sugar. Serve warm or at room temperature.

Cherry CRISP

This ain't your grandma's cherry pie! I add zip to this classic American dessert by adding a little chili powder to the crumble on top and fresh thyme leaves and balsamic vinegar to the cherries. I like to use frozen and fresh cherries together to add dimension to both the texture and flavor. Serve this with a scoop of Sour Cream Sherbet (page 39) and your grandma will be asking you for the recipe. **SERVES 6**

FOR THE CRUMBLE TOPPING

⅓ cup sliced almonds (35 g)

⅓ cup rolled oats (35 g)

½ cup plus 2 tablespoons all-purpose flour (78 g)

1 teaspoon ground cinnamon (2 g)

½ teaspoon kosher salt (2 g)

½ teaspoon freshly ground black pepper (1 g)

¼ teaspoon chili powder

6 tablespoons (¾ stick) cold unsalted butter, diced (85 g)

¼ cup raw (turbinado) sugar (80 g)

FOR THE FILLING

1 tablespoon olive oil (15 g)

1 tablespoon unsalted butter (14 g)

1 pound thawed and drained frozen sour cherries (454 g)

⅓ cup confectioners' sugar (40 g)

1 tablespoon balsamic vinegar (15 g)

1 teaspoon vanilla extract (5 g)

1 pound fresh Bing cherries, halved and pitted (454 g)

1 tablespoon cornstarch (9 g)

Leaves from 4 sprigs fresh thyme

To make the crumble topping, put the almonds and oats into a food processor and pulse until coarsely ground. Transfer the mixture to a mixing bowl. Add the flour, cinnamon, salt, pepper, and chili powder and stir to combine. Add the butter and turbinado sugar and, using your fingers, mix the butter into the flour mixture until well combined and large clumps form. Spread the crumble out into the bowl and freeze while you make the filling or for up to 1 day.

To make the filling, in a large, deep skillet, heat the olive oil and butter over medium heat. Add the sour cherries and confectioners' sugar and cook for about 5 minutes, until the juice thickens and reduces slightly. Add the vinegar, vanilla, and fresh cherries and cook for 1 minute. Remove from the heat and let stand until room temperature. When the filling is completely cool, stir in the cornstarch and thyme leaves until the cornstarch is dissolved.

Preheat the oven to 325°F.

Using a slotted spoon, divide the cherry mixture among six 6-ounce ramekins or scoop into a 1-quart baking dish. A little juice is okay, but you don't want the cherries to be too soupy. Scatter the frozen crumble mixture evenly over the tops of the dishes and put them on a baking sheet. Bake for 35 to 40 minutes, until the filling is bubbling and the crumble topping is golden brown. Let the crisps stand for at least 10 minutes before serving warm or at room temperature.

CHAPTER 7

YEAST DOUG

HS

Recipes with yeast in them undoubtedly cause more stress to home bakers than just about any others. But the payoff is big—doughnuts, croissants, cinnamon rolls, brioche, and Danishes. Yeasted pastries and breads are the backbone of bakery shelves and hotel pastry kitchens all over the world and are made by the millions every day. The dough may be temperamental to work with, but damn, does it taste good. Have no fear; as with anything, the more patience and practice you have working with yeasted doughs, the more success you'll achieve.

SUBSTITUTING YEAST TYPES

One .6-ounce (17 g) cake of fresh yeast has the rising equivalent of one ¼-ounce (7 g) packet of active dry yeast, the standard package weight.

If you switch from fresh yeast to active dry, remember that the dry yeast must first be activated in liquid.

If you are using bulk active dry yeast from a jar, there are 2¼ teaspoons in one standard ¼-ounce (7 g) packet.

The most important parts of working with yeasted dough are the mixing of the dough and proper proofing (a kitchen term that simply means letting your dough rise). Many yeasted pastries have a breadlike texture and so require longer mixing times than cakes or cookies. Not only does the yeast need to work its magic to create a tender, airy pastry, but the gluten (protein) in the flour also needs to be developed by kneading it. Once the yeast rises in the heat of the oven creating air pockets in the dough, the dough itself, with strong protein strands after kneading, has the proper structure and strength to hold the air and set it in place. Some softer doughs, like doughnuts, need less mixing time so that when you bite into them they remain tender. Other doughs, like brioche bread, need lengthy time in the mixer so that the bread has that fluffy webbed texture when you tear into it. As a result, it's important to pay close attention to the mixing times and visual cues given in yeasted dough recipes.

Yeast is a living organism, and seeing your dough rise in the bowl is very satisfying. To ensure that happens, double-check that the yeast you work with is alive in the first place. I tend to work mostly with fresh yeast, which is much easier to deal with when you are mixing dough. Fresh cake yeast can be thrown right in with the dough ingredients, provided there is enough moisture to activate it. The problem, though, is that you have no idea whether the yeast is actually alive until you see the dough begin to crawl up the sides of the bowl. In contrast, active dry yeast, which is in powdered form, must always be activated with moisture, before being mixed with the flour. Most recipes with active dry yeast require you to sprinkle it into lukewarm liquid until it gets foamy; this is the sign that the yeast is alive and will expand in the dough, causing the dough to rise. Some recipes in this chapter use fresh yeast and some use active dry yeast—in one case you can choose between them.

Always remember to check the freshness date on the package; if either type is past its prime, its rising properties can be really diminished or, at worst, gone completely, and you will have wasted a few hours of time. That said, recipes with yeast in them are nothing to be afraid of. As with any pastry or dessert, the more you make them, the better they will turn out.

➡ *Tips for* WORKING *with* YEAST:

- For best results, work *only* with either fresh cake yeast or active dry yeast. Skip the "instant" yeast or "rapid-rise" packages you'll find in the baking aisle. These were developed mostly for bread machines, and using them, to me, is an oxymoron—why do you want to speed up the process that makes risen, yeasted baked goods so tasty in the first place? A long, slow rise, preferably overnight, helps develop both flavor and texture in bread and pastry doughs containing yeast.

- Fresh yeast has been increasingly difficult to find in supermarkets. There are several different brands, with different-sized packaging, but just make sure the one you choose, when unwrapped, is soft, free of dry spots, crumbly, and has that distinctive smell of yeast.

- It is crucial to have a scale to weigh fresh yeast—sometimes the products you'll find vary in size, so you'll need to weigh the yeast to make sure you use the correct amount. Too much yeast and the dough will overproof, causing large air bubbles to develop, which in turn make the structure inconsistent throughout the bread. Too little yeast, and the final product will be dense and chewy. I worked mostly with a brand of fresh yeast that comes in .6-ounce cubes for this book.

- To activate dry yeast, use a small amount of the liquid called for in the recipe, whether it is milk or water, and heat it until lukewarm (just slightly warm to the touch). Sprinkle the dry yeast over it and let stand for about 10 minutes; it should start to foam and bubble, which means the yeast is alive and working. You can proceed with the recipe, adding the yeast mixture to the recipe with the rest of the liquid. If using fresh, it can be crumbled and whisked into the liquid called for in the recipe.

- Store *all* types of yeast in the refrigerator and pay close attention to freshness dates.

- Any dough with yeast in it benefits from some time resting in the refrigerator. This helps develop deeper flavor and better structure. Most of my recipes suggest overnight resting in the refrigerator, so plan ahead.

BRIOCHE

This dough can be used to make cinnamon rolls or baked and then turned into French toast or bread pudding. It's great for savory dishes as well, like sandwiches. You might think this takes a lot of elbow grease, but it's really simple provided you have a standing mixer to do the work for you. Plus, there's nothing better than the smell of buttery home-baked bread. **MAKES TWO 8½-INCH LOAVES**

½ ounce fresh yeast, crumbled (14 g)

Scant ½ cup whole milk (102 g)

2 cups bread flour (266 g)

½ cup all-purpose flour, plus more as needed (63 g)

3 large eggs

14 tablespoons (1¾ sticks) unsalted butter, softened (196 g), plus melted butter as needed

3 tablespoons sugar (36 g)

1 teaspoon kosher salt (4 g)

In a standing mixer bowl, whisk the yeast into the milk until dissolved (1). Add the flours, attach the bowl to the mixer along with the dough hook, and turn the mixer on to low speed (2). Slowly add the eggs, one at a time (3), stopping occasionally to scrape down the bowl and hook with a rubber spatula, mixing for 4 to 5 minutes, until the ingredients are incorporated and the dough begins to come together (4).

Increase the mixer speed to medium. With the mixer running, slowly add the butter, a couple of tablespoons at a time (5), waiting until the butter is incorporated before adding more. Once the butter is fully absorbed, continue mixing for 15 minutes, stopping to scrape down the bowl and hook occasionally. This will develop the gluten in the flour and create a light, airy structure in the bread.

MAKING DOUGH

With the mixer still running, add the sugar and salt and continue mixing until the dough is very smooth and elastic, 5 to 8 minutes. Stop the mixer periodically and scrape down the dough hook and bowl.

To test the dough to see if it is ready, grab a handful (about ½ cup) of dough in the bowl. Use both hands to pull the dough into a "window pane" (6); you should be able to stretch out the dough until it is thin enough to see through without tearing. If it tears easily, continue mixing for a few minutes and then test it again.

Grease a large bowl or plastic container with butter and transfer the dough to it. Cover the bowl tightly with plastic wrap and refrigerate for at least 6 hours, but preferably overnight.

Grease two 4½ × 8½-inch loaf pans with butter. Lightly flour a work surface and turn the cold dough out onto it. Evenly divide the dough in half. Using your hands (flour them lightly if the dough sticks)

and the pan edge, press 1 portion of dough into an even rectangle about 2 inches thick; try to form the rectangle as perfectly even as possible (7). Using a bench scraper or sharp knife, cut the rectangle in half lengthwise and then cut it crosswise into 6 equal portions (8). You will have 12 equal-sized pieces of dough (9). If any are smaller than the rest, take pieces of dough from other portions to even them out—the more evenly shaped the dough balls are, the more even the brioche loaf will be. (Weighing them on a scale is the best way to ensure they are all equal.) Repeat with the remaining dough.

Working with one at a time, place a dough piece on a very lightly floured wooden board and cup your fingers over it as if it were a tennis ball. Simultaneously roll the dough on the board in your hands while lightly pressing the bottom of it with the heel of your hand. You want to apply enough pressure to the dough while you roll it to form a perfectly round ball. If the dough sticks a little to the work surface while you roll, the ball will form more

recipe continues

easily. If there is too much flour on the surface and the dough just slides around, it will be harder to get a perfectly round ball. Transfer the ball to the corner of one loaf pan. Continue rolling dough balls until each pan has 12 balls in it. Evenly position them in each pan so they rise evenly (10).

Cover the pans loosely with plastic wrap and set them in a warm spot in the kitchen. Let stand until the dough has risen to the level of the pan rim, which takes from 45 minutes to 2 hours, depending on the temperature of your kitchen.

Preheat the oven to 350°F.

Unwrap the loaves, brush them gently with melted butter (11), and bake on the center rack for 30 minutes, rotating the pans after 20 minutes. Reduce the oven temperature to 325°F and continue baking the loaves until they are golden brown on top and sound hollow when you tap on the bottom of the unmolded loaf, 25 to 30 minutes more.

Immediately remove the bread from the pans and transfer to a cooling rack to cool completely.

Note: *This bread freezes beautifully: Wrap it tightly in plastic wrap and put it into a resealable plastic food bag. You can unwrap and slice it while frozen with a large serrated knife and use it as you need it, rewrapping and freezing any unused bread.*

FORMING BRIOCHE

BUTTERMILK BRIOCHE

This brioche is richer, softer, and more tender than the preceding recipe and is great for making sweet rolls like cinnamon rolls or sticky buns. The switch from regular milk to buttermilk gives the dough a tangy richness that will taste very much like those cinnamon rolls you buy at the mall, only better. It also makes a terrific dinner roll: Just form the dough into balls as for the regular brioche recipe and place them barely touching on a greased baking sheet; let them rise and then bake them until deep golden brown. Or form this dough into loaves just like the plain brioche and use it for some killer French toast.

MAKES TWO 8½ × 4½-INCH LOAVES, 24 DINNER ROLLS, OR 1½ DOZEN CINNAMON ROLLS OR STICKY BUNS

.6-ounce fresh yeast, crumbled (17 g)

½ cup low-fat buttermilk (120 g)

2¾ cups all-purpose flour, plus more as needed (343 g)

2 large eggs

2 large egg yolks

½ pound (2 sticks) unsalted butter, softened, plus more as needed (225 g)

¼ cup sugar (50 g)

1 tablespoon kosher salt (12 g)

Prepare the dough as for the Brioche (page 292), replacing the milk with the buttermilk. Let the dough rest overnight as instructed and form the dough according to the recipe you're making.

Pecan-Caramel STICKY BUNS

Sticky buns are one of the loves of my life, but also my sworn enemy; I can't walk past a sticky bun without having it. The combo of the rich chewy dough, the sweet filling, and the crunchy nuts is irresistible to me. This is one of the few desserts I enjoy eating that is on the sweeter side. These rolls have several components and take a bit of time to prepare, but I guarantee they'll be the best sticky buns you'll ever eat.

MAKES 1½ DOZEN BUNS

FOR THE FILLING

½ cup (packed) light brown sugar (116g)

6 tablespoons (¾ stick) unsalted butter, softened (84 g)

2 tablespoons light corn syrup (34 g)

2 tablespoons honey (40 g)

1½ teaspoons ground cinnamon (3 g)

1 teaspoon ground ginger (2 g)

1 teaspoon ground star anise (2 g)

½ teaspoon kosher salt (2 g)

1 cup pecan halves, toasted (see page 142) and chopped (100 g)

FOR THE ROLLS

3 tablespoons unsalted butter, melted, plus butter for the pans (42 g)

About ½ cup Demerara sugar, for the pans

All-purpose flour, for rolling

Dough for Buttermilk Brioche (page 295), rested overnight in the refrigerator

FOR THE CARAMEL

1 cup heavy cream (240 g)

¼ teaspoon kosher salt (1 g)

½ cup granulated sugar (100 g)

2 teaspoons light corn syrup (12 g)

1 tablespoon water (15 g)

2 tablespoons (¼ stick) cold unsalted butter, diced (28 g)

To make the filling, put the brown sugar, butter, corn syrup, honey, cinnamon, ginger, star anise, and salt into a bowl and beat together with a wooden spoon until well combined.

To make the rolls, grease two 8-inch cake pans with butter. Generously dust the pans with Demerara sugar, tapping out the excess. Line a baking sheet with parchment paper.

Lightly dust a work surface and rolling pin with flour and roll the cold dough out into an even rectangle about 12 × 20 inches and ⅛ inch thick. Pull the dough lightly at the corners to make the rectangle even so the rolls will be uniform in size. Using an offset spatula, spread the filling evenly over the dough, leaving a ½-inch border along the bottom edge. If the filling is too stiff to spread, add hot water, a tablespoon at a time, and stir until it is softened and spreads easily. Sprinkle half of the pecans evenly

recipe continues

over the filling. Brush the exposed dough along the bottom with some of the melted butter.

Working from the top edge down, roll the dough tightly into a cylinder and pinch the seam together where the dough roll meets the bottom edge. Roll the cylinder lightly several times on the counter to seal the edge and gently press with your hands while rolling to elongate the dough roll; keep rolling until it is 27 inches long. Bend the dough into a horseshoe shape and transfer it to the lined baking sheet. Cover with a towel and refrigerate for at least 30 minutes.

Meanwhile, make the caramel. In a saucepan, gently warm the cream and salt over medium-low heat. Fill a large bowl with cold water.

Put the sugar, corn syrup, and water into a large saucepan. Make a wet caramel, following the instructions on page 139, and cook until deep mahogany brown and the caramel is emitting white smoke. Reduce the heat to low and carefully whisk in the warm cream a little at a time (the sugar will bubble up), whisking well between additions. Once all the cream has been added, whisk well to dissolve any sugar lumps that appear. Remove the pan from the heat and whisk the butter into the caramel a little at a time, until very smooth. Dip the bottom of the pan into the bowl of cold water to cool off the pan and caramel, which should be cool but still pourable.

Once cool, divide the caramel between the sugared pans, swirling them to evenly coat the base of each pan. Sprinkle the remaining pecans evenly into each pan.

To assemble the rolls, remove the dough roll from the refrigerator, slice it in half to make two 13½-inch logs, and roll each log lightly on the work surface to straighten it. Slice each cylinder into 9 slices, each exactly 1½ inches thick, and reshape them with your hands until very round and even if necessary. Place 1 slice, cut side down, onto the caramel directly in the center of each pan. Arrange 8 more slices so that the sides are barely touching in each pan. Brush the rolls with the remaining melted butter, cover with a towel, and let stand in a warm spot until the rolls are puffy and doubled in size, 45 minutes to 1½ hours.

Preheat the oven to 350°F. Bake the rolls for about 40 minutes, rotating the pans halfway through, until golden brown.

Let cool in the pan for 5 minutes. Run a knife around the edges of the pan to release any rolls that are stuck before inverting them onto serving platters. Serve warm.

PANETTONE

Every Christmas when I was growing up, there was a big panettone on the table, as is the custom with so many Italian families, that we nibbled on all through the week. Since it's so labor intensive, I make it only during the holidays. I much prefer this light, airy sponge cake studded with boozy dried fruits to doorstop American fruitcakes. Panettone is very much like brioche, made the same way, but has more yeast and is lighter and fluffier. I bake this in heavy ovenproof paper baking molds that you can find online or at cake supply stores. Guaranteed, your office mates won't regift these next year. **MAKES 10 INDIVIDUAL LOAVES •**
SPECIAL EQUIPMENT: 10 ONE-CUP PAPER BAKING MOLDS

.8 ounce fresh yeast (25 g)

¼ cup water (60 g)

1½ cups all-purpose flour, plus more for shaping (190 g)

7 ounces mixed dried fruit, such as apricots, cranberries, cherries, currants, golden raisins, and figs, chopped into ¼-inch pieces (200 g)

1 cup Cognac (240 g)

1 cup bread flour (133 g)

2 large eggs

2 tablespoons orange flower water (30 g)

¾ cup (1½ sticks) unsalted butter, softened, plus melted butter for brushing (168 g)

½ cup granulated sugar (100 g)

1 teaspoon kosher salt (4 g)

Coarse sanding sugar, as needed

Whisk the yeast and water together in a medium bowl. Add ½ cup of the all-purpose flour and stir until a rough dough forms. Cover the bowl tightly with plastic wrap and refrigerate overnight.

Put the fruit into a small bowl. Heat the Cognac in the microwave or in a saucepan until almost boiling; pour it over the fruit, cover tightly with plastic wrap, and let stand overnight at room temperature.

Stir the yeast mixture to deflate the air and then transfer to a standing mixer bowl. Add the remaining 1 cup all-purpose flour, the bread flour, eggs, and orange flower water and attach the bowl and dough hook to the mixer. Mix on medium-low speed for about 5 minutes, until the ingredients are mixed and

the dough is rough and shaggy (1). Scrape down the bowl and hook with a rubber spatula.

With the mixer on medium speed, add the butter, about 2 tablespoons at a time, and mix until completely incorporated before adding more. Stop the mixer frequently and scrape down the bowl and hook. When the butter is completely mixed in, with no lumps, add the granulated sugar and salt and continue mixing for 8 to 10 minutes, until the gluten is developed and the dough is elastic and smooth. Stop the mixer and press the dough down into the bowl if it crawls up the dough hook.

Meanwhile, drain the soaked fruit in a strainer set over a pitcher; press on the fruit very firmly with a

recipe continues

rubber spatula to remove as much liquid as possible. Reserve the liquor for another use (like a shot in some hot tea).

To test the dough to see if it is ready, grab a handful (about ½ cup) of dough in the bowl. Use both hands to pull the dough into a "window pane"; you should be able to stretch out the dough until it is thin enough to see through without tearing (see photo on page 293). If it tears easily, continue mixing for a few minutes and then test it again.

When the dough is ready, with the mixer on low speed, add the soaked fruit (2) and mix for just a few rotations of the dough hook; remove the bowl from the mixer and finish mixing the fruit in by hand, kneading it directly in the bowl (3). Cover and refrigerate the dough for at least 1 hour and up to overnight.

Turn the dough out onto a lightly floured work surface and pat the dough into a rough rectangle. Cut the dough into 10 equal pieces, about 3½ ounces (100 grams) each (4). Cup your hand over a portion of dough and roll it on the surface until it is a rough round ball (5); transfer it to a 1-cup paper baking mold, making sure any seams are on the bottom

of the dough ball in the cup (6). Repeat with the remaining dough. Set the molds on a sheet pan, cover loosely with a light towel, and set the pan in a warm spot in the kitchen. Let stand until the dough has risen three quarters of the way up the sides of the molds and is puffy to the touch, 45 minutes to 1 hour.

Position a rack in the lower third of the oven and preheat the oven to 350°F.

Brush the surface of the risen panettone with melted butter (7) and sprinkle a layer of coarse sugar (8) over each. Bake the panettone on the lower rack for 30 minutes.

Reduce the oven temperature to 325°F, rotate the pan, and continue baking until golden brown on top and the bread is hollow sounding when you tap on the bottom of a loaf, 30 to 35 minutes more.

Cool the panettone completely in the paper molds (remove when you serve the bread). Wrap tightly in plastic wrap and store at room temperature until ready to serve, or for up to 2 weeks. The panettone can also be frozen, tightly wrapped, for up to 1 month.

See technique photos, pages 300–301

Cinnamon ROLLS

When I was young, I had a secret girlfriend. My parents didn't know about her, so I had to sneak around to see her. Her name was Little Debbie. She made me cinnamon rolls. Like a lot of kids, we used to mow lawns to make money, so my brother and I would use the money we made to buy candy and hide our sweet tooth from my mother. I would always buy one of those big cinnamon rolls and eat it before we got home. I still have a soft spot for cinnamon rolls, only now I make them myself. **MAKES 1½ DOZEN ROLLS**

FOR THE FILLING

½ cup raisins (70 g)

2 tablespoons spiced dark rum (30 g)

1 tablespoon water (15 g)

1 cup (packed) light brown sugar (232 g)

1 tablespoon ground cinnamon (5 g)

¼ teaspoon ground allspice

¼ teaspoon freshly ground black pepper

¼ teaspoon kosher salt

⅛ teaspoon ground cloves

3 tablespoons (¼ stick) unsalted butter, melted (42 g)

FOR THE ROLLS

All-purpose flour, for rolling

Dough for Buttermilk Brioche (page 295), rested overnight in the refrigerator

4 tablespoons (½ stick) unsalted butter, melted, plus butter for the pans (56 g)

FOR THE ICING

4 ounces cream cheese, softened (113 g)

¼ cup whole milk, at room temperature (60 g)

1 teaspoon vanilla extract (5 g)

½ teaspoon kosher salt (2 g)

3 cups confectioners' sugar, sifted (360 g)

To make the filling, put the raisins, rum, and water into a small microwave-safe bowl and heat in the microwave for 30 to 40 seconds on high (or heat the mixture in a small saucepan) until hot. Set aside to cool. In a small bowl, mash the brown sugar, cinnamon, allspice, pepper, salt, cloves, and butter together with a fork until well combined.

To form the rolls, lightly dust a work surface and rolling pin with flour and roll the cold dough out into an even rectangle about 12 × 20 inches. Brush the surface of the dough with half of the melted butter. Sprinkle the filling evenly over the surface of the

dough and press the filling lightly into the dough. Drain the raisins and scatter them evenly over the filling.

Proceed, rolling the dough as for Pecan-Caramel Sticky Buns (page 297), omitting the caramel and pecans. Once the rolls are cut and placed in the pan, brush the surface of the rolls with the remaining melted butter before covering and letting the dough rise.

Preheat the oven to 325°F.

Bake the rolls for 45 to 50 minutes, rotating the pans halfway through, until the rolls are firm to the touch and light golden brown. Transfer the pans to a rack to cool.

While the rolls are cooling, make the icing: Put the cream cheese into the bowl of a standing mixer fitted with the whisk and whip on medium speed until creamy. Add the milk, vanilla, and salt and whisk well to combine. With the mixer on low speed, slowly add the confectioners' sugar and whisk until very smooth.

When the rolls have cooled and are just barely warm, spread the icing evenly over them and serve immediately.

Fresh Yeast

Doughnuts

FRESH YEAST DOUGHNUTS

Gauging by all of the artisanal doughnut shops popping up everywhere, everyone loves a good doughnut as much as I do. Here's a great basic doughnut recipe—how you fill it is up to you: creamy custard, sweet sticky jelly, or perhaps light, refreshing ricotta cheese. Try any of the puddings or pastry creams in this book or your favorite fruit preserves. **MAKES ABOUT 2 DOZEN DOUGHNUTS**

¾ cup water (157 g)

1.8 ounces fresh yeast (51 g)

4 cups all-purpose flour, plus more for rolling (500 g)

Vegetable oil cooking spray

⅓ cup whole milk, at room temperature (80 g)

4 tablespoons (½ stick) unsalted butter, softened (57 g)

⅓ cup sugar, plus more for rolling (65 g)

5 large egg yolks

1½ teaspoons kosher salt (6 g)

¼ cup nonfat dry milk powder (30 g)

Canola oil, for deep frying

In a medium bowl, whisk together the water and .3 ounce (8 g) of yeast until the yeast dissolves. Add 2 cups of the flour and stir with a rubber spatula until the flour is evenly moistened. Spray a large bowl with cooking spray and transfer the dough to it. Cover tightly with plastic wrap and refrigerate overnight.

Put the milk, butter, sugar, egg yolks, salt, remaining 1.5 ounces (43 g) yeast, remaining 2 cups flour, and the milk powder into the bowl of a standing mixer fitted with the paddle. Mix on low speed until the ingredients are combined and form a dough, 2 to 3 minutes. Switch to the dough hook, add the refrigerated yeast mixture, and mix on medium speed for 6 to 7 minutes, until the dough is smooth and not sticky. Spray a large, clean bowl well with cooking spray, transfer the dough to it, and cover with plastic wrap. Refrigerate for 2 to 3 hours.

Turn the dough out onto a floured work surface and, with a floured rolling pin, roll the dough until it is ½ inch thick. Using a traditional doughnut cutter

or a plain 2¼-inch round cutter, cut out rounds of dough, rerolling as necessary, until the dough is used up. Line a baking sheet with parchment paper and lightly flour it. Transfer the dough rounds to the sheet, cover them with a clean towel, and let them rise in a warm spot in the kitchen until doubled in size, 45 minutes to 1 hour.

To fry the doughnuts, fill a large pot with oil to a depth of 3 inches and heat it to 360°F. Line a baking sheet with paper towels and fill a pie dish with sugar for rolling. Fry the doughnuts in batches, turning frequently, until golden brown on all sides, 4 to 5 minutes total. Monitor the temperature, being sure it remains around 360°F through the frying process.

Drain the doughnuts briefly on the paper towels. Roll them in sugar before they cool. Serve slightly warm or at room temperature.

FOCACCIA

A savory type of bread, focaccia is an important member of the yeasted bread family. Here is a basic and straightforward recipe for a thin, crisp, and crunchy focaccia that is open to your creative spin. You can sprinkle caramelized onions, grated Parmesan, chopped herbs, or sliced tomatoes over the top just before baking. This bread is perfect torn into pieces as a snack, drizzled with a little more oil over the top, or sliced in half horizontally for sandwiches. **MAKES ONE 12 × 17-INCH PIECE; SERVES ABOUT 12**

Scant 2 cups lukewarm water (480 g)

2 teaspoons active dry yeast or .3 ounce fresh yeast (8 g)

2 tablespoons olive oil, plus more as needed (24 g)

4⅓ cups all-purpose flour (545 g)

2 tablespoons sugar (25 g)

2 tablespoons kosher salt (24 g)

Maldon sea salt, for sprinkling

Red chile flakes, for sprinkling

Put ½ cup of the water into a small bowl and sprinkle the active dry yeast over it; let stand for about 10 minutes, until foamy. (If using fresh yeast, whisk it in the water until dissolved.)

Put the yeast mixture, remaining scant 1½ cups water, and the 2 tablespoons oil into the bowl of a standing mixer and whisk well until the yeast is dissolved. Attach the bowl to the mixer along with the paddle and add all of the flour at once. Mix on low speed for about 5 minutes, until the dough comes together, stopping the mixer and scraping down the bowl and paddle several times with a rubber spatula.

Switch to the dough hook and, with the mixer on medium-low speed, add the sugar and kosher salt. Increase the mixer speed to medium and knead the dough until it is very smooth and elastic but still sticky, about 8 minutes. The dough will be very wet. Cover the bowl and refrigerate for at least 1 hour and up to overnight.

Oil a large mixing bowl and transfer the dough to it. Cover with plastic wrap and set in a warm spot in the kitchen until the dough has doubled in size. Depending on the temperature, this can take up to 2 hours.

Pour a generous amount of olive oil into a 12 × 17-inch rimmed sheet pan to cover the base with a thin layer of oil. Transfer the dough to the pan, drizzle a little oil over it, and press it out evenly to fill the pan and the corners; be sure the entire surface of the dough has a light coating of oil. Cover the pan with plastic wrap and let stand in a warm spot until the dough has risen to the level of the pan edge, about 1 hour.

Preheat the oven to 375°F.

Using your fingers, dimple the focaccia by pressing your fingertips into the dough all over the surface. Sprinkle a light layer of Maldon salt and chile flakes over the dough, to taste, and transfer to the center rack of the oven. Bake for 35 to 40 minutes, rotating the pan halfway through, until golden brown at the edges and light golden on top.

Cool completely in the pan before cutting or tearing into pieces.

Note: *If you like a thicker, spongier focaccia, this recipe can be baked in a 9 × 13-inch cake pan, which produces a bready focaccia about 1 inch thick. It will take roughly the same amount of time to rise as the thinner sheet but may need an additional 5 to 10 minutes in the oven to finish baking.*

KOUIGN-AMANN

I fell in love with kouign-amann (*coon-yah-mahn*) while working at Ladurée in Paris. I ate one every single time I stepped foot in the door. It is unlike any other pastry—crispy caramelized sugar on the outside, fluffy, buttery, and light on the inside, with lots of layers, like puff pastry. Every bite has a different taste and texture as you tear it apart. If a palmier and some brioche had a baby, it would be like a kouign-amann. This is not the simplest of pastries but is well worth the effort. The recipe here is adapted from one Pierre Hermé shared with me during my time there as a *stagiaire* (an apprentice). They are baked in bottomless 3-inch pastry rings you can find at cake supply stores, but in a pinch, use greased nonstick jumbo muffin tins. Baking them inside a mold holds the dough together to make the crunchy caramelized edges with a tender center; they need walls to hold them in or they will spread and not be as delicious. **MAKES 12 PASTRIES • SPECIAL EQUIPMENT: 12 RING MOLDS, 3 INCHES IN DIAMETER AND ¾ INCH TALL**

⅔ cup lukewarm water (160 g)

1½ teaspoons active dry yeast (5 g)

2 teaspoons kosher salt (8 g)

2 cups plus 2 tablespoons all-purpose flour (266 g), plus more for rolling

½ pound (2 sticks) unsalted butter, softened (226 g), plus more for the pastry rings

1½ cups sugar (300 g), plus more for the pastry rings

Pour about ½ cup of the water into a small bowl and sprinkle the yeast over it. Let stand until foamy, about 10 minutes.

Pour the remaining water into a standing mixer bowl, add the salt, and stir well to dissolve it. Pour the 2 cups plus 2 tablespoons flour into the bowl on top of the water. Dice 2 tablespoons of the butter and toss it with your fingers in the flour in the top of the bowl until it is coated in flour. Pour the yeast mixture over the top and attach the bowl and dough hook to the mixer. With the mixer on medium-low speed, mix for 2 to 3 minutes, until the mixture forms a ball. Remove the dough from the mixer and knead it on a work surface until smooth. Form the dough into a thick rectangle, wrap it tightly in plastic wrap, and refrigerate for at least 1 hour and up to overnight.

Meanwhile, lay a 12 × 18-inch piece of parchment on a work surface with a long side facing you. Put the remaining 14 tablespoons butter on one side of the parchment (1), and mash it with the ball of your hand until very soft and malleable (2). Using a large rubber spatula or your hands, spread the butter into an evenly thick 7 × 10-inch rectangle on one side of the parchment. Fold the paper over the butter again and transfer it to a sheet pan; refrigerate until firm.

Remove the butter from the refrigerator and let stand at room temperature for 10 minutes. Lightly flour a work surface and a rolling pin and roll the cold dough (3) out into a 12 × 16-inch rectangle with a long side facing you, making sure to square the sides with the rolling pin or your hands. Invert the parchment sheet

recipe continues

of butter, a long side facing you, onto the right side of the dough, leaving a 1-inch border of uncovered dough at the edge and centering the butter on the dough from top to bottom (4). Roll across the paper once with the pin to adhere the butter to the dough and then carefully peel the parchment off and discard it. Fold the unbuttered dough flap on the left side up over the butter like a letter fold (the crease should be where the butter begins). Then fold the buttered dough side over the 2 layers of dough (5) until the right-side edge meets the left-side fold, like folding a letter. If the butter is too firm to fold over, wait for 10 minutes and try again. It should be soft enough to move with the dough without cracking. Adjust the dough lightly to make sure the fold and top edges meet and are even.

Turn the dough 90 degrees (the long side will now be facing you again), sprinkle about 2 tablespoons of the sugar on the work surface, set the dough on top of it, and sprinkle about 2 tablespoons of the sugar on top of the dough. Roll the dough out again to a 12 × 16-inch rectangle (6). Sprinkle another 2 tablespoons of the sugar on the work surface and over the top of the dough. Fold the dough again into thirds as

described above, making sure all of the edges meet squarely. Press on the dough a few times to adhere the seams and sugar and transfer it to a baking sheet. Refrigerate for 10 minutes. Do not leave in the refrigerator for more than 15 minutes or the sugar will begin to melt.

Preheat the oven to 350°F. Butter the pastry rings, coat them in sugar, and set them on a silicone mat- or parchment-lined baking sheet.

Sprinkle about 2 tablespoons of the sugar on the work surface and lay the dough lengthwise on top of it (a long side is facing you). Sprinkle about 1 tablespoon of the sugar on top of the dough and roll it into a 12 ×16-inch rectangle. Cut the dough into twelve 4-inch squares (7) and sprinkle about ½ teaspoon sugar over each square.

Working with one at a time, fold the corners of each dough square into the center to create a rough circle (8) and press on it firmly with your palm to adhere the dough and sugar. Sprinkle a little more sugar over each dough round and fold the 4 "corners" into the center of each piece of dough again (9); press on them firmly to adhere the dough. Lay each circle inside a pastry ring (10). Set the baking sheet in a warm spot and let the pastry rise until it is 50 percent higher, 30 to 45 minutes.

Transfer the kouign-amann to the oven, reduce the temperature to 325°F, and bake, rotating the pan halfway through, until puffed and golden and the sides and bottom are caramelized, 45 to 50 minutes. Cool completely on the pan before removing the rings. Store them in an airtight container at room temperature for up to 3 days.

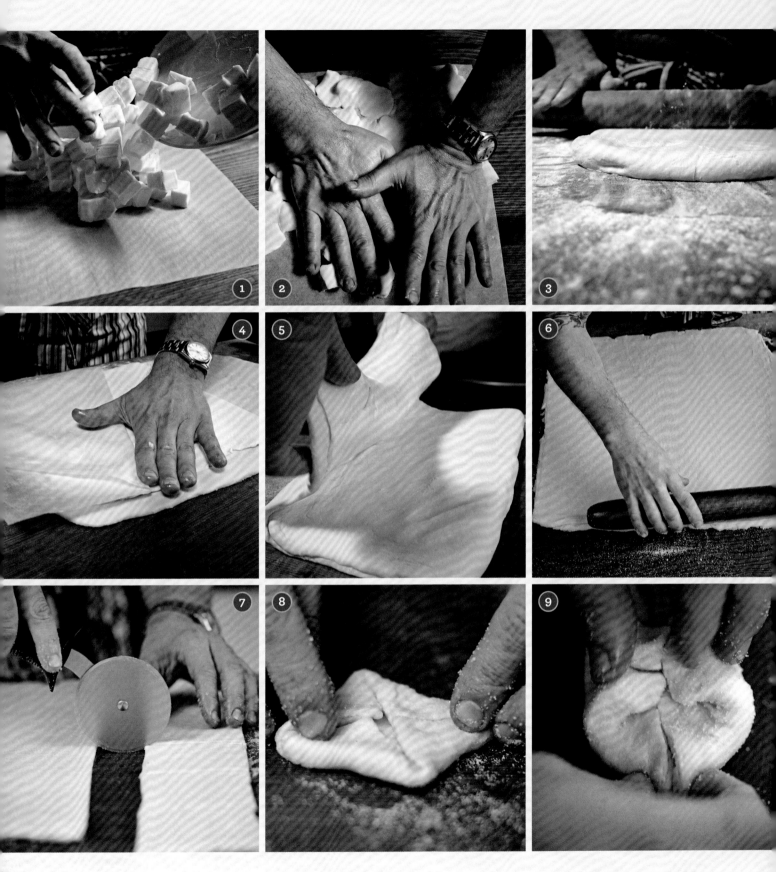

CHAPTER 8

GLAZES,

FROSTINGS, FILLINGS, and SAUCES

Now it's time to take off the training wheels and have some fun. I've given you a lot of basic recipes for cake, tarts, cookies, mousses, and more; now here are a few more components that can help you elevate them and make you the envy of your friends. Within this chapter, you will find fillings, glazes, and toppings that can be paired with the custards, cakes, tarts, and pastries in this book.

There are both basic flavors and a few more exotic combinations that will push the envelope a bit. Try Miso Buttercream (page 321) on a plain vanilla cake and cover it with crushed Candied Hazelnuts (page 143); it will be a sweet yet salty dessert like you've never tasted. Or try a spoonful of Spiced Pineapple (page 331) over some Piña Colada Pastry Cream (page 45) with Ginger-Curry Sugar Cookies (page 225) on the side. You'll be immediately transported to the Caribbean.

Use these recipes as a jumping-off point, adding flavors you like and combining them with your own favorite recipes. Perhaps you'll create new desserts that become family favorites.

MISO

VANILLA

COFFEE

RASPBERRY

SALTED DULCE DE LECHE

GREEN TEA

CHOCOLATE

VANILLA BUTTERCREAM

The most stable, silkiest buttercream is made with Italian meringue; it tends to hold up better in the heat than most buttercreams made with egg yolks and is also easier to pipe and style on a cake. Once you've made the recipe a couple of times, you'll practically be able to make it with your eyes closed. The key to making silky buttercream is to make sure your meringue is completely cool before adding room-temperature butter. This is an emulsion, and the strongest emulsions are made when the ingredients are all at the same temperature.

MAKES ABOUT 7 CUPS

---

5 large egg whites

2 cups sugar (400 g)

Seeds from 1 vanilla bean

Pinch of cream of tartar

¼ cup water (60 g)

1¼ pounds (5 sticks) plus 2 tablespoons unsalted butter, softened and cubed (593 g)

Put the egg whites, 2 tablespoons of the sugar, the vanilla seeds, and the cream of tartar into a standing mixer bowl and whisk well to combine. Attach the bowl and whisk to the mixer and turn it on to low speed.

Put the remaining sugar and the water into a medium saucepan. Stir it with your finger until sandy; wipe the sides of the pan down with a wet finger and put the pan over medium heat. When the sugar is melted and begins to bubble, brush down the sides of the pan with a clean pastry brush dipped in cold water.

When the sugar reaches a rolling boil, increase the mixer speed to medium. Continue cooking the sugar, brushing the pan sides if any crystals form, until it reaches 250°F (soft-ball stage).

Increase the mixer speed to medium-high. The whites should be fluffy and shiny but still soft. Carefully pour the hot sugar syrup in a slow, steady stream into the mixer—pour it directly onto the whites between the mixer bowl edge and the outer

reach of the whisk. Increase the mixer speed to high and whip the meringue for 6 to 8 minutes, until cool to the touch.

Begin adding butter, a little at a time, whipping until completely combined before adding more. If you see the butter melting, stop adding butter and whip the meringue longer until cool. Continue gradually adding the butter. When all of the butter has been added, the buttercream should be very smooth and fluffy. The buttercream is now ready to use.

Buttercream can be refrigerated in an airtight container for up to 3 days; let stand at room temperature and rewhip it in a standing mixer until it is smooth and fluffy again before using. Buttercream can also be frozen in an airtight container for up to 1 month. Thaw the buttercream overnight in the refrigerator and then let stand until room temperature before whipping until smooth.

Plain Buttercream

Simply omit the vanilla seeds from the recipe for Vanilla Buttercream.

Citrus Vanilla Buttercream

Although I do love bits of citrus zest in mousses and frozen desserts, it is not pleasant in silky buttercreams. Instead, I use essential oils—lemon, lime, orange, et cetera—which can be found in cake supply or craft stores. They are very potent, so be careful. Start by adding ¼ teaspoon oil to the finished Vanilla Buttercream in the mixer and whip it; taste and add more depending on how strong you want the flavor to be.

Salted Dulce de Leche Buttercream

Dulce de leche continues to be a favorite flavor on many dessert menus, and I love its caramel-like taste. But it can be overwhelmingly sweet, so a balance of salt that you can actually taste makes this buttercream truly awesome—and much simpler to make than real caramel.

Put 1 cup Dulce de Leche (page 329) into a medium bowl, add 1 teaspoon kosher salt, and whisk well to combine and dissolve the salt. Add about 1 cup of the Vanilla Buttercream and fold it gently until combined to lighten it. Add the lightened dulce de leche to the batch of buttercream and whip it until evenly combined. Use immediately.

Chocolate Buttercream

This is a simple way to make silky chocolate buttercream, but you must make sure that both the melted chocolate and buttercream are at room temperature. If one or the other is too warm or too cool, the chocolate can seize and you'll have lumpy buttercream.

Melt 4 ounces (113 g) unsweetened or extra bittersweet (72% cacao or higher) chocolate and cool. Put the chocolate into a large bowl and add about ½ cup of the Vanilla Buttercream. Using a large rubber spatula, fold the two together until well combined and homogenous. Add another ½ cup of buttercream and fold again until well combined. Add the chocolate mixture to the buttercream and whip it until smooth and creamy with no streaks of white. Use immediately.

Coffee Buttercream

I drink at least a couple of espressos every day and love the flavor of coffee. Using it in buttercream is great because it cuts the sweetness of the frosting, but be sure to use a good-quality espresso powder like Medaglia d'Oro to make it.

Once you have added the final bits of butter to the whipping Vanilla Buttercream, dissolve 1 tablespoon (6 g) instant espresso powder in 1 teaspoon of hot water; cool. Add the liquid to the finished buttercream and whip until incorporated. Taste the icing and add more if you like a real espresso punch.

Raspberry Buttercream

Put ¼ cup (75 g) Raspberry-Mint Jam (page 316) or other seedless raspberry jam in a medium bowl and add 1 tablespoon hot water; whisk well. Check the consistency—it should be the same thickness as the buttercream. If too stiff, add a little more hot water. Put about 1 cup of the room-temperature Vanilla Buttercream into the bowl and whisk until well combined. Add the raspberry mixture to the remaining buttercream and whip in the mixer with the whisk until well combined.

Miso Buttercream

This probably sounds a little wacky, but since I like really pronounced flavors and usually include salt in my dessert recipes, it makes perfect sense. The umami-salty zip of white miso paste is a great partner for sweet buttercream. You can find miso paste in the refrigerated section of good natural grocery stores or Asian supermarkets. This frosting is great for cakes that are rich and dense or are nut based.

In a small bowl, whisk ½ cup (130 g) white miso paste and 2 tablespoons (30 g) hot water together until very smooth. Using a rubber spatula, press the mixture through a fine-mesh strainer into a clean medium bowl. Press on the solids firmly to strain as much liquid paste from the mixture as possible. Discard the solids; let the paste cool to room temperature.

Add about ½ cup of room-temperature Plain Buttercream to the miso paste and whisk to combine. Add this mixture to the remaining buttercream and whip until well combined. Use immediately.

Green Tea Buttercream

Put ¼ cup (28 g) matcha (green tea powder) into a bowl and pour 6 tablespoons (90 g) boiling water over it; whisk very well until no lumps remain. Pour the mixture through a fine-mesh strainer set over a clean bowl; let cool to room temperature. Put about 1 cup of room-temperature Vanilla Buttercream into the green tea paste and whisk well until evenly combined. Add the green tea mixture to the remaining buttercream and whip in the mixer with the whisk until well combined.

Whipped Caramel CREAM

This is not as rich as buttercream, but it's every bit as luxurious. Use it on chocolate or nut cakes or on any dessert where you want a kick of caramel flavor. It is also great as a crepe filling. **MAKES ABOUT 4 CUPS**

---

2 cups heavy cream (480 g)

½ cup sugar (100 g)

1 tablespoon water (15 g)

Pinch of kosher salt

4 tablespoons (½ stick) unsalted butter, diced (57 g)

Warm 1 cup of the cream in a small saucepan over low heat.

Put the sugar, water, and salt into a medium saucepan and stir with your finger until sandy. Wet your fingers and wipe down the sides of the pan; set it over medium heat and cook until the sugar is dissolved. Brush the sides of the pan with a clean pastry brush dipped in cold water and continue cooking, swirling the pan as necessary, until the sugar turns a deep mahogany brown.

Very carefully and slowly add the warm cream—it will bubble up. Reduce the heat to low and stir until well combined. Add the butter, a little at a time, stirring between additions.

Pour the caramel into a bowl and stir in the remaining 1 cup cream. Let stand until room temperature and then refrigerate overnight or for up to 1 day.

When ready to use, whip the caramel cream in a mixer until soft peaks form.

Cream Cheese–Tahini FROSTING

This is a grown-up icing that tastes great on chocolate cakes, nut cakes, or citrus baked goods. The sesame paste adds an earthy, rich, nutty flavor. It's also a quick filling for crepes—spread a thin layer over them and then warm them slightly so the filling gets gooey. **MAKES ABOUT 3½ CUPS**

8 ounces cream cheese, at room temperature (227 g)

½ pound (2 sticks) unsalted butter, softened (226 g)

¼ cup tahini (sesame paste) (60 g)

1 teaspoon kosher salt (4 g)

1 tablespoon fresh lemon juice (15 g)

½ teaspoon vanilla extract (2 g)

2 cups confectioners' sugar, sifted (240 g)

Put the cream cheese, butter, tahini, and salt into a standing mixer and whip with the paddle on medium speed until creamy and smooth. Add the lemon juice and vanilla and whip well; with the mixer on low speed, slowly add the confectioners' sugar, stopping to scrape the bowl with a rubber spatula occasionally.

Once the sugar has all been added, increase the mixer speed to medium and whip for about 1 minute until very fluffy. Use immediately or refrigerate in an airtight container for up to 1 week, being sure to let stand until room temperature and rewhipping until fluffy before using.

Orange CURD

The flavor of fresh orange is irreplaceable in multilayered desserts. I like to pair it with chocolate or nuts, such as almonds or hazelnuts; it adds dimension without being overly sweet, just like its cousin the lemon. This curd is tart and lip smacking and great for filling cakes, cupcakes, or tarts. **MAKES ABOUT 3½ CUPS**

1⅔ cups fresh orange juice (from about 4 oranges) (400 g)

2 tablespoons fresh lemon juice (30 g)

8 large egg yolks

3 large eggs

½ cup sugar (100 g)

14 tablespoons (1¾ sticks) unsalted butter, softened and diced (196 g)

Finely grated zest of 4 navel oranges

2 tablespoons orange liqueur, such as Grand Marnier (30 g)

Put the orange juice in a small saucepan and bring to a simmer over medium heat. Cook for 12 to 15 minutes, until the liquid has reduced by half.

Meanwhile, fill a saucepan one-third full of water and bring to a boil over medium heat. Prepare an ice bath in a large bowl.

Pour the reduced orange juice into a large heatproof bowl, whisk in the lemon juice, and let stand until cool to the touch. In another small bowl, whisk the egg yolks, eggs, and sugar until well combined; pour into the cooled juice and whisk until combined. Set the bowl over the simmering water, making sure the bowl does not touch the water, and stir constantly with a large rubber spatula for about 10 minutes, until the mixture is very thick and hot to the touch (180°F).

Press the mixture through a fine-mesh strainer into a clean medium bowl and set it in the ice bath. Cool, stirring frequently, until the temperature has lowered to slightly above body temperature, about 104°F. Do not let the egg mixture get too cool or the butter will not incorporate properly.

Meanwhile, put the butter into a medium bowl and mash it vigorously with a rubber spatula until it is smooth and malleable. Add the orange zest and mix well. The butter should be smooth but not too soft. Remove the egg mixture from the ice bath and add about a third of the softened butter to it; mix it well with the spatula until it is thick and well combined. Add another third of the butter and mix well; once incorporated, add the remaining butter and the orange liqueur and fold with the spatula until very smooth and no lumps of butter remain. Press a sheet of plastic wrap directly on the surface of the curd and refrigerate for at least 2 hours and up to 3 days before using.

ALMOND CREAM

This is a classic French recipe, used to fill tart shells or breakfast pastries, like croissants, before they are baked. It can be frozen for up to 1 month; thaw in the refrigerator before using. **MAKES ABOUT 2 CUPS**

8 tablespoons (1 stick) cold unsalted butter, diced (113 g)

½ cup sugar (100 g)

1 teaspoon kosher salt (4 g)

1 cup almond flour (95 g)

3 tablespoons all-purpose flour (24 g)

2 large eggs

1 teaspoon vanilla extract (5 g)

Put the butter, sugar, and salt into a food processor and pulse until evenly combined and no lumps of butter remain. Add the almond flour and all-purpose flour and pulse until just combined. Scrape down the bowl with a rubber spatula. Add the eggs, one at a time, pulsing between additions, until combined. Add the vanilla and process until the mixture is combined and smooth. Transfer the cream to a bowl, cover the surface with plastic wrap, and refrigerate for up to 3 days or freeze for up to 1 month.

Raspberry-Mint JAM

This super-thick jam, on its own or when mixed with buttercream, makes a delicious macaron filling; It's sweet, herbaceous, and tart all at once. In that case, you may want to color your cookies a shade of red, pink, or mint green to hint at the filling. **MAKES ABOUT 2 CUPS**

18 ounces raspberries (about 4 cups) (510 g)

1 (packed) cup fresh mint leaves (38 g)

1½ cups sugar (300 g)

2 tablespoons powdered apple pectin (24 g)

½ teaspoon citric acid

Purée the raspberries and mint together in a blender. Strain the mixture through a fine-mesh strainer over a medium saucepan, pressing on the solids with a rubber spatula to remove as much liquid as possible. Discard the solids. Set the pan over medium heat and bring the purée to a simmer.

Meanwhile, stir together the sugar and pectin. When the temperature of the raspberry purée reaches 219°F, stir in the sugar mixture. Bring the mixture to a boil, reduce the heat so that it simmers, and cook for 5 minutes.

Remove from the heat and stir in the citric acid. Return the pan to low heat and cook until the jam sets, 5 to 6 minutes. Test it by dropping a bit onto a frozen plate—if the mixture gels within 5 seconds, it is ready. Remove from the heat and cool to room temperature.

Store in an airtight container in the refrigerator for up to 3 weeks.

CHOCOLATE GANACHE FILLING

This is a thick, chocolate ganache that can be used to fill macarons or other sandwich cookies or spread into the bottom of a tart shell and topped with fruit or a nut caramel. Use it while it is soft and spreadable, before it sets up completely. **MAKES ABOUT 1 CUP**

¾ cup heavy cream (200 g)

4 teaspoons light corn syrup (25 g)

8 ounces bittersweet chocolate (70% cacao), finely chopped (227 g)

1 tablespoon unsalted butter, softened (14 g)

Heat the cream and corn syrup in a small saucepan over medium heat until very hot and just about to boil. Put the chocolate into a large bowl and make a small well in the center. Pour about a third of the hot cream into the center of the chocolate. Using a rubber spatula, stir in very small circles in the center, until the liquid is smooth in the center. Add another third of the hot cream and stir in small circles again, this time expanding the circle to halfway to the sides of the bowl. Stir until the liquid is smooth. Pour the remaining cream into the center of the bowl and stir from the center out, pulling any remaining chocolate pieces into the liquid. Continue stirring, scraping the sides of the bowl, until the ganache is completely smooth and shiny. Stir in the butter and mix until very smooth.

Let stand until cool; once the ganache is firm enough to hold its shape, it can be used to fill macarons or tart shells and allowed to stand at room temperature until firm.

SHINY CHOCOLATE GLAZE

This is a deep, rich chocolate glaze that dries very shiny and can be used to glaze éclairs or cakes or to top cupcakes by dipping them into it. Be sure to let the glaze cool to room temperature and thicken before using it so it isn't too thin and runny. **MAKES ABOUT 2 CUPS**

4.25 ounces bittersweet chocolate (70% cacao), chopped (120 g)

1 cup Simple Syrup (page 333) (300 g)

6 tablespoons plus 2 teaspoons dark cocoa powder (40 g)

Put the chocolate into a medium bowl.

Bring the simple syrup to a boil over medium-high heat. Slowly whisk in the cocoa powder until dissolved; return the mixture to a boil.

Make a small well in the center of the chocolate and pour about a quarter of the syrup into it. Using a rubber spatula, stir the mixture in small circles in the center of the bowl until the chocolate liquefies.

Add another quarter of the syrup and stir in tight rotations in the center of the bowl, slowly working outward to pull in more solid chocolate; mix until smooth in the center. Add the syrup in 2 more additions, stirring from the center out, pulling in more solid chocolate, until the glaze is very smooth and shiny.

Let stand until room temperature before using.

DULCE DE LECHE

This ingredient has made a real impact on pastry menus, in ice creams, and even cookies. It is simply caramelized sweetened condensed milk and is really easy to make. It lasts for weeks in the refrigerator and is great to mix with whipped cream as a filling or to fold into buttercream for a roasted caramel flavor.

MAKES ABOUT 3 CUPS

2 (14-ounce) cans sweetened condensed milk

Put the cans of condensed milk *unopened* into a deep saucepan and cover them with hot water. Bring the water to a boil over medium-high heat and then reduce the heat to maintain a simmer; cover the pan. Simmer the cans, moving them occasionally in the pot and making sure they are always covered with simmering water, for 3 hours. This will caramelize the milk solids in the can and produce a buttery, thick paste.

Remove the cans from the water and let cool completely before opening and transferring the dulce de leche to an airtight container. Store in the refrigerator for up to 3 weeks.

Note: *If cooking unopened cans on the stovetop makes you uneasy, you can also make dulce de leche in a double boiler. Bring a saucepan filled three-quarters full of water to a rolling boil. Pour one 14-ounce can sweetened condensed milk into a deep metal bowl big enough to rest tightly on top of the saucepan. The boiling water should touch the bottom of the bowl to speed cooking time. Cook, stirring the milk frequently with a rubber spatula and adding more water to the saucepan as it evaporates, until the milk is very thick and has turned a deep nutmeg brown, 2½ to 3 hours. Cool the dulce de leche completely before transferring to an airtight container. Makes about ¾ cup.*

Fruit GARNISHES

I don't use a lot of fruit coulis or puréed fruit sauces with my desserts; I prefer using lightly stewed or roasted fruit, either whole or chopped, because it adds another layer of texture and freshness. This is where in-season fruit is crucial—if you toss very ripe fruit with a little juice like orange, cranberry, or other fruit nectars, it makes a great accompaniment for cakes, tarts, and frozen creamy desserts.

I like to pair fruits with like-flavored liquids; I'll toss the fruit with the juice, warm it briefly so the fruit releases juice and softens, and then sometimes add a splash of citrus or other acid to brighten the final flavor. Here are some suggestions for quick fruit compotes that can liven up a sliced dessert or turn a dish of ice cream into something fresh and special.

I'll also sometimes stew or roast fruit briefly to bring out its juiciness. Tossing or steeping fruit in simple syrup is a great way to preserve the fruit's texture while pulling out more flavor and sweetness.

Stewed Raspberries

MAKES ABOUT 1 CUP

Heat about ¼ cup (60 g) cranberry juice and a used vanilla pod, if you have one, in a small saucepan until hot. Add about 1 cup (140 g) raspberries and toss them gently with a large spoon over the heat to warm up the fruit, abut 30 seconds. Remove the pan from the heat and stir in a little finely grated lemon and lime zest. Use warm or at room temperature.

Macerated Strawberries

MAKES ABOUT 1½ CUPS

Hull and quarter about 12 ripe strawberries. Drizzle about 1 teaspoon (20 g) honey and 1 teaspoon (5 g) balsamic vinegar over them. Add a little chopped fresh tarragon and finely grated lemon zest. Toss well and let stand for about 10 minutes. Before using, squeeze a few drops of fresh lemon juice over the berries and toss.

Stewed Blueberries

MAKES ABOUT 1 CUP

Heat about ⅓ cup (80 g) orange juice in a small saucepan with a pinch of sugar and a small piece of cinnamon stick until warm. Add 1 cup (140 g) blueberries and heat for 3 to 4 minutes, stirring frequently, until the liquid begins to simmer and the blueberries just begin to pop. Do not overcook them or they will release pectin and get gummy. Stir in some finely grated orange zest and use warm or at room temperature.

Citrus Compote

Peel and cut oranges, blood oranges, tangerines, lemons, limes, and grapefruit or any mixture into segments and squeeze the excess juice from the membranes left over into a measuring cup. Mix equal parts Simple Syrup (page 333) and the juice in a saucepan and bring just to a boil. Pour the hot liquid over the citrus segments and toss in a sprig of fresh thyme; let cool. This is great for granola or is a good accompaniment for rich, creamy, fatty desserts like frozen mousse or ice cream because it cuts the richness.

Spiced Pineapple

Put about 1 cup (300g) Simple Syrup (page 333) into a saucepan and add some coriander seeds, whole black peppercorns, and a handful of fresh cilantro leaves. Bring the mixture to a boil, remove from the heat, and let stand for 10 minutes. Strain the warm syrup over cut fresh pineapple in a bowl and let the mixture stand for 10 to 15 minutes. This is great for tropical desserts or cakes, ice creams, or mousse containing coconut.

Roasted Apples

Toss peeled wedges of Granny Smith apples in a little Simple Syrup (page 333) and then roll them in sugar. Roast them on a baking pan lined with parchment paper or a silicone mat in a 250°F oven until they are soft and "fudgy" but still hold their shape, 15 to 18 minutes. They are great on French toast, stuffed into crepes, or used in a parfait or trifle.

Exotic Melon Compote

I don't like melon that has been heated or cooked, so I make a fragrant "stock" to soak it in. Put about 1 cup (300 g) Simple Syrup (page 333) in a small saucepan and add half of a scraped vanilla bean with its seeds, some kaffir lime leaves or large strips of lime zest, a few whole cloves, a whole star anise, a small piece of cinnamon stick, and some strips of orange and lemon zest. Bring the mixture to a boil, remove from the heat, and let stand until just slightly warm. Pour the mixture through a fine-mesh strainer over very ripe diced honeydew or cantaloupe in a bowl. Make sure the syrup is only slightly warm so the melon doesn't get mushy. Let the compote stand for 10 to 15 minutes before using.

Candied CITRUS PEEL

When I need a little tart bite to a dessert to cut sweetness or to balance creamy, rich fillings, candied citrus peel is just the ticket. You can use finely diced candied lemon or lime zest to sprinkle on iced cakes or serve very thin slivers of candied orange peel with chocolate desserts. The technique for candying any peel is the same; just keep an eye on it and never boil the blanching water or the syrup so the peel remains tender and the bitterness is coaxed out of it. **MAKES 1 TO 2 CUPS, DEPENDING ON THE FRUIT**

CHOOSE ONE OF THE FOLLOWING

2 navel oranges

2 lemons

3 limes

1 cup kumquats

2 cups Simple Syrup (opposite)

½ cup sugar, or as needed, for coating (100 g)

Halve the oranges, lemons, or limes lengthwise and, with your hands or a large spoon, pull out the flesh and membranes; reserve for another use. If using kumquats, slice them lengthwise and use a melon baller to remove the flesh and seeds.

Slice the orange, lemon, or lime peels lengthwise into ¼-inch strips. Leave the kumquat halves intact; they can be sliced later if desired. Put the peels into a large saucepan and cover them completely with cold water. Set the pan over medium-high heat until the water is just beginning to simmer; do not boil. Drain the peel, return it to the saucepan, cover with cold water, and repeat the process 2 more times.

Return the drained blanched peel to the saucepan along with the simple syrup. Set the pan over medium-low heat and cook gently, never allowing the mixture to boil, until the peels are translucent throughout but still firm. This can take anywhere from 15 to 45 minutes, depending on how thick the citrus peel is. There should be no white pith visible once the peel is candied. Remove from the heat and cool in the syrup; drain and reserve the syrup for another use, like brushing on cakes.

Toss the drained candied citrus in the sugar until well coated. Spread the citrus on a rack set over a sheet pan and let stand at room temperature for at least 1 day to dry it. If any of the peel looks wet, toss again in sugar and dry it completely on the rack. Store in an airtight container for up to 3 months.

Note: *Candied citrus peel can be dried as above or stored in the syrup in the refrigerator. If you want soft, moist pieces, do not coat it in sugar; just drain it thoroughly before using.*

Simple Syrup

MAKES ABOUT 4 CUPS

It's a good idea to always have some
simple syrup around. It keeps nearly
forever in the refrigerator, and you can
flavor it with spices, vanilla, citrus zests,
et cetera, to use for brushing on cakes or
cupcakes, or for tossing with fruit for a
quick garnish. Plus, it is handy to have
around when you are whipping up last-
minute cocktails at home. Sometimes I
use a little more sugar than water, which
makes the syrup a bit thicker. It delivers
sweetness without making things soggy if
you plan on using it to flavor cakes.

Put 3 cups (600 g) sugar and 2 cups
(480 g) water into a saucepan and heat
over medium heat, stirring a few times,
until the sugar is dissolved. Store in an
airtight container in the refrigerator.

CHAPTER 9

BUILDING *a* BALANCED DESSERT

Hands down, the most satisfying part of the past two decades of my career has been the process of creating plated desserts. Nothing, except maybe a ride on a track on my Ducati, is more exciting to me than pulling together flavors and textures that make people flip. It's why we chefs do what we do; in the end, it's about pleasing people, especially with dessert, which they might not make at home.

What makes a dessert great is a balance of contrasting texture, flavor, and, sometimes, even temperature. Think about the perfect dish of mac-and-cheese covered in toasted bread crumbs; there is creaminess, saltiness, sweetness, crunchiness, richness. Every bite is different, depending on what you scoop onto the spoon, which keeps you going back for more. Desserts should offer the same experience—every bite should keep you engaged and wanting more.

When I devise a new dessert, I start with one single element or dominant flavor—the star of the show. Sometimes the headliner is driven by what seasonal ingredients are available. When it is strawberry season, I run with it, creating textures and flavors around the sweet, juicy berry that complement it and do not overpower it. In my years in restaurants, I've worked with everything from chocolate and caramel to tomatoes and sassafras root.

Then I look for compatible flavors and textures, as well as contrasting ones, all to showcase the star. If you start with something sweet, like a berry, find some sour or tart flavors to pair with it. If you are working with creamy textures like mousse, sabayon, or ice cream, pick some crisp items like crumbled cookies or streusel or crushed candied nuts to serve alongside. Adding extra textures and flavors to a dessert keeps the palate alive. But know when to show restraint: Too many elements of texture and flavor can confuse the palate and take away from the overall experience. Everything on the plate should enhance the main ingredient.

After many years and literally thousands of recipes in restaurant kitchens, I found the most streamlined way to create new desserts is with a chart, where I have lists of cakes, mousses and creams, crunchy elements, and seasonal flavors. You can easily do the same thing at home, using the recipes in this book. Pick a flavor or ingredient and go from there. If you find beautiful, ripe plums at the farmer's market, you can build a cake or tart around them and add creamy, crunchy, hot, and cold elements to the plate. As you master different cakes or tarts and base flavors, either from these pages or elsewhere, keep track of them. It gets easier and more fun to create desserts when you can easily recall all of the tools you have to work with. This is the fun part and what your friends and dinner guests will remember long after the party is over.

Within this chapter are a few suggestions and creations I came up with using the recipes in this book. But I want you to think outside of this box and create desserts that excite you, keeping texture, flavor, temperature, and visual appeal in mind. There really is no wrong answer when putting together a dessert. Some tries will taste better than others; that's how you learn. But even if you don't knock it out of the park, I'll wager that no one is going to push your dessert away and not eat it. Pull the flavors together that enthrall you and that you will be eager for your friends and family to try.

Go big or go home.

OLIVE OIL CAKE *with* STEWED BERRIES

- Olive Oil Sponge Cake (page 201) pieces

- Stewed berries (page 330)

- Citrus Sabayon (page 87)

- Tarragon leaves

TROPICAL PAVLOVA

- Individual Swiss meringue crunchy "nests" (see pages 72–73)

- Mango Lassi Pudding (page 63) lightened with whipped cream

- **Diced tropical fruit:** star fruit, mango, pineapple, kiwi, papaya, and passion fruit seeds

PLUM MOUSSE TRIFLE

- Brown Sugar–Molasses Cake (page 183) rounds

- Honey Roasted Plum Mousse (page 92)

- Plum brandy–flavored whipped cream

- Crunchy Meringue Cookies (page 80) pieces

TRIPLE CHOCOLATE MOUSSE TORTE

- Flourless Chocolate Meringue Cake (page 205)

- Bittersweet Chocolate Mousse, Milk Chocolate Mousse, and White Chocolate Mousse (pages 88, 90, and 91)

- Cocoa powder and confectioners' sugar

- Crushed cacao nibs

PEAR, CARAMEL, *and* ALMOND ROULADE

- Thin Almond Sponge Cake (page 198)

- Whipped Caramel Cream (page 322)

- Caramelized pears (see page 140)

- Crystallized almonds (see page 145)

VANILLA-BANANA CARAMEL CAKE

- Vanilla Sponge Cake (page 202)

- Banana-Rum Mousse (page 95)

- Caramelized bananas (see page 140)

- Candied Hazelnuts (page 143)

CITRUS POUND CAKE
with EXOTIC MELON

- Toasted warm Citrus Butter Loaf Cake (page 175)

- Sour Cream Sherbet (page 39)

- Exotic Melon Compote (page 331)

ACKNOWLEDGMENTS

I need to thank Rica Allannic and Marysarah Quinn, my editor and designer, for their hard work on our second and more elaborate book together. Thank you for truly helping me to refine my vision and create something so very special that will be a great resource for generations to come. I'm very proud of it.

Many, many thanks to Joy Tutela and David Black, my literary agents, for believing in me and fighting for me over the years, no matter what. You supported my decisions and you helped me realize my true ambitions with this huge piece of work. *Grazie mille.*

To my pal and partner in sweet baking crime, Wes Martin, my cowriter: Man, this project turned out to be way bigger than either of us expected and I am blown away by your dedication and professionalism. I couldn't imagine having done this with anyone else. You did a great job translating my energy and ideas into the words in this book. Bravo.

To Michael Spain-Smith and Frank Angel (Team Cupcake), for a mammoth photo shoot under the strangest of conditions. Thank you for understanding my vision and for thinking outside of the box every time you snapped a shot. Your creativity and talent shine through with every picture.

I have been fortunate in my career to develop so many wonderful relationships, ones that I will always cherish, and friendships that will last a lifetime. Without them this book wouldn't be as fantastic as it is.

I owe a huge debt of gratitude to Beth Robinson of KitchenAid and my friends at Digitas for going above and beyond as usual. I couldn't imagine what life was like before this equipment existed. Truly one of the best!

To Avi Kendi of Metal Dimensions, for his generosity and for lending his amazing artistic and creative touch and textures to help make the photos in this book extraordinary.

I have been working with All-Clad and Lisa Callahan for more years than I want to admit. The cookware speaks for itself; it's been in every top restaurant I have ever worked in and it's definitely what I cook with at home.

My friend Brooks Morrison and the team at Moore & Giles helped me make some of the images in this book really reflect my personality and lifestyle through the use of their fantastic leathers.

A pastry chef is fanatic about organization and OXO makes my favorite storage containers as well as extremely useful hand tools. Gretchen Holt has become a dear friend over the years.

I'm always looking for new textures and iSi North America, Inc., changed the game for so many of us with their cream whippers and soda siphons. Plus I can't live without their silicone mixing bowls now.

Thanks to Waring and Daniel DeBari, for producing unique, small, and powerful equipment that makes a chef's life much easier both at work and at home. Definitely came in handy in our test kitchen.

Thanks to Danni Kaplan and Marcee Katz of Chef Works for supplying all my colorful aprons and so many great chef jackets over the years. High quality, well fitting, and long lasting—the perfect recipe.

Thanks to Valrhona chocolate for being such a mark of excellence and Eric Case, a great friend of mine for so many years.

Thanks to Brooklyn Slate for kindly loaning me so many gorgeous and exquisite slates that added the earthy and organic feel I was looking for in the photography.

You can always tell a quality establishment because they are using Steelite tableware. I love how the tableware presented my food in this book and on my table at home.

Thanks to my great local purveyors whom I've worked with for many, many years: Riviera Produce, Dairyland, The Chefs' Warehouse, Paris Gourmet, Mr. Recipe, and Terra Spice.

To Alison Attenborough, Hadas Smirnoff, Alex Leonard, Jo Keohane, and Janine Kalesis, thank you for your styling assistance with the photos, and to Daniel Petix, for your artistic eye.

To the culinary school students and graduate volunteers at the photo shoot—Anthony Michael Contrino, Rachel Herbert, Laura Lozano, Mandel Lum, Madhuri Sharma, Julie Eisenberg, Emily Jacobs, and Chloe Bean—your help and dedication was invaluable. Special thanks go to Janet "Eskimo Miffy" Lo, who kept everything running smoothly on and off set.

Last but not least I need to thank the man who keeps my smile intact, the mac of all tooth daddies, Dr. Uri Levy.

—Johnny Iuzzini

To Johnny: Working on this mountain of a project with you has been an amazing experience. I'm grateful for the huge amount of knowledge I gained; you're truly a world-class talent. But even more than that, I'm thankful for the brotherly bond that grew as we baked together. Cheers, my friend.

—Wes Martin

INDEX

ABOUT THE AUTHORS

JOHNNY IUZZINI, winner of the James Beard Award for Outstanding Pastry Chef and recognized as one of the 10 Most Influential Pastry Chefs in America by *Forbes,* was the executive pastry chef of the world-renowned Jean-Georges restaurant in New York City for ten years and also the head judge of *Top Chef: Just Desserts*. He currently runs his own pastry and culinary arts consulting company named Sugar Fueled Inc.

WES MARTIN is an accomplished cook, writer, culinary producer, food stylist, and media consultant. He has worked with many of the biggest names in the television and food publishing world, both as a full-time cook and stylist at the Food Network and for two years as Martha Stewart's kitchen manager and TV chef on her daytime talk show.

MICHAEL SPAIN-SMITH is an award-winning lifestyle advertising photographer known for capturing images of vibrant intensity. Like Johnny, Michael has a passion for motorcycles, travel, and dessert, which helped make working on *Sugar Rush* a sweet success.